sour/the magical element that will transform your cooking

For Chris, Ian and Stuart – the oldest and best of friends

Publishing Director Sarah Lavelle
Commissioning Editor Susannah Otter
Art Director Claire Rochford
Design Matt Cox at Newman+Eastwood Ltd.
Photographer Mark Diacono
Props Holly Bruce
Ceramics Ella Hookway, Tasja Pulawksa
Production Director Vincent Smith
Production Controller Nikolaus Ginelli

Published in 2019 by Quadrille, an imprint of Hardie Grant Publishing

Quadrille
52–54 Southwark Street
London SE1 1UN
www.quadrille.com

Cataloguing in Publication Data: a catalogue record for this book is available from the British Library.

text © Mark Diacono 2019
photography © Mark Diacono 2019
design © Quadrille 2019

ISBN 9781787132269

Printed in China

sour/the magical element that will transform your cooking

MARK DIACONO

Hardie Grant

QUADRILLE

CONTENTS

INTRODUCTION

Despite a seventies and eighties childhood largely dedicated to sugar and potatoes in all their glorious forms, it is the sour I remember fondest. Of those quarter-pounds of sweets decanted from sweet-shop jars to be secreted in my blazer pockets for mid-lesson pleasure, most were sharp; acid drops, sherbet lemons, rhubarb and custards and soor plooms among them. There's a yoghurt I can still almost taste, despite the decades passed.

It may have been made by St Ivel. The stubborn foil peeled back on a layer of chocolate – hard and thin as ice on a winter puddle and the colour of cheap cigars. I'd teaspoon through to the pale, sour sea beneath – properly sharp and that fawn of lads' jackets and car interiors of the time. I may have imagined a further layer of chocolate at the base. My God it was good: sour enough to set the back of your jaw alight and, as John Shuttleworth's cup-of-tea adage goes, one was never enough and two was one too many. Salt and vinegar crisps were *the* crisp. Vinegar on chips, lemon juice on pancakes, sherbet dip dabs, a post-illness half-grapefruit (admittedly under a rubble of granulated); sour was everywhere.

And then everything drowned in an avalanche of sugar.

Thankfully, as our wild affair with sugar shows signs of calming to a more manageable fumble, our appreciation of the sour is returning. The increasingly available range of naturally sour citrus, rhubarb, cherries, tamarind and sour spices are reaching a more inquisitive audience, while more of us are embracing sour fermented foods such as sourdough, kefir and kombucha, which we owe to the resurgent skills of artisan bakers, cheesemakers and fermentistas.

My daughter is an unwitting supporter of my feeling that we are born loving sour and mostly sweeten ourselves away from it. As much as she shares my love for all things Toblerone, her enthusiasm for sourness remains: at 13 she still sucks lemons, steals a slice of the Bramleys I'm peeling for a crumble and prefers the least ripe of the kiwis in the fridge. I cook and eat more sour foods than ever thanks to her enthusiasm for the sharp. Last weekend, salvaged from the depths of a cold-knuckle freezer forage, a tub of gooseberry purée allowed me to make a fool of something, reversing life's usual trajectory. My daughter and I shared it, a proper two-spoons-in-a-bowl kind of pudding, the clack of metal against metal, all creamy-toothed smiles. Gooseberries are a perfect example of how sourness can be celebratory, and how just a little by way of balancing, complementary flavours – in this case, elderflower and a dash of honey – can magnify gooseberries' delightfully sour essence.

Almost everything you eat can and should be acidified in some way. What are brown sauce, ketchup, piccalilli, or vinegar if not happy-making ways of souring a chip? That slice of lemon in a gin and tonic, a slack spoonful of yoghurt or crème fraîche with the chilli, a gloss of dressing on salad leaves: sourness is there, every day. Often it isn't entirely necessary, but unnecessary embellishments are what transform fuel into food, and feeding into eating. Sourness brings contrast, balance, variety, zing – pleasure. And who couldn't go for a little more of that.

Of course, sweetness has most of us in its gorgeous grasp, and that can affect our disposal towards sourness; not that sourness is in any way less of a pleasure, but we are tuned too tightly towards sweetness' pleasing immediacy and the endorphin rush. To quote the magnificent Julian Cope, 'It takes no strength of character to love the summer'; so too sugar. Where sugar (and salt to a degree) is all lustful, instant gratification, sour is more quietly, deeply rewarding. Gradually falling in love with sour is like realizing the friend who's been standing so close all along is actually the one for you.

It can take a little effort to ease back on sweetness. A few years ago I stopped adding sugar to apple, rhubarb or gooseberries in a crumble, and allowed the fruit to be characteristically sharp and the topping suitably sweet: the difference was remarkable. Both elements and the whole were so much improved; the sourness was there yet never too much thanks to the sweetness against – rather than in – it. I'm not suggesting anyone give up sugar – Hell's teeth, I love a Double Caramel Magnum like April sun – but if eating a little less of it (while enjoying every mouthful) and embracing the sour means a chance of living a little bit longer, a little bit healthier, and more rewarding food, then all to the good. Allowing bitter to be bitter, sweet to be sweet and sour to be sour widens the experience and pleasure in what we eat, and reminds us of the importance of contrast and variety.

As I hope these pages will convince you, sourness is where so much of food's magic is. It goes far beyond taste into the genuinely life-enhancing. As well as being a satisfying thread we can sow through much of what we eat, sourness can be unquestionably good for us as the avenue through which we can engage with the genuinely incredible microbial world, and teach us the understanding to cook well.

Sourness pulls a number of health-giving carriages. Sourdough bread, where the activity of specific bacteria ferment the dough to our sensory and gustatory pleasure; high levels of vitamin C in citrus; the microbiome-enriching qualities of kefir; and more: each among the many sour foods offering real, tangible benefits to go with the pleasure and flavour. As you'll discover, the skills required in creating and using these life-enhancers are easy to acquire.

Acidity – so closely related to sourness – also offers any number of preserving opportunities. Most of us are, thank heavens, largely beyond the need for actively preserving food – fridges and freezers slow the trajectory of decay to suit our speed of consumption – but the pursuit of flavour, texture and the joy in the doing ensures that making and using pickles, ferments, vinegars and other foods with an extended lifespan is as popular as ever.

Sourness comes in many forms, from citrus and vinegars to lesser known spices and pickles. As well as the familiar, I will encourage you to investigate ingredients that might be new to you: my bet is that once you've tasted dried passion fruit powder (somehow even better than it sounds), you'll be dusting everything from chops to the end of a wet finger with it, and that after you've made the tamarind pork ribs and mixed yourself a ginger tamarind mojito (see pages 170 and 280), you'll come up with other ideas for where tamarind's spectacular spicy sourness will work.

As rewarding as it is to get to grips with the wide range of sours, much of the pleasure is in developing an understanding of sourness as a transformative tool in the kitchen. Sour has the rare ability to both distinguish and to harmonize: used thoughtfully, it draws more clearly into view every key ingredient in a recipe. It makes other flavours finer, and allows them to offer more of themselves. It balances fat, salt and sweet, yes, but critically it makes tomatoes more tomatoey, it pulls garlic from the (delightful) fog of slow cooking, it reveals and burnishes in exactly the same way the grain in wood rises with a little white spirit and wax. Try a few drops of vinegar on apricot halves before roasting and you'll see how it brings out their glorious acidity and yet amplifies their sweetness too. When you're looking to bring out an ingredient's or dish's qualities or lend it something new, vinegar, citrus, tamarind, verjuice, sumac or any of the many other sours are likely to be the answer.

Despite all these possibilities, most of us use sourness in a limited way. I suspect much of this is down to confidence; some of it might be time. I hope this book will imbue you with the first and convince you that – at least sometimes – investing a little time in what you eat rewards you heavily, both in the doing and the result.

The heart of this book is divided into two sections: the souring skills and the recipes. The former familiarize you with all you need to create kombucha, sourdough, kimchi and more that are not only wildly superior in flavour to those you can buy, they also enrich and nourish your digestive system, and in so doing can positively influence your life in many other ways. Once you have some familiarity with the methods, the recipes that come from them are endless, and endlessly delicious. Of course, you can buy any of these delicious sours – please do – but there are pleasures to be had as much in the creating as the eating. This is the path into an extraordinary world: every time sourdough rises, every time kombucha fizzes it feels mildly miraculous. Unseen armies of fermentation are being lightly marshalled to your (and their) benefit: it's genuinely magical. It is like gardening in so many respects: you never quite lose the sense of wonder that the seed germinates, that life springs.

There is a delicious unpredictability that comes with this glorious alchemy that you should embrace: it is all part of the dance. One of the gifts of engaging with the souring skills and in using sour ingredients well is that it helps you to develop a sense of feel and understanding: while there are steps to follow, so much of the reward is in falling into the music. Even if you only make sourdough occasionally or paneer only once, you will be richer for it. These are real life skills, life pleasures, and you may find (as I do) that what you once thought of as palaver is now very much how you want to spend a little of your time.

USING SOURNESS

As the great writer Loudon Wainwright Jnr said, 'Maps are just excuses for the journey they set us on'. And what are recipes if not culinary maps. The beauty of sour is that it encourages us to be dynamic with our food, to engage and be adventurous with what we eat; to perhaps follow the map at first, but to be prepared to fold it away once we understand the landscape a little better.

Sourness can bring pretty much anything you want to what you eat. Some of our favourite recipes are defined by it – vindaloo, ceviche and lemonade among them; others are guided by a lighter hand, sometimes even the invisible influence of a dash of white wine vinegar or a spoon of yoghurt to brighten a soup, a late dusting of sumac on a chop or chip, a drizzle of intense pomegranate molasses on roasted apricots. I could go on. I will go on. Because even when you don't notice it's there, sourness can transform in the pan and on your plate.

Using sourness well is not just about flavour: vinegar tenderizes as well as flavours the beef in the sauerbraten, a sea of citrus 'cooks' and sharpens the fish in the ceviche, the coming together of sweet, rich kulfi and sweet–sharp rhubarb is set alight by a little tamarind and, of course, the naturally souring activities of bacteria in sourdough, kimchi and other ferments bring health benefits too.

While sourness can be its own reward, there are times when just a little can be a powerful transformer. Yes, the naked shock of the Tom Collins (see page 276) is, as friend and chef Val Warner says of the perfect martini, 'an elegant brick through the window of your day' – and there are times when a proper wince is exactly what's required, but as much as anything, sourness is a creative tool. As a result, some of the recipes here are, in truth, not so sour at all. Mojito marmalade (see page 122) is sweeter than it is sour, but without the glorious sharpness of the lime the mint would be lost in a sea of sweetness, the whole diminished. Some recipes will have you adding acidity early as a way of building complexity, or late to punctuate and refresh; many will have you doing both, layering the sours as you go. In her superb *Salt, Fat, Acid, Heat*, Samin Nosrat distinguishes these as Cooking Acids and Garnishing Acids, not because (for example) vinegar can't be both, but as a way of understanding what sourness can bring at different stages in the process. The squash soup (see page 127) illustrates beautifully how adding sour early can build depth and complexity, whereas late lime freshens the whole and shines a light on to each of the soup's constituent parts.

There are many sources of acidity: citrus fruit including limes and lemons; fruit harvested early, before fully ripe, such as mangoes and tomatoes; sourness as the result of bacterial activity that gives us sourdough, vinegar, kefir and others; and naturally sharp ingredients such as hibiscus flowers, tamarind, passion fruit and gooseberries. Some are available in numerous forms: pomegranate, for example, can be used as the seeds of the fruit itself, as molasses, juice, or dried and powdered. Each offers something unique, and while they all bring sourness, the intensity, depth and volatility varies considerably: all the instruments may play an E, but each differs in the impression it leaves. What I hope this book does is offer invitations to play those different sours, to encourage inquisitiveness and experimentation, to build familiarity, to cook better and to take pleasure in the process and the results.

Perhaps the intimidating part for some is that using sourness well necessitates an element of feel, an almost unconscious understanding in the hands and mind that comes with relaxed attentiveness and a little familiarity. Sourness can vary with time, season and many other variables: that lemon you bought on Saturday morning may be wildly different in flavour after a week in your fridge, the bacteria present in my kitchen may make my sourdough rise more reluctantly than yours, and so on. When you are not the only living organism involved in the recipe, don't be surprised (or alarmed) if you're not the only one affected by temperature, light levels and the simple randomness of being alive.

And of course, we experience sourness differently, as much as if some of us have a sour tooth to go with our supposed sweet one. The combination of natural preferences (if they exist), habit and culture, makes food a delightfully singular, personal pleasure, so go with it, while challenging those habits. Like most worthwhile pursuits, developing a feel for what you are doing – which is as much about learning to observe and trust yourself as anything – is exactly what leads to the richest rewards.

Using sourness well requires you to be present: a thimble of vinegar can transform the plainest of leek and potato soups, stews and more into a delight, literally sharpening not only the flavour but the distinction between its constituent parts; behold, leek *and* potato, rather than their alloy. Drive down that road too far and the effect is lost so that you end up with leek and potato and vinegar soup; you must tweak and taste and interact. And while there is a place for each of them, remember that homemade vinegar, the supermarket staple and the finest artisan vinegar are only broadly similar. A teaspoon of each may have considerably different results, so taste you must, and then taste again. The only 'right' answer is yours.

The ability of acidity to change the structure and consistency of proteins is one to celebrate. In the raw fish of ceviche (see page 182), the acidity – in this case citrus – tenderizes the fish by causing the proteins to unravel in such a way that they are forced to create new bonds that tighten the flesh, in effect 'cooking' the fish without heat. The dairy souring skills (see pages 39–45) take advantage of acidic liquids' ability to separate milk's proteins (the curds) from the rest (the whey) to create all manner of cheeses. In a subtler way, a few drops of acidity are used to help set the egg white around the yolk more neatly than it would without when poaching an egg: the proteins coagulate before the simmering water can pull them apart, resulting in neater, more evenly cooked eggs. Some add vinegar to the poaching water for this, but I prefer a few drops of lemon juice on the just-cracked egg (see Turkish eggs on page 218) to prevent any hint of the flavour changing.

Sour ingredients – especially lemon juice and vinegar – can also affect the colour and texture of food, and while strictly speaking this doesn't happen as a result of their sourness, it's as well to know that there may be other implications to adding these sours to your food. Most of us use some kind of acid – lemon juice, most commonly – to prevent vegetables and fruit such as apples and celeriac discolouring as a result of enzymes oxidizing once cut, while adding vinegar early when cooking green vegetables makes their bright chlorophyll turn army surplus green. Happily, acidity brightens red foods as they cook (e.g. in braised red cabbage), as the anthocyanins they contain appear more intensely red in acidic conditions, and bluer in alkaline;

for the same reason, pickled red cherries are wildly vivid, and muffins made with cherries stay redder when buttermilk is used in the batter than if not.

A little acidity can also help prevent pasta from sticking: a tablespoon of lemon juice or vinegar to acidify the water is all it takes; a too-thick sauce releases its grip with just a touch of lemon juice to break down the starchy chains of flour without the dilution in flavour that more water would bring; an acid in the form of a pinch of cream of tartar or a few drops of vinegar eases the coagulation of proteins when whisking egg whites – just enough so that those responsible for the graininess in (say) meringues can't form.

Timing can be all-important too: a little vinegar or citrus in a bean dish – such as a cannellini stew – will brighten and clarify the flavours as well as retain some bite in the beans if added late, when the beans are half-cooked; if added early, the acid can toughen the skins and extend the cooking time.

I hope that sets the picture of how powerful sourness can be in creating really good food, and how perhaps the most crucial part of using it well – in whatever form – is observing, tasting and being inquisitive.

The main thing I hope to encourage in using sourness is a little less tension in the hands with no less attention in the mind. Whether you are creating a dressing, making sauerkraut or adding a little vinegar to a soup, you must taste, trust your judgment, interact: there are few absolutes, and as intimidating as it may seem, this is the very quality that will uncurl your fingers from rigidly adhering to a recipe and really get you cooking. A map is only a map. And maps are just excuses for the journey they set us on.

WHAT IS SOURNESS?

On the face of it, sourness is a simple measure of acidity that can be observed on the pH scale: pH 7 is neutral (pure water has a pH of 7), with higher values considered alkaline, and anything lower, incrementally acidic.

The list below offers a comparison of relative acidity in foods we consider sour. It's important to note that the pH scale is logarithmic, which means a difference of 1 on the pH scale implies 10 times the strength, so lemon juice is ten times more acidic than pomegranate, and so on.

Lemon juice	pH 2
Lime juice	pH 2
Vinegar	pH 3
Pomegranate	pH 3
Gooseberries	pH 3
Rhubarb	pH 3.2
Grapefruit	pH 3.4
Sauerkraut	pH 3.5
Apple juice and wine	pH 3.5
Raspberries	pH 3.5
Oranges	pH 4
Green mangoes	pH 4
Yoghurt and buttermilk	pH 4.5
Tomatoes	pH 4.5
Milk	pH 6.5

The figures take no account of what can be considerable variations in ripeness, differences between varieties, types of vinegar, etc, but they offer a quick means of comparison at least.

As one of the core building blocks of flavour and how we experience food, sour – like bitter, sweet, salt and umami – helps us understand what we are eating. It can inspire involuntary reaction – google the lemonade scene from the *Detectorists* to see the glorious power of the properly sharp. Even in low intensity it causes us to salivate – it is literally mouth-watering – possibly to counteract the potential for the acidity damaging our teeth, but let us not lose too much romance to science. It helps us perceive where this mouthful might be on that sliding scale of ripeness, of spoilage and more, but it is only useful to a point, as so much of sourness is experiential.

In many ways, sourness illuminates the distinction between taste and flavour: taste is what our five food sensitivities – sweet, sour, salt, bitter and umami – tell us about what we are eating, while flavour is a more complex interaction of taste, smell, texture, experience and expectation. Our understanding of sour as a flavour is dependent as much on our relative consumption of sugar, the frequency with which we use vinegar, lime, lemon and other sour ingredients, as the pH itself. So while pH is a useful indicator, sourness in its widest sense goes beyond an awareness of where we are on the pH scale between 'lemon face' and a glass of water: it is our experience of acidity, a personal take rather than an absolute. Our relative preference for sourness involves cultural, genetic, experiential, fluke, taught and instinctive factors: it is ours, and yours is likely to be different to mine.

Sourness is always relative. While salt imparts a very definite character that may only be reduced by dilution, our experience of sourness is partly defined by the balance of acidity with sweetness, and readily influenced and moderated by salt and bitter too. Context is everything. Interestingly, sugar has a pH of 7, so in using it to balance and contrast with sour we are doing so for flavour only, rather than neutralizing the acidity itself. If it were all about chemistry, about acidity, then in balancing and complementing sourness it would seem to make sense to add alkaline ingredients, and yet rarely is this the case: in making a dressing we might blend lemon juice (pH 2), honey (pH 3.9) and olive oil (pH 4) – each acidic – and yet the whole feels right. My point is that absolute acidity – i.e. taste – is not the crucial thing here; how we read and experience sourness is. So I hope you'll excuse me if I do away with too much more chemistry and focus on flavour, and the experience and pleasure that comes with cooking more thoughtfully with sourness.

BACTERIA AND SOURNESS

A good part of this book is in many ways the story of spoiling, of encouraging or allowing things to go 'off' in a way that suits us: for fruit to become alcohol that acidifies to vinegar; for milk to become yoghurt, cream or cheese, and so on. That we have made a simple craft of these gentle dilapidations is quite something.

These sours are the result of the beautifully effective action of particular beneficial bacteria. In specific yet very easily replicable conditions, these bacteria transform raw ingredients into the artisan – sourdough, vinegar, kombucha, kimchi among them – each with an element of sourness that reflects the process of acidification that the bacteria bring about.

Many fermented foods owe their sourness to lactic acid bacteria that multiply in anaerobic conditions (i.e. in the absence of oxygen), converting sugars into lactic acid. The change is more profound than flavour: in many cases, the composition of the raw ingredients is altered in such a way so as to align more completely with how our body can assimilate them, and in doing so we introduce our gut to representatives from the bacterial community that promote healthy digestion and physical and mental wellbeing. The combination ensures we assimilate more of the nutrients in what we eat. We are, simply, made to thrive on these foods.

The beneficial microorganisms that live in – and are introduced by fermented food to – our gut are known as probiotics. They aid digestion in numerous ways, and establishing and maintaining a flourishing population plays a crucial role in our health. As with all living organisms, probiotic bacteria need food, and their preferred diet is of plant fibres known as prebiotics. Probiotics eat prebiotics. This is useful to remember: eating probiotics promotes a healthy gut, and eating prebiotics helps ensure probiotics are able to thrive. Foods high in fibre tend to be laden with prebiotics: root vegetables, avocados, apples, bananas, asparagus, whole grains and cold rice are excellent sources.

There are any number of benefits attributed to fermented foods and drinks – a stronger immune system, reduced dietary intolerances, improved mood and energy levels among them – but even if all it gives us is delicious, nutritious food that also enables us to get more from everything we eat, that's more than plenty for me.

All of these foods require us to embrace the presence and activity of invisible microbes that are working in our culinary interest. You would not be alone in feeling slightly intimidated by the prospect of consuming fermented foods: we are more used to hearing of bacteria doing us harm than being essential to our existence. Fear not: these are foods that most cultures have been eating in one form or another for millennia. You may be familiar with some of sauerkraut, kimchi, miso and kombucha; it is only comparatively few (primarily Western) cultures where fermented foods are rare. It is estimated that a third of the food we humans consume globally is fermented. In many ways, sourness in the form of fermented foods is the medicine we have been denying ourselves while we ran off to spend all our time with sugar. Let me encourage you towards culinary polygamy.

Please don't be afraid of bacteria. Or at least, not all bacteria: our daily bread and our evening intoxication owe much to bacteria whose activity we have learned to harness to our advantage. Familiarity is everything here: likely as not, buying kefir grains or a starter for kombucha feels a little more intimidating than a packet of dried yeast. I felt the same. Jump in the pool, the water's fine.

Now you've taken the plunge, a word of caution: if you are new to fermented foods, take an enthusiastic yet steady approach at first. Introducing a diverse population of health-giving bacteria to a digestive system unused to them can bring a little turmoil if not done with care. Start little and often. Frequency is the thing: a little once a day, is exactly the way to go. You are inoculating yourself with beautifully beneficial bacteria, but allow them to colonize your gut slowly and you'll enjoy their goodness without upset.

When you are dealing with living entities, predictability is at a premium. The methods of fermentation that give you vinegar, sourdough and more give you a process to follow, but only to a point. You will need to develop a familiarity for what you are doing, a feel. Your ferments may turn out exactly as the method suggests – in many cases they will – but when you are dealing with different seasons and temperatures, with milk and sugars from different origins, don't be surprised if it affects the timing and nature of the outcome. This is to be celebrated; it is how it should be. It's the same when dealing with any living creature: sometimes the dog comes when called, sometimes not; often the cat wants to be stroked now, sometimes in its own sweet time. The fact is, it works; you just need to be present enough to observe, to choose and to enjoy. However, if the largely invisible processes of bacterial transformation are of little interest, ignore them: it matters less what happens, than that it does.

A FEW WORDS...

You will notice other peoples' names scattered through the book. As much as this book has been a creative process of refining methods and writing recipes like songs, I have unquestionably felt like a DJ as well as a songwriter. You may write your own melodies but you can't help but be influenced by those whose words and rhythms make your ears prick up. It has been a joyous time of trialling others' sourdough methods and kimchi recipes, of wondering if so-and-so's recipe for X might work beautifully with grapefruit in place of Sevilles, and of bending the ear of others about vinegars I should investigate or about whether that sour curry is really worth trying. Sour is such a deliciously addictive element of cooking – both in flavour, its ability to enhance and in the practice of souring – that it's impossible not to acknowledge and revel in others' take on it too.

That said, this is very much *my* rather than *the* book of sour. As happily influenced and inspired as I will always be, the prejudices, preferences and enthusiasms herein are mine: while this kitchen is never without lemons, cranberries appear once in a while, and there is no cottage cheese as I shall have no hand in encouraging anyone to eat liquid polystyrene; these biases, preferences and randomnesses are reflected in these pages. It is, of course, impossible to do anything other than draw an arbitrary circumference around what to celebrate about sourness; here's mine.

NATURAL SOURS

I'm not sure which came first: losing my virginity or my first real lemon. Before that life-changing event (the latter), Pancake Day was all about the coming together of sugar and lemon, but the lemon was plastic: a squeezy Jif. Yellow and shaped like a lemon, a cartoon fruit. Squeezing it cast a glorious, fine, sour rain over the rolling tundra of sugar that landscaped my pancake. Once exhausted of juice, the Jif made the best and most easily concealed of nuisances with which to fire cold water at a younger sister.

This plastic lemon wasn't a substitute; it was lemon, as far as I and many were concerned. I genuinely have no recollection of citrus (beyond baggy oranges or half grapefruits when I was ill) being available until the early eighties, and even then they were mostly to look at: it was the Lucozade that got me better. 'There's fruit in the house, and no one's ill' is still my favourite definition of middle class.

Even at that age, I was already in love with sour, but I knew it largely from 'unnatural' sources, from sweets and drinks rather than the fruit itself: lemonade, sherbet lemons and rhubarb and custard sweets among them. When the real deal was finally tasted, it was quite a revelation. I must have been just into my teens when a friend walked out of a greengrocer's with a bag of satsumas: if he'd carried a koala in his arms I would have been less surprised. We shared the fruit. Eating those first few, I discovered the back of my jaw – the fruit were sour as hell with a dash of lifesaving sweetness right at the end that allowed you to unsquint an eye without the aid of fingers.

The world has shrunk in the decades since, and so limes, mandarins, Sevilles, delightfully gnarled lemons, tamarind, sour mangoes, redcurrants and more have come to brighten our plates. Let's enjoy them. There is no shortage of these natural sours – raw ingredients that have a sharpness largely thanks to the presence of one or more acids, be they citric, ascorbic, malic, tartaric, oxalic or others. Citric acid unsurprisingly dominates with citrus fruit but is also a contributing acid in others, including strawberries, raspberries and gooseberries. Malic acid brings sharpness to apples and many of the stone fruit including nectarines and cherries. Tartaric is the main acid in grapes and tamarind. Other acids appear less commonly and/or in lower concentrations – benzoic acid sharpens a cranberry; quinic acid is present in kiwis – but at the end of the day, it matters little which acid lends sourness.

The recipes later in the book include many fruit that bring sourness, either thanks to their inherent sharpness – citrus, cranberries, gooseberries among them – or those that are often harvested before they reach a naturally sweet peak, such as apricots and mangoes. Few vegetables or herbs are sour, though sorrel is a delightfully lemony exception. Perhaps the most rewarding, or at least never-ending, pleasure of exploring how to use naturally sour ingredients, are the spices. Many are unfamiliar to most cooks: sumac, and the spice blend za'atar to which it lends itself are increasingly popular, but few use kokum or black lime. While each of these natural sours is unique and distinctive, their shared sour character offers every opportunity to substitute one for another – tamarind for kokum, anardana for sumac, and so on – that will be interestingly different to the original. As with most fine things, there is always something else to explore and that way discoveries lie.

Allow me to introduce you to a few sour spices, in case you are unfamiliar.

Tamarind

I've come to tamarind rather too recently, and it is one of those flavours that can make you enter a slightly daydreamy state, imagining how it might suit this or complement that. Once you start cooking with tamarind, it is as if you have discovered a special music or favourite author previously unknown to you. The weeks following may easily be lost in enthusiastic exploration, and that 'what else can I do with this?' feeling never quite leaves you when it comes to tamarind.

Tamarind comes from a tropical tree of the same name, likely to originate from Madagascar. Its brown pods look not unlike broad beans after a long weekend and in need of a shower and a glass of water; they contain a dark sour pulp that is extracted from the desiccated pods when ripe and squeezed into blocks, or strained of seeds to make a paste. In either form, it is used in curries, stews, drinks, chutneys and more throughout the Middle East and Asia, as well as Worcestershire sauce and brown sauce in the UK. As much as it is used for its distinctive and complex flavour – perfectly described by Niki Segnit in *Lateral Cooking* as 'like a lemon that's sucked a date' – tamarind brings a distinctly characterful souring that just works in so many dishes.

The concentrated paste is pretty good and widely available; the block version is superb and available online and from Asian food shops. Tamarind block involves the tiny faff of adding a little boiling water and encouraging it to dissolve, for which – as is usual for a little culinary effort – you are more than proportionately rewarded in flavour.

Although tamarind adds a unique spicy-sour tone, if you are without, then use vinegar or lime juice in a similar quantity (and then amend to taste) to add the required sourness.

Amchur

This seriously marvellous powder is made from dried, unripe, green mangoes. The mangoes are peeled, sliced thinly and dried, traditionally in the sun. If you are lucky enough to be somewhere – northern India or China ideally – where you can buy amchur as crunkled beige sheets before they've been ground into a powder, then please get me some too. As well as being the core ingredient in chaat (see page 96), amchur in its pure form adds a honeyed tartness to dishes. As is entirely usual, spices have an affinity with other plants and dishes of their region: amchur's gently sweet, strongly sharp flavour lights up sour curries, pickles, vegetable samosas, desserts and dals, adding depth as well as brightness, and can even be used to tenderize meat. That said, don't be shy of introducing amchur to food from other cultures: a sprinkle to the skin of chicken, roast potatoes and fruit salads is just wonderful.

If you have it, go easy at first: fresh, it is intense and pokey. As you would salt, add a little, taste and adjust to suit. If you are without, lemon and a little of its zest gives a ballpark of what amchur brings. Available online and from specialist food shops.

Hibiscus

Hibiscus grows wildly in many parts of the world where there's proper heat, and its flowers are widely used to make hot and cold drinks, many of which have subtly different recurrences around the world: zobo in Nigeria (see page 277) is similar to sorrel in the Caribbean, and so on. The crimson-pink flowers, most commonly available dried, bring colour, a beautifully intense and perfumed sourness and vitamin C in water, with a flavour not too far from cranberries. They are also purported to be high in antioxidants and apparently help lower blood pressure. You'll be able to source them online and from some health food shops.

Once you use hibiscus flowers a little, you'll find your imagination turning them to ever more uses: they make an excellent tea; I use them with raspberries when making water kefir; they make a good and sharp sorbet with strawberries; and whizzed in a blender in a ratio of 20:2:1 hibiscus to sugar to citric acid powder, they make a phenomenal sherbet. Have a play.

Anardana

Sometime last year I discovered anardana, and everything – most frequently a moistened finger – has been dipped in or sprinkled with it ever since. Anardana is dried pomegranate seed and is most widely available as a powder, though if you are fortunate enough to find a supplier, you may be able to get it in its unground state. As with fresh pomegranate seeds and pomegranate molasses, anardana brings a rich depth with its sourness. I tend to use it late on, as you might a final flourish of lime, to add zing and life before serving, though if the cooking time is minimal, as with the pheasant main course on page 168, its effect isn't lost. Available online and from Asian food shops.

Although a little less sweet than pomegranate molasses, you can use anardana as a substitute, especially where adding more liquid to a dish isn't required. Try two-thirds of the volume, so 2 teaspoons of anardana in place of 3 of pomegranate molasses. Its sweet, rich sharpness works really well with both autumnal fruit and spices (a sprinkling over star anise plums and yoghurt, for example) or to add the finest of sour intensities to chicken skin, finishing its brittle transformation on the barbecue.

Think of it as sour salt: play with it.

Sumac

Sumac is made from the dried, crushed red-brown berries of the sumac bush that grows on high ground in the Mediterranean's heat, perhaps most notably in Sicily, as well as in Iran and Turkey. Picked slightly unripe, the berries are dried and ground into a powdered form that is perfect for adding a very citrusy sourness to anything from fish to poultry to vegetables. What sumac lacks in zing compared to lemons, it makes up for in balance, bringing a slightly less combative sourness than lime or lemon, while enhancing flavours in the way that salt does. As with the other sour spices, it doesn't add liquid to a recipe, which makes it perfect for the sumac duck recipe (see page 166), for sprinkling over hummus, or as a late dusting for added punch – try it on fruit, salads and chops, for instance. If you are lucky enough to lay your hands on the dried berries, they can be torn and soaked in hot water (as kokum commonly is) and the gloriously sour liquid used in drinks such as zobo (see page 277). You'll find sumac in an increasing number of supermarkets, online and from specialist food shops.

In Iran and neighbouring countries, it is perfectly usual for it to be on the table, alongside salt and pepper, to use as you wish: I greatly encourage you to do the same.

Dried passion fruit powder

As much as I love the other sour spices, if you let me have only one with which I may spend a day in a locked room with nothing but a small spoon, this would be it. Intensely flavoured and full of aromatic sour and sweetness, passion fruit powder is a great ingredient to have to hand as a final sprinkle, or for flavouring yoghurt, sorbets, custards, fools, ice creams and biscuits. And so much more. For more of a nibble experience, you may be able to source dried passion fruit as small rubbled pieces 2–5mm across, or even in sugar-cube size, though both are less widely available than the fine powder. I've only ever seen dried passion fruit powder available online.

Black lime

Black limes are mini, burnt-out honeycomb planets, light as a sneeze, carrying only an unpromising ghost of a fragrance, yet with their crust cracked their latent sourness is released, transforming whichever sea they find themselves in. Black limes are created by boiling and then sun-drying familiar or Persian limes; they are widely used throughout Iran and neighbouring countries even as far as northern India. Available online and from Asian food shops.

I use them mostly whole and just punctured, left to infect stews (try the rhubarb khoresh on page 178 with black lime in place of the molasses), curries – the Persian fish stew (see page 192) shows exactly what they can add to a spicy dish – and soups. They're also good to grind into a powder to dust over grilled meat either before or after cooking (or indeed both) as you might sumac. Black lime is also quite special in summer drinks, and makes a great alternative in the zobo instead of the hibiscus flowers.

Kokum

Kokum trees are evergreens found throughout much of India and neighbouring countries producing red-purple fruit, not unlike plums. Once harvested, the fruit – also known as mangosteens – are sun-dried to intensify their flavour and prolong their shelf life. They are available online or from specialist shops in a form that looks not unlike dusty fruit pastilles that have been run over some time ago. Soaked in warm water and encouraged to break up by determined fingers, kokum releases a sweet–sour, slightly earthy flavour that, while not wildly powerful, finds a way of being present when used to sour dals and curries, especially fish curries, as its other name 'fish tamarind', rightly suggests. I love it in drinks: a handful of dried kokum blitzed with the boiling water in which they've soaked with a little sugar, soda water and crushed ice refreshes beautifully on a hot day. Kokum also works perfectly in place of the tamarind in zoom koom (see page 272) and instead of the hibiscus in zobo (see page 277). Easily sourced online.

SOURING SKILLS

After another of those runs where I came home and wondered when – if – I'd ever experience that elusive post-exercise euphoria, I flopped into the sofa with half an ear to Radio 4. An unnamed guest spoke eloquently about the largely unknown world that lies within each of us: the gut, and its apparently fascinating microbiome. It sparked a chain of small revelatory discoveries that quietly changed my life.

Perhaps like many, I unthinkingly pictured the internals of digestion as a slightly refined tangle of bicycle inner tube leading to a hot water bottle of a stomach, in which all the sorting of Useful from Useless took place, before another slightly more direct inner tube took the Useless to be reunited with the outside world. In my post-run melting, my awareness that the gut must be something more complex than inner tubes and hot water bottles was transformed into a sense of wonder. Not only are we apparently forested with living organisms working to our benefit, research increasingly indicates that our physical and mental wellbeing owes much to the vitality and diversity of this remarkable ecology. The guest assured us that in the same way that mental health was little spoken of three decades ago, yet its importance is now appreciated as it should be, so too our internal microbiome would come to be recognized as a world as fascinating and undiscovered as outer space.

I listened again online the next day, taking notes. I bought the book; I devoured the book; I went from occasional intermittent fermenter to avid reader and experimenter. I listened to the few fascinating fermenters I knew, I spent a day with Sandor Katz, I listened ever more intently to the brilliant Gaby and Hans Wieland from the Neantóg Kitchen Garden School in Ireland, I lapped up so much of Naomi Devlin and Dearbhla Reynolds' bright, fresh takes on fermenting, I subscribed to The Sourdough School, I drank my wife's unbeatable kombucha – the fruit of her own inquisitive dabblings. I was hooked.

The pages on souring skills will familiarize you with a series of simple transformations that create exceptional flavours, ingredients that while sour in themselves also provide the starting point for so many recipes. Each of the nutritious, bacterial sours in these pages come about by offering a gentle guiding hand on a natural process that would happen without you, encouraging the largely invisible activity of bacteria to work to our advantage. These skills take little of your time, they are particular yet simple, and the results are extraordinary.

The process of creating these sours is also good for the soul. Being able to make sauerkraut or kombucha is a life-enriching pleasure in itself, as much as the eating and drinking of it. Even if you only make sourdough or kombucha once in a while, the fact that you can makes you more of a free-range human, and that can only be a good thing.

You can, of course, buy all the sourness you need. Whether it's natural sours like limes and sumac, or the products of fermentation like sourdough and water kefir, you can find them in most supermarkets, otherwise online. Do – many of them are excellent. And yet, I'm not going anywhere until I've encouraged you to try making your own too.

You may feel you are too busy, too idle or perhaps intimidated by the idea of working with bacteria or the inexact nature of fermentation: put these concerns to one side. Of course, making sourdough or ricotta takes a little time, but really not so much: I'm ok with that.

We are the only species that cooks. While entirely unnecessary to our survival, cooking brings us the luxury of time: when you aren't spending half your day chewing an almost endless pile of food into a digestible slurry, you have time to get beyond the basics of staying alive; to develop, to settle into communities, to build civilizations, to express yourself artistically. Cooking made us what we are. We don't cook because we are clever and creative; we are clever and creative because we cook. It is all too easy to whittle simple pleasures out of our

lives in search of convenience – and in so doing create more time to ponder how to bring a little joy back into our day-to-day. So why not dedicate a little of that time that cooking created for us in the first place to one of the few compulsories of life: eating well. And by eating well, I don't mean expensively; I mean by dedicating just enough time to get the most flavour, nutrition, pleasure and love from what you eat. As Billy Bragg sang, 'most important decisions in life, are made between two people in bed', but it is still around that kitchen table where most of those decisions are played out, where life is lived, where love is quietly shared.

Of course, there are times I'm as idle as the next person and I'm by no means advocating a life of self-sufficient fundamentalism: if you never make sourdough or vinegar but enjoy the recipes herein, then happy days. But why not gamble a few minutes and try each skill once: you have nothing to lose and all to gain. The skills are simple to acquire, utterly adaptable to individual expression and personal preference, and each enables you to do one of the things that turns existing into living: feeding yourself and your loved ones well.

Thankfully, we are simple creatures: in the end pleasure wins us over. If you are even mildly inquisitive about what you eat, there are only so many times you can enjoy a jar of kimchi or pay a fiver for an excellent loaf without coaxing yourself through the turnstile of culinary adventure. Whether making your own fermented fruit and vegetables, bread, vinegars and assorted dairies is new to you or not, you will find methods that I hope you'll enjoy for the pleasure of the doing, as well as for the creation of unique ingredients that, delicious as they may be in themselves, can be employed yet further in all manner of recipes.

If this book does one thing, I hope it is to encourage you to taste and trust yourself, to relax and play a little in the kitchen. You'll get most out of this book, the recipes and cooking (and maybe life) if you develop a bit of a feel for it. We are used to following exact instructions leading to predictable outcomes, and while there are very definite methods, they are open to a number of variables that make developing a feel for what you're doing an essential part of the process. Embrace this. Your sauerkraut will be unique to you, your kitchen, the time of year, where you live and your tastes. While accuracy is important in places, timings will vary with season, temperature, the freshness of the vegetables and more. We are not baking; we are interacting with the natural world. Taste, compare and enjoy the fun.

Treat these methods as blueprints. I have a rule I try not to break: the first time I make someone's recipe, I do it to the letter; thereafter, I'll embellish as I please. I see it as the right thing, what the author would have wanted. If it's not the original song I'm listening to, I want to hear it done differently while keeping its spirit, so once you know the tune, sing as you like.

And this is the beauty of sourness: the pleasures and flavours compound. The eating of a sourdough loaf is a splendid thing, yet never as pleasing as following its life cycle from creating and nurturing a sourdough starter, to folding and forming a dough and encouraging natural processes to develop it into a tight dome of delicious nutrition, to be the hand that judges when it has lived long enough under fierce heat to have the perfect balance of crust and crumb, to failing to resist the urge to slice into it, still warm, armed with too much salty butter.

If, like me, you are the sort to prevaricate over everything, from adopting a new fitness regime that will at last turn you into a specimen worthy of objectifying to what to do on your day off, you may take some persuading to make a loaf or to risk a jar of kombucha fermenting in your kitchen: if that's you, hop to the recipes, and I'll take a bet that you'll be quietly persuaded to venture back to these early pages eventually, because flavour and pleasure always win, in the end.

SOURDOUGH

I often have a book on the go that I dip into once in a while, rather than read front to back. At the moment, there's a Sinatra biography, some short stories and the one that turned my mind in more ways than one, *The 100-Year Life*. Its premise being that the linear climb of life expectancy over time is now such that if you were born in a Western country this century, you have a 1 in 2 chance of living to 100. My daughter has a 50:50 chance of a telegram from the monarch.

That steady upward slope also implies that perhaps her father might have a little longer than he was taught at school: he, I, might be only halfway through. The thought is quite refreshing: now is not the time to give on up those things I haven't got around to yet. It is precisely the moment (isn't it always?) to resolve to populate life with simple everyday pleasures.

So, I resolve to make it to 99. I'm already at the point in life where few things thrill more than a cancelled arrangement, so dodging a 100th birthday party should bring a special, final glee – and the prospect of another half century leaves me with no excuse not to fill it with the pleasure of exceptional bread. I suggest you do too.

Not all mass-produced bread is entirely terrible: there are days when I crave a doughy, soft white loaf to carve into doorsteps, to toast and eat hot, sodden with salted butter. Acquiring a full stomach through deeply pleasurable eating is a joy denied many humans past and present, and we should revel in every last mouthful. That said, most mass-produced bread has the nutritional value of a bath mat. I think we can aim a little higher than that, at least sometimes.

Well-made sourdough is full of nutrition, vitality and – having been properly fermented before baking – arrives in your stomach ready to be digested; ready to nourish you.

If you are used to making bread in a machine using yeast, or have yet to try baking a loaf, the idea of making sourdough can seem a little intimidating; fear not. Yes, it is a step up from baking with yeast – much like painting rather than colouring in – but if you relax, are attentive and use your nose, eyes and hands thoughtfully, you'll be making special bread in no time.

I'm not interested in making good-for-you bread that lacks anticipation. Wherever that loaf is along the spectrum from soft, white, mild sourdough to deeply sour, dark rye loaves, the thought of eating it has to give me enough of a kick-start to lift my arse from the sofa to make it. Of course, as ever, I would encourage you to explore beyond your usual tastes, but do remember that there is no 'better' bread, other than that which you prefer, but if you find one that's both delicious and highly nutritious, you win twice.

There are as many methods for making sourdough as bakers, some much more complex than others. I've adopted and adapted many, always in search – as I am with exercise – for the way that gives the best results while not crossing into the tedium that makes me resent doing it. The way I make sourdough owes much to ex-River Cottage baker Daniel Stevens, Emmanuel Hadjiandreou and Vanessa Kimbell. Their advice given via books, The Sourdough School (see page 24) and in conversation has helped me improve the consistency of my bread as well as my understanding of the process. There are many avenues for the inquisitive sourdough maker to investigate, from hydration levels to the influence of different flours, and while I'm all in favour of palaver, I'm also in favour of making and eating the best bread most often. Hence the two methods I've given here are easy to adopt, readily adaptable to your day and, if the idea of kneading or washing up a mixer fills you with inertia, you'll be glad to know that both involve only a little stretching and folding instead. Both methods result in unfailingly excellent bread.

Why sourdough is better

Bread requires only four ingredients: flour, water, salt and yeast. Check the ingredients of a shop-bought loaf and you'll see quite a collection of unnecessaries. Supermarkets want to make bread as quickly, cheaply and with outcomes that are as predictable as possible, and that list reflects those aims.

Make your own bread and you have the luxury of using flour full of vitality, good mineral-rich sea salt, filtered water and natural yeasts that allow the bread to develop slowly and fully. This allows the flour to ferment well, to release carbon dioxide and to rise naturally as a result, making more of the flour's nutrients available to us and creating a more readily digestible loaf. Equally importantly, it has a deeper flavour, and – to many – a more satisfying texture.

With surprisingly little practice, you can easily and repeatedly make remarkable bread. Perhaps even with your first try. And in doing so, you'll uncover another pleasure: the easy palaver of mixing, folding, stretching and shaping makes those of us who do it feel – for a few moments at least – quietly content.

From a health perspective, the argument for eating sourdough above other bread is compelling. Blood sugar and insulin levels increase slowly and modestly after eating sourdough, compared with the pronounced spikes in both after eating most other bread. The likeliest explanation is that in allowing the bread to ferment over time, the starches in the flour are more slowly digested and assimilated into the body. This acidification (or souring) of the dough thanks to lactic acid also seems to improve the availability of beneficial minerals for our bodies to take up. All of this is useful to us directly, but long fermentation also makes the grain more digestively accessible to the microbiome of bacteria in our gut, the organisms responsible for helping us get the best from the food we eat: in effect, sourdough feeds us twice.

It seems probable that allowing the dough to ferment over time, so that the active bacteria has to work for longer to ferment outside the body rather than in it, produces bread that many people find more easily digestible. Anecdotally, my experience is that for many with low-level issues as a result of eating bread, such as bloating, intestinal discomfort and sleepiness afterwards, eating sourdough proved a revelation. As with all such things, if you are one such troubled, I'd advise cautious experimentation to see whether your symptoms are alleviated. You should at least get to eat some excellent bread.

A note on ingredients

Making your own food from scratch is your opportunity to be in control of what goes into your body, to feed yourself and loved ones as you see fit. Dilute the quality if practicality and inclination dictates, but please be aware that there are very good reasons why organic whole flour, filtered water, pure salt and wild yeast are the best starting points you can find.

Of course, making sourdough with ordinary ingredients is going to still be better than eating most other bread, so if what you have is flour that's nearing its best-before date, tap water and fine table salt, make the loaf.

Flour

Organically produced wholemeal flour, used as soon after it is milled as possible, is most beneficial to us. It is richest in a wide spectrum of antioxidants – compounds that act against free radicals that contribute to ageing effects and cancers – including vitamin E, carotenoids (readily converted in the body to vitamin A), flavonoids and ferulic acid. The last of these is a hugely powerful antioxidant associated with lower levels of heart disease, cancer and reduced cholesterol levels, and is found in greatest quantities in the outer layers of grain, which is why wholemeal flour is most beneficial to us. These elements degrade as the flour ages. Most often, I use strong white and wholemeal bread flours in varying proportions, although I have an affection for rye and spelt which I enjoy greatly, if less frequently than my standard loaf. When using other flours, be prepared to adjust the volume of water needed, as flours take up water in varying amounts.

Salt

The proportion of salt to other ingredients in most loaves is, you'd think, too small to warrant much attention: other than bringing a little crucial saltiness to the party, what else can a few pinches of salt contribute? A whole world of trace minerals and elements – magnesium, manganese and zinc among them – that are essential to bodily function, and ideally taken in small, repeated, confined doses. Spending your money on mineral-rich sea salts from artisan producers not only supports independent small businesses, it is giving your body more of what keeps it healthy over time. Importantly, these salts are without added chemicals, anti-caking agents and so on: you get the real deal. Salt also acts to draw the protein molecules in sourdough more closely together, giving a tighter, more stable dough.

Water

Tap water comes replete with chlorine and fluorine, both of which are intentionally disagreeable to most microbes, including natural yeasts. A water filter removes most and allows the natural yeasts to thrive; in the absence of a filter, leaving a bowl of tap water open to the air for a few hours or overnight allows most of the chlorine to degrade.

Sourdough starter

The first time I was given a pot of sourdough starter, I looked on it as I might a sample that a friend had asked me to deliver to the hospital: to be held at arms length, with suspicion, in case it made me ill. This is not the way to be with your starter: it should be your favourite pet, to be loved, attended to and enjoyed.

Where most shop-bought bread uses yeast to enliven the process, sourdough uses a starter, a simple mix of water and flour, on which bacteria act. This starter – like the starter motor on your car – is what gets the main process of breadmaking underway.

You can use any container for the starter and you can choose from a variety of flours: I'll tell you what I do, and you can go from there.

I should also say that if idleness or impatience gets the better of you, you can buy very good starters online: I've had most success with a starter from The Sourdough School.

Creating a starter is simple, keeping it alive similarly straightforward – but both are particular. Here's how.

Creating your starter

I use a 1 litre (1¾ pint) glass Kilner jar: the starter never takes up more than a third, but the open top and space makes stirring easy. A knickerbocker glory spoon makes the perfect stirrer. You'll need enough muslin to cover the jar's opening – this allows air in, nothing else.

250g (9oz) strong bread flour or rye flour
250ml (9fl oz) warm water
1 organic apple

Stir the flour into water that is just too cool to tolerate if it were tea until thoroughly combined. The consistency should be quite like expensive emulsion paint. You know the brand I mean.

Grate half the apple and stir into the emulsion. It has to be organic (to be unsprayed) and unwashed, as the wild yeasts living on the skin will thrive in the flour paste and kick-start the microbial activity on which all bread relies.

Cover the opening with muslin and secure with an elastic band or use the lid to keep it in place. Keep it somewhere warmish – comfortable room temperature is fine.

Over the next 12 hours or so, bubbles will start to form at the surface: this is a good sign. Carbon dioxide is being produced as the bacteria get to work.

After 24 hours, the yeast needs more to feed on. Tip half of your starter away: don't be tempted to keep more as it's crucial to build up a lively population of active bacteria, and tipping away half allows you to refresh the starter with new 'food' in the form of flour and water without accumulating an ever-increasing volume of starter.

Repeat this tipping away and refreshing for two more days. At the end of this cycle, your starter should be mature and ready to use. A good way to be sure is to carry out a float test: carefully spoon a dollop of starter on to the surface of a glass of water – if it floats, it's ready. If not, continue refreshing.

Maintaining your starter

Your starter is a living thing. It's a palace of majestic microbial activity, albeit one very well disguised as a pot of paint. Like you and I, it needs feeding to flourish.

How and when you feed your starter depends on how frequently you want to use it, but before adding more flour and water, you should reduce the volume of the starter either by using it (see sourdough pancakes and pasta on pages 71 and 72) or pouring some away.

I make a loaf every couple of days, so more days than not I stir in a little flour (60g/2¼oz or so) and as much warm water – usually a roughly equivalent weight – as needed to retain that consistency. If you are a once a week or less frequent baker, you have the choice of pouring away a little starter and refreshing on most days, or keeping your starter in the fridge (this slows down microbial activity) and taking it out, ideally the day before you intend to bake, and refreshing the starter.

Resurrecting a starter

Once in a while, you may leave your starter too long unloved. It may, like Chris and Gwyneth, consciously uncouple into a floury fudge drowned in a thin vinegar known as hooch. Almost certainly, it lives. Stir like crazy until a smooth incorporation is achieved. Take a clean jar and pour in a few generous tablespoons of the starter – 50ml (2fl oz) or so – and stir in 240ml (8fl oz) water and 200g (7oz) organic strong white bread flour. If you use wholemeal, rye or another flour, you may have to adjust the water a little to make a smooth, easy emulsion.

Leave your refreshed starter somewhere at normal room temperature – you don't need heat nor other enliveners. Bubbles should be apparent within around 12 hours. If it looks good and lively, it's ready to use. If you've used white flour, do a float test (see opposite). If after 36 hours you are not convinced it is resuscitated, pour away two-thirds, add the same quantities of water and flour and allow that to ferment for another 36 hours, after which it should be nicely recovered. In cases of extreme negligence, you may have to persevere for a week.

Everyday sourdough

This method is about the least you can do to create excellent sourdough yourself. It's all done over a short day, involves a floury kitchen surface only once and for a short time, and the results are consistently marvellous. It's even easy to tweak so that you do the first steps before work, and finish it off when you get back.

I've included two approximate timetables, to give a picture of how the process might be integrated into your day: one for if you are in, the other if you are out for the day. The timings are only indicative: tweak them to suit you. Don't let the start-to-finish times put you off, as your active time is minimal: perhaps 10 minutes to start, and another 5 minutes to shape and pop in the oven later.

Timetable

8am	Weigh, mix and fold
8.10am	Leave to autolyze
8.40am	Add salt and fold
9.15am	Fold and leave to ferment
1pm	Final fold and shape
1–2pm	Final rise
2.20pm	Refrigerate the dough
2.40pm	Bake
4.30pm	Ready to eat

Or, if you are out for the day:

7am	Weigh, mix and fold
7.10am	Leave to autolyze
7.40am	Add salt and fold
8.15am	Fold and leave to ferment somewhere cool
5pm	Final fold and shape
5.10–6.10pm	Final rise
6.10–6.30pm	Refrigerate the dough
6.30–7.15pm	Bake
8pm	Ready to eat

Ingredients

150ml (9 tbsp) starter
350ml (12fl oz) warm water
500g (1lb 2oz) strong bread flour
12g (½oz) salt
A little flour for dusting; rice flour is best

Weigh everything and have it to hand. Pour the starter into the large bowl, add the water and stir to dissolve the starter thoroughly. Tip the flour into the watery starter and mix together using your hand. It should come together into a sticky but workable ball. Don't worry if it appears to be bread with the worst cellulite – in no time it will be altogether smoother. Allow it to rest for 30 minutes, covered with a damp tea towel, to autolyze: this is the process whereby the flour properly hydrates and the gluten starts to develop as enzymes in the flour get to work.

Sprinkle the salt over the dough – this is not added earlier as it inhibits the autolyze stage.

Now for the folding. Wet your hands and take the furthest edge of the ball and stretch/pull it over and towards the nearest edge, trapping air (and incorporating the salt) as you do so. Rotate the bowl 90 degrees and repeat. You may need to anchor the main body of the dough with your other hand as you stretch the furthest edge towards you. Do this until you have rotated the bowl by 90 degrees 16 times, in other words you have completed four circles of the bowl. Leave the dough to rest for 30 minutes, covered with a damp tea towel.

Repeat the 16-time folding and turning steps with wet hands, and take a photo of the dough with your phone before you cover with a damp tea towel. Leave at room temperature (18°C/65°F or so) to ferment, until the dough has reached 1.5 times its original size - the photo helps you compare: this is likely to take somewhere between 3–5 hours if your starter is reasonably lively. Don't worry if it takes longer. If you are leaving the house for the day, place the dough in a cool room (or the fridge in the summer) to slow the process.

When the dough has reached the required size, carefully tip the dough on to a floured surface. Repeat the 16-time folding and turning steps with wet hands.

Next, the shaping. This is simpler in practice than it reads. Have your palms up and at 30 degrees to the counter, with little fingers starting against opposite edges of the dough (i.e. 3 o'clock and 9 o'clock). With a gentle pressure against the join between the dough and the work surface, push your left hand away from your body, with your right pushing towards you, in such a way as to slightly tuck the edge under the base – the dough should rotate clockwise as you do, creating a pleasing tight dome, while the gentle tension at its base helps steer how the loaf develops in shape as it bakes.

If using, lightly moisten a banneton (a house plant mister is ideal for this) and dust with flour to prevent sticking – I find rice flour, fine as it is, is best for this. Carefully lift the dough into the floured banneton (or a colander lined with a clean tea towel) so that the surface that was uppermost during shaping is down in the bowl of the banneton. Just before you cover it with a damp tea towel, take a photo with your phone. Allow the dough to rise to almost twice its size – this should take 1–2 hours.

Once it has risen (use the photo to compare), turn the oven on full, place a baking sheet (or baking stone if you have one) in the oven and put the banneton in the fridge for 20 minutes – this helps to stabilize the loaf ahead of baking.

Remove the baking sheet/stone from the oven and carefully tip the loaf from the banneton. If it sticks a little, a gentle shake usually works; employ a finger otherwise. Using a razor blade or a truly sharp knife, make four slashes around the top in the shape of a hashtag – this allows the bread to burst in a controlled way as it expands. Return the sheet/stone to the oven and very quickly mist the loaf with the water squirter – this creates a humid environment, which encourages the formation of that magnificent crust you're after.

Bake for 15 minutes before turning the temperature down to 200°C/400°F/gas mark 6 and baking for a further 25 minutes. It may take a little longer: the loaf is done when it sounds hollow when you tap the underside. Test again after 5 minutes if needs be, and again 5 minutes later if required. Allow to cool completely on a wire rack before cutting open.

Cast-iron sourdough

So-named as this method is both foolproof and as the loaf is baked in a lidded cast-iron pot which both retains steam, which gives a superb crust, and encourages the bread to rise rather than spread too far laterally.

This knead-less method uses more starter and less flour than the other, and is particularly handy if you have a lot of starter and want to save on flour, if your loaves tend to come out a little low, or if the timings suit your routine better than the first method. The addition of more folding and a longer, slower fermentation give a loaf that's usually a little more complex in flavour than the Everyday method, and one that is more fully fermented. There is, of course, nothing to stop you mixing and matching here: by all means use a cast-iron pot with the Everyday method, and/or try the rye as part of the overall weight of flour.

Timetable

6pm	Weigh, mix, fold, shape
Overnight	Refrigerate to ferment and develop
7am	Remove from fridge
8am	Bake
9am	Ready to eat

Or, if you are out for the day:

7am	Weigh, mix, fold, shape
10am	Refrigerate to ferment and develop
6pm	Remove from fridge
7pm	Bake
8pm	Ready to eat

Ingredients

300g (10oz) starter
350ml (12fl oz) warm water
430g (15oz) strong bread flour
100g (3½oz) rye flour
14g (½oz) salt
A little flour for dusting; rice flour is best

Weigh everything and have it to hand.

Pour the starter into the large bowl, add 325ml (11fl oz) of the water and stir to dissolve the starter thoroughly. Tip the flour into the watery starter and mix together using your hand or scraper. As it starts to come together, add a little more water if needs be to create a ball; it should be sticky but workable.

Cover with a damp tea towel and allow it to rest for 30 minutes. It should just be showing signs of swelling and bubbling a little. Add the salt and incorporate it by taking the furthest edge of the ball, pulling it over and rotating the bowl 90 degrees. Repeat until you have completed the circle a few times.

Allow the dough to ferment and develop under a damp tea towel for 3 hours, repeating the folding process every 30 minutes.

Now, for the shaping. Lightly dust a work surface and the banneton with flour. Scrape the dough on to the work surface; it will be quite tacky. Repeat the folding technique using floured hands or a scraper, pulling the far side of the dough over the centre and towards you, rotating the loaf 90 degrees and repeating until you have been around the dough twice. Flip the loaf so that the folds are on the bottom.

Have your palms up and at 30 degrees to the counter, with your little fingers starting against opposite edges of the dough (i.e. 3 o'clock and 9 o'clock). With a gentle pressure against the join between the dough and the counter, push your left hand away from your body, with your right pushing towards you, in such a way as to slightly tuck the edge under the base – the dough should rotate clockwise as you do, creating a mushroom-shaped dome, while the gentle tension at its base helps steer how the loaf develops in shape as it bakes.

Lightly flour the dome and – using the scraper to help – lift it into a floured banneton (or a colander with a clean tea towel inside) so that the dough's base is pointing upwards.

Place this in the fridge for 8 hours to retard the loaf – in other words to slow the fermentation and proving process down, while developing a more flavoursome loaf with a superior crust.

Remove the loaf from the fridge and allow it come up to temperature for at least an hour at normal room temperature (18°C/65°F or so).

Turn the oven on full and place a cast-iron pan with its lid on the top shelf. When it has reached temperature, remove the pan and carefully tip the dough in. Using a razor blade or a truly sharp knife, slash the surface of the dough four times in the shape of a hashtag to allow the bread to burst in a controlled way as it expands. Mist the loaf with the water squirter – this creates a humid environment, which encourages the formation of that magnificent crust you're after – then put the lid on and place in the oven.

Bake for 25 minutes before turning the temperature down to 210°C/410°F/gas mark 7, removing the lid and baking for a further 15–20 minutes. The loaf is done when it sounds hollow when you tap the underside. Test again after 7 minutes if needs be, and again 5 minutes later if required.

Allow to cool completely on a wire rack before cutting open.

DAIRY

A jug of milk is a vessel of potential, of magic waiting to happen. As much as we might ordinarily try to stop it from turning sour, if we allow or direct it to, the results can be extraordinary.

This white amalgam of proteins, enzymes, vitamins, fat, minerals and lactose can be steered in seemingly endless directions using bacteria, heat, rennet, acidity and patience to create yoghurt, creams, cheeses and more. Here, I've included my favourites, where the result or the process are defined by acidity.

All the dairies in this chapter are at least mildly sour, but it's the souring process and the ability to take the sourness further by allowing more time or introducing more acidifier that allows them all under the radar of my inconsistently applied rules.

If you've not made your own dairy before, tip a pot of yoghurt into a muslin and allow it to give up its liquid overnight; the resulting soft cheese, labneh – perhaps with a little honey, toasted almonds and a torn fig or two – will convince you that this way deliciousness lies. So much for so little effort.

Of course, not all cheeses and creams are sour, but many result from a souring process that is reflected in that familiar tang, however gentle, and happily, many are simple to make at home. I include my favourites, each the result of an acid directing the milk to separate into its constituent curds and whey. Ricotta, paneer and queso fresco are, in many respects, different bus stops in the same town: all it takes is a change of acidifier (vinegar or lemon), whether you leave the milk on the heat or not, and whether any squeezing pressure is applied that decides which is your outcome. For me, ricotta is best made with lemon juice and without heat; the best paneer involves vinegar, no salt and gentle heat when curdling; queso fresco (a sort of halfway house) uses lemon, heat and a good deal of salt. Despite such small distinctions in method, you'll find each cheese is differently delicious.

By all means substitute lemon for vinegar and vice versa, add the acidity a teaspoon at a time until the degree of split you require has been achieved, stir or don't stir as the curds are forming, allow the curds longer or shorter to drain; it's really up to you. It's all cheese, even if it doesn't have a name. You'll notice that lemon juice may add a gentle citrusy note to the cheese, whereas vinegar usually leaves a more neutral flavour.

Why make your own dairy
The techniques are so simple, the results so fine, and despite anything I say about rules, it's quickly apparent that once you have a little confidence, it is all there to be tweaked and played with as you like. If you are the contrary sort, by all means extend the fermentation time, allow a longer period of draining, add or leave out salt and/or herbs, and so on, and see if you like what you create. You may find you prefer my method, and at least I can say I told you so.

Either way, within a short time, you'll find that the yoghurt, the sour creams and the cheeses reflect exactly what you want to use them for. And being able to make your own yoghurt, cheese, milk kefir, creams or buttermilk is almost as happy-making as doing so. And it builds understanding, which is at the heart of cooking – and living – more rewardingly.

Buttermilk

Some of the finest foods are the leftovers, the by-products, the less-favoured bits. Devilled kidneys, chicken stock and fig leaf liqueur are enough to bring the judge's gavel down on that one. And so too, with buttermilk.

Buttermilk isn't something most have hanging around in the fridge, but it is very much worth getting to know. Aside from the delightful tartness that it adds to pancakes, soda bread and cakes, its acidity initiates a reaction with the baking agent that causes an effervescence, a release of carbon dioxide that lightens a cake, pancake or bread. Although a little of the sourness and some of the probiotics are lost in the cooking process, a gentle tang endures.

There are three similar yet significantly different entities known as buttermilk. There's 'traditional' buttermilk – the liquid 'leftover' of butter making; cultured buttermilk, created by introducing a bacterial community to milk; and a buttermilk substitute, created by adding a small amount of lemon juice to milk. Each has its advantages.

Traditional buttermilk is as simple to come by as making butter: whisk 500ml (18fl oz) full-fat cream until the fats grip the whisk, forming an untidy ball in the centre of its wire cage; what lies in the bowl is buttermilk. This form of buttermilk is barely sour and has little impact on a raising agent, but can be used in place of milk in most recipes. If you have an electric mixer, it takes just a few minutes on a medium setting. Strain the buttermilk through muslin to catch any remaining globules of butter and squeeze the globules and the mass of butter together in the muslin to extract all the buttermilk, which is now ready to use. To finish the butter, rinse it under cold water, then submerge it in iced water, kneading it to force out any remaining buttermilk. Repeat this 4–6 times with fresh iced water until it runs clear, then knead a little salt into the butter, form into a block and use as normal. Historically when making butter, the milk was sometimes allowed to rest at room temperature before whisking, allowing naturally occurring lactic acid bacteria to set to work partially fermenting (and lightly souring) the milk – essentially a halfway house between the traditional and cultured methods.

Cultured buttermilk is much more akin to sourdough or kombucha, in that a lactic acid bacteria 'starter' is added to milk to feed on the milk's lactose, and in so doing sour it. The starter comes in liquid or powdered form and instructions vary, but for most liquid starters add 100ml (3½fl oz) cultured starter to 400ml (14fl oz) milk (or any quantities that respect the 1:4 ratio) in a Kilner jar or similar, seal and allow to stand at warm room temperature for 24 hours. The result is quite yoghurt-like, thick and usually sourer than with traditional buttermilk, and is really wonderful eaten as you might yoghurt, or used in cooking. You can use it immediately, or it will keep for a few weeks in the fridge. Keep a little of the new buttermilk to be used as the starter for the next batch.

If time and circumstance dictate, you can shortcut to a buttermilk substitute simply by adding lemon juice to milk (15ml/1 tbsp lemon juice to 250ml/9fl oz milk), which has the effect of curdling and souring it. What this method lacks in subtlety, probiotic goodness and cultural richness, it half makes up for in expediency.

You can also buy buttermilk in an increasingly wide variety of outlets and online, and so too starters for cultured buttermilk (see above).

Yoghurt

Some things are so familiar that we no longer see how ludicrous they are. A few years ago, when explaining to a group of Dutch gardeners that you can start seedlings off in the airing cupboard, I was met with confused looks. It seems that airing cupboards aren't a thing in the Netherlands. 'So...' the nearest asked, '...you wash your clothes, you dry your clothes and then you fold them up into a small stuffy cupboard...?' I nodded. 'And you think this makes a difference?' I nodded. The group folded up like the aliens in the seventies Smash advert. 'You English, always making us laugh so many hard with your crazy ways'. An airing cupboard is a ridiculous notion, but if you are looking for somewhere to create yoghurt (and you don't live in the Netherlands), this may be the best place.

You may well be one of the sane ones wondering why you should bother making your own yoghurt. I promise, I used to be one of you. The reason is because you can, because it is such a great thing to be able to make, and because it is just that little bit better than bought yoghurt that you'll want to do it at least once in a while. I confess, I never saw myself as a yoghurt maker. This wasn't how it was meant to be. It's not exactly rock 'n' roll, yet somehow, and (surely) having exhausted every single other thing I've ever wanted to do, I found myself making yoghurt. And now I love to. Whatever next.

This is a fine recipe to do in the evening while preparing a meal – all it takes is a few minutes and a kitchen thermometer – so that you can leave the yoghurt to activate the milk overnight. Milk powder makes the yoghurt a little thicker, but I tend not to use it as I like the consistency without it, and as it seems a shame to add something processed and that I don't usually have around.

Makes approx 1.1 litre (37fl oz)

1 litre (1¾ pints) whole milk

100g (3½oz) organic yoghurt

5 tbsp milk powder (optional)

Slowly warm the milk in a pan, stirring occasionally to prevent it catching on the bottom, until it reaches around 45°C/113°F. Whisk in the milk powder, if you are using it. Add a couple of spoonfuls of the warm milk to the yoghurt in a cup to thin it and warm it through. Stir the thinned yoghurt into the milk.

Cover the pan with a warm tea towel and put it in a warm place overnight – perhaps in the, err, airing cupboard.

The next day, transfer to the fridge and let it chill thoroughly.

Crème fraîche and soured cream

Sour cream is one of those ingredients I've been tempted to think I can do without: yoghurt and double cream will cover most bases. Except when they don't, they really don't. Chilli with yoghurt rather than a splodge of sour cream is like a weak G&T; seemingly similar but really not. And while double cream can take care of the silky end of cooking with dairy, sour creams bring finesse and piquancy.

You'll find sour cream in the shops sold either as crème fraîche or soured cream: the last two letters of 'soured' are important. They signify intent; the souring was meant. In most cases, lactic acid bacteria have been introduced to cream to work their way through the sugars, enriching the result with probiotics and moving the pH into the acidic.

The difference between crème fraîche and soured cream is a wedge on the price, a little exotica in the name, and the degree of sourness and fat content. Crème fraîche is thicker than soured cream, a little less sour, and its higher fat content makes it more resistant to curdling. It is particularly useful when wanting to bring a little silky acidity or creaminess to soups and stews. I tend to use soured cream for when I want that tangy dairy next to, rather than within, a dish – on baked potatoes, with chilli or in dressings – and I use crème fraîche more for cooking.

As with buttermilk and cheese making, there are methods whereby you introduce bacteria as a transformative culture, or you can acidify the cream with vinegar or lemon juice. The choice depends largely on your time, inquisitiveness and desire for probiotic goodness via the bacteria. This method is weirdly simple.

My default homemade sour cream is perhaps more similar to crème fraîche than soured cream, but you can alter that easily: either shift the proportions in the recipe in favour of milk and less to cream (reducing the fat content, and making it more like soured cream), and/or you can allow the cream to stand on the kitchen counter for longer to extend the souring process.

Makes 380ml (13fl oz)

80ml (3fl oz) whole milk

1 tsp white wine vinegar

300ml (10fl oz) double cream

In a jar large enough to comfortably accommodate the ingredients, stir the cream and vinegar together, then add the milk, pop on the lid and shake well.

Undo the lid and cover with a piece of muslin held in place by a rubber band.

Leave it at room temperature for around 24 hours, then stir and taste. It may well be too thin, not sour enough, and in need of more time. Mine usually takes 40–45 hours to be how I want it. When it is as you'd like, stir, do up the lid and refrigerate. It will keep for a week or so.

Milk kefir

Think of milk kefir as drinkable, intensely healthy, delicious yoghurt. It's inexpensive and once you get used to the simpe process it is relatively predictable too. As with water kefir (see page 64), milk kefir is made using 'grains' – gelatinous, raisin-sized communities of bacteria and yeasts that feed on the milk's sugar (primarily lactose), producing lactic acid, a little ethanol and carbon dioxide in the process. The lactic acid lends a sour flavour and the carbon dioxide brings a soft fizz.

The grain will ferment batches of milk indefinitely if looked after. The grains can be stored for a few weeks in their liquid in the fridge. Slowly, the grains will multiply: this allows you to ferment larger batches, to give some to others to start their own kefirs, or to discard.

As well as the nutritive benefits of milk, kefir brings a wealth of probiotics. The fermentation process also breaks down the lactose in milk, which is one of the primary sources of dairy intolerance. I'm not overly enthusiastic about the flavour of milk kefir, but I am keen on its health-promoting qualities, so I use it in smoothies or stirred into yoghurt-y breakfasts.

Depending on how long you ferment the milk for, and the conditions in your kitchen, you may see the usual yoghurt-like appearance of kefir begin to separate into something more akin to curdled milk: this is normal. You can strain the curds from the whey and use them normally, or stir briskly to recombine.

As with most ferments, temperature is one of the variables that make this process as much about developing a feel rather than a reliance on the stopwatch. Room temperature can commonly vary between 17–24°C (63–75°F) and the impact that has on the pace of fermentation is considerable, so trust your eyes and nose rather than written timings. As a rule, the longer the ferment the more sour the result, and the more lactose is consumed in the process. If in doubt or just inquisitive, allow the fermentation a little longer – the grains won't be harmed and you might like it. If not, you'll find where your line is best drawn. Be aware too that seasonal changes, moving the grains to a new place or the randomness of life can cause thin or thick kefir, a shorter or longer ferment and so on: this is perfectly usual.

While milk kefir fermentation is anaerobic (it doesn't require air), you don't need to keep anything submerged in the way you might with sauerkraut, as the milk creates its own surface barrier of sorts and most of the grains sit low in the jar during fermentation.

Although creating milk kefir is possible using most kinds of milk, go for as high a fat content as you can (full-fat organic, ideally raw, is where they do their best work). Oh, and avoid UHT; along with 'never eat a biscuit that floats', this is as good a rule for life as I know. Goat's milk kefir is delicious, though a little funkier in aroma and flavour than cow's, as you'd expect. I've not tried other animal milks but if you enjoy their milk in its unfermented state, give it a go – it will work.

Makes 750ml (1¼ pints)

1–2 tbsp milk kefir grains

750ml (1¼ pints) organic whole milk

Place the grains in a 1 litre (1¾ pint) jar, add the milk, cover and allow to ferment at room temperature for 24–48 hours. Strain through a plastic sieve into a jug, using the grains to start the next batch. You can use the kefir in the jug immediately, or jar and keep in the fridge. You may also want to extend the fermentation a little by allowing the jarred, grain-free kefir another 24 hours at room temperature.

Ricotta

I never had a huge amount of time for ricotta until I made my own. I'd always found it a pleasing enough bus for driving bigger flavours about, but the freshness, the creaminess and the subtle flavour and texture of homemade ricotta elevate it into more of a delicacy to be appreciated for its gentle delights. It is so utterly rewarding to make, so entirely simple, with results disproportionately marvellous to the effort spent.

Historically, ricotta is made from the whey left over from making mozzarella, created from the proteins that mozzarella ignores, but given that few of us have access to it, and that mozzarella isn't a 'sour' cheese, this is an excellent version.

Makes 320g (11oz) or so

2 litres (3½ pints) whole milk

50ml (2fl oz) lemon juice

1 tsp sea salt

Gently warm the milk in a large non-reactive pan, stirring frequently, until just below a simmer. A food thermometer should read 88°C (190°F) or so. Remove from the heat, add the lemon juice and salt and stir quickly but gently in figure-of-eight swirls for half a minute.

The milk will start to separate and form curds. Allow the curds and whey to cool for at least an hour; if you're watching a match, longer is fine.

Line a colander with muslin and pour in the curdled milk. Leave to drain for anywhere from an hour to overnight, depending on how firm you fancy the cheese. If you are the impatient sort or short of time, you can twist the ends of the muslin to squeeze out more liquid after an hour of draining.

It's ready to use immediately or will last in the fridge for a week or so.

Paneer and queso fresco

On an overly Novemberish Saturday in late March, I made my first paneer. It cheered what would otherwise have been a grey weekend: there is a soft thrill in recognizing that you are doing something for the first time that you know you'll repeat again and again.

One of the things I love about homemade paneer is that it impersonates halloumi so well too, in flavour, texture and in refusing to melt despite heat's persistent knocking. I use it more as I would shop-bought halloumi – in salads especially – than as paneer might traditionally be used. Fried in a little olive oil, heavily dusted in harissa powder, it manages to retain its delicacy while taking on just the right amount of halloumi's squeakiness.

It is mildly sour: as my wife said the first time I made it, it tastes and smells 'a little miffy, in a good way', but the soft milkiness of its origin remains.

The proportions of milk to acidity are the same as for ricotta, but I don't add salt while making paneer, I add it afterwards if at all, as I prefer the texture.

For queso fresco, follow the same process below substituting the vinegar for lemon juice and stirring in 2 teaspoons of salt as you add the juice.

> ### Makes around 350g (12 oz)
> 2 litres (3 ½ pints) whole milk
>
> 50ml (2fl oz) cider vinegar

Pour the milk into a large non-reactive pan and bring it slowly to 88°C (190°F), just below a bare simmer, stirring (with a non-metallic spoon) once in a while to prevent the milk catching on the base.

Reduce the heat to low and sprinkle the vinegar over the surface. Stir for a minute or so, as quickly as you can while being gentle and not creating waves.

Turn off the heat and allow the milk to separate into curds and whey for 10 minutes or so.

Using a slotted spoon or sieve, lift the curds into a colander lined with muslin. Twist the muslin into a tight bag around the cheese and use a peg to secure it. In a large roasting tray or in the sink, place the muslined cheese between two chopping boards and weigh it down with a couple of cans of beans or similar. Allow the whey to drip out for 15 minutes.

Undo the muslin bag and place the cheese into a large bowl of cold water for 20 minutes to cool and set the cheese a little more.

Lift out of the water and store in a sealed container in the fridge. You can use it immediately, though it will last for a week or so.

VINEGAR

If the definition of being a proper grown-up is having booze in the house that isn't being drunk today, then having a few vinegars in the cupboard that we use thoughtfully must be a sign of higher consciousness.

It is, of course, a wonder we ever discovered vinegar, as it derives from alcohol; alcohol we don't consume. If you are one of the many who has dedicated long hours to ensuring that that exact set of circumstances never comes around, bear with me.

Almost everyone has vinegar in the house. Even my father, who had more of a short rota of evening meals than a repertoire, had a bottle of malt for unspecified deployment – it may have spent more time in the larder past its 'use by' than before it, but still. And yet few of us investigate vinegar beyond a bottle of red or white wine, or cider and (if we're feeling a little swish) maybe a balsamic. It is perhaps the great under-utilized ingredient of our kitchens. I hope to persuade you to use vinegar more frequently, that in exploring a wider variety of vinegars you'll discover flavours and subtleties that transform the simplest of creations such as salad dressings, and I aim to convince you to make your own. It's remarkably simple.

Most ingredients naturally high in sugar – such as fruit and rice – can become vinegar in a two-stage process, whereby naturally occurring (or introduced) yeasts consume the sugar and ferment it into alcohol, before acetic acid bacteria consume the alcohol and ferment it into vinegar. The name itself derives from the French *vin aigre*; literally 'sour wine'. Making your own vinegar allows you to jump in at either stage: the cider vinegar recipe on page 78 begins with the booze rather than the apple; the banana vinegar on page 82 thankfully starts with the fruit rather than drawing you into the frankly dark prospect of banana wine.

While acetic acid dominates vinegar (it usually makes up 4–8 per cent of culinary vinegars) thanks to the action of acetic acid bacteria in its creation, different fruit also contribute particular acids to the creation of the sour whole: for example, red wine vinegar carries tartaric acid, which is so much a part of red wine's profile, while cider vinegar inherits the more appley malic acid.

Vinegars tend to vary with geography and climate: where red wine dominates, so too its vinegar, with the same true of sherry, white wine, champagne and so on. This is reflected in regional recipes: sherry vinegar is a must for Catalonian romesco sauce, red wine vinegar for the chicken sauce in so many bistros in southern France, and so on. By all means though, swap one vinegar for another if you fancy or don't have the traditional one in the house. I'm much more disposed to white wine vinegar than to red, and my cooking reflects this.

Developing the urge to make your own vinegar, and to use a greater variety of (and better quality) vinegars goes hand in hand with a love of using vinegar enthusiastically. There are recipes herein where vinegar is very much prominent – the sauerbraten, most of the pickles, the chicken au vinaigre and more – but even a tablespoon or two can make a serious difference to what you eat. France taught me the gentle influence that vinegar can invisibly exert in making something taste somehow more of itself; just one day into a primary school trip

across the Channel (blushing brightly having been hauled before the pre-tea assembly not so much for eating a friend's TUC biscuits but for my denials), I sat dipping my spoon into a beige-orange soup; this wasn't anything I knew that answered to the name of soup. We had it to begin every evening meal that week and gradually I got to know and love it, but I didn't have the wherewithal to decode it. Years later, picking grapes south of Lyon, lunchtimes came with soup that rang so many bells from my childhood; my cheeks even flushed with recalled embarrassment. This time I could pick apart what was behind this quiet revelation: faint bitterness thanks to a hint of lovage, and a certain distant acidity. The cook enlightened me: 'If it's hot soup I use a splash of vinegar, if it's cold I use lemon'. Perhaps in my quiet desperation to appear continental and interesting, I have adopted this seasonal seasoning too.

Next time you make soup, try a tablespoon or two of vinegar stirred in just before serving and behold how it brightens and adds clarity to the flavours.

That same couple of tablespoons of vinegar, thoughtfully employed, help turn a glass of water into a deeply refreshing switchel, enable you to make a cheaty soda bread (see page 68) when the shops are shut, to create soured cream (see page 41), help retain a firm texture when cooking beans, and to make the white gazpacho (see page 130) the glory it is.

In Harry Rosenblum's excellent *Vinegar Revival* he urges us to 'sprinkle vinegar on dishes you normally wouldn't', including rice, kale and so on. And he's so right: try it on everything. Roast potatoes with a splash, a capful in scrambled eggs, a teaspoon on a fried egg – there's no end to the inquisitive pleasure. It's easy to get quietly obsessed with using just a tweak of vinegar here and there, and you'll find your food all the better for it – even for knowing where it doesn't quite work: too much in that leek and potato soup and the leeks draw out almost enough to give you squeaky teeth.

Quality is important. Vinegar should taste of the alcohol from which it derives; ideally, it should bring to mind the fruit that was its grandparent. You should relish the flavour of a capful. There are a couple of sherry vinegars in particular that I'm unable to use without taking a little nip of myself. Of course, as with olive oil, there is little sense in using an expensively acquired, special vinegar when it will be cooked at high temperatures for a long time or when large quantities are used, but if it's for a dressing for leaves or being used in its raw form with some finesse, you'll notice the difference a good-quality vinegar makes. I've included some excellent suppliers on page 282, but do investigate more widely and don't die having never made your own: it is simple and the results almost always superb.

Vinegar does require a little care. It may be strong, it can even burn; treat it as you would chilli, sucking the tiniest of dabs from your little finger first, before moving on to a small sip on the tip of your tongue. As with wine, draw air in almost a reverse-whistle: this aerates the vinegar, and has the effect of shaking its component flavours out. A little concentration at this point should reveal something more complex than delicious acidity – its fruity origin, possibly woody notes from any time spent in a barrel maturing, bright citrus and any number of subtleties. Just take a moment to let it collapse on your tongue and unravel its flavours – that should help you come up with ideas for how you might use it.

Why make vinegar

In the same way that run-of-the-mill wine may get you tiddly with little accompanying pleasure, an okay vinegar will offer acidity but lack finesse, subtlety and the ability to bring depth or character. While adding sharpness, it will often only do so much to enhance the flavours with which it sits. Avoiding disappointment is relatively straightforward: spend just a little more on a good vinegar (see page 282), or dedicate a few short minutes to making your own.

There's so little to making your own vinegar that it makes you wonder why on earth we aren't all doing it as a matter of course: if you possess the ability to place a jar in a cupboard and forget about it for a short time, you have the necessary skills to make astonishing vinegar.

While reasonable quality vinegars are widely available, many are pasteurized – rid of the bacteria that created them. Search for a raw vinegar, ideally 'with mother'. This signifies that some of the bacterial community (the mother) that turned the alcohol into vinegar is still present. This is what you need in order to start your own batch of vinegar, as well as being beneficial for your own consumption.

Homemade vinegar is a living entity, with beneficial bacteria involved in its creation as well as enriching every glug with probiotic goodness. There are any number of medical benefits associated with vinegar consumption – believe those you wish – but from the wealth of evidence, it seems highly plausible that vinegar's amino acids at the very least help moderate blood lactic acid levels, and in so doing boost energy levels and reduce muscle stiffness.

The process of making your own is simple. Leaving a jug of non-fortified alcohol exposed to the air encourages acetic acid bacteria to start working on the slow conversion to vinegar. This can take many months, so rather than simply waiting, we can introduce a culture by way of the mother – very much as you do with a sourdough starter when making a loaf – that will kick-start the process. A pleasure of making your own vinegar is that these days, with the easy availability of alcohol from other parts of the world, you can celebrate your own culture – cider into cider vinegar is the default here in my native Devon – or dress up in another's.

Making your own vinegar also gives you control, allowing you to arrest the fermentation process when the flavour suits. As soon as you bottle the vinegar, oxygen is taken out of the equation and bacterial activity slows to a halt, though the flavours mature and develop still. Bottling vinegar to allow it to mature allows you to taste and compare different vintages, to identify where along the line of their development you like them best.

Of course, even when you have made vinegar, the experimentation needn't stop there: vinegar readily takes on flavours left to infuse in its acidity. Elderflowers, raspberries, tarragon and rosemary are four of my favourites, each easily made, following the principles outlined in the recipes on page 81. There is really little more to it than allowing a flavour you enjoy to surrender some of itself to the vinegar, over anything from a few hours to several months. As long as you taste regularly so that you can remove the infusing flavour at a good time, it's hard to go wrong.

The process
Nature wants us to have vinegar, and who are we to argue. Leave a glass of wine out for long enough and you'll end up with vinegar.

This is the end of a delightful process whereby sugar transforms into alcohol, which in the presence of air becomes vinegar. It means that pretty much anything heavy with sugar – from apples to tomatoes to honey – can become vinegar. Practically speaking, it is much easier to start making vinegar with non-fortified, non-distilled alcohol than with its parent fruit. Cider, white wine, ale and red wine are the easiest, offering fairly reliable and delicious outcomes.

The essential process is little more complicated than covering a wide-necked jar of alcohol with muslin – this allows air and acetic acid bacteria in, while excluding bugs. Acetic acid bacteria, present almost everywhere, consume the ethanol in booze and convert it to acetic acid: this is what makes vinegar sour.

It is not just the ethanol in alcohol that contributes to the process: along with micronutrients present, good levels of tannins tend to give consistent and high quality results, hence red wine, dark beers and cider are among the easier vinegars to make well.

As vinegar is created, a cloud of cellulose forms at the meeting of liquid and air; an indication that the bacteria are doing their work. This cloud may even become a slippery rubbery disc, and in either form is known as the 'mother'; it may grow, perhaps even have 'children' in the form of extra discs. Should the mother sink, weight is likely to be to blame: fish it out, carefully peel any children from it – they grow on top – and use them for other vinegars or pass them on to friends.

Make sure you decant your vinegar once it has completed its transformation, otherwise you may end up with a jar of cellulose and little liquid.

While making vinegar is a delightfully imprecise process that's as much to do with feel, your taste and the particularities of your kitchen, there are a few very important guidelines.

Your starting alcohol should be no more than 8 per cent ABV. If it's higher, then you should dilute with water to reach 8 per cent or lower. To work out how much water to add, it's all about proportions.

> Here's an example, using 1 litre (1¾ pints) of 10 per cent ABV wine:
> • The wine's ABV is 2 per cent higher than the maximum 8 per cent allowed, i.e. the wine is 25 per cent too strong (2 is 25 per cent of 8).
> • Therefore, to dilute your alcohol to 8 per cent you should add 25 per cent of the volume of wine, as water: 250ml (9fl oz).
> • So adding 250ml (9fl oz) of water to 1 litre (1¾ pints) of wine gives you 1.25 litres (2¼ pints) of diluted wine that has 8 per cent ABV.

There are two core methods of making your own vinegar. The first is for when you want vinegar from a single original – cider vinegar, red wine vinegar and so on. This 'single estate' results in a vinegar that unambiguously reflects its parent. The advantages of this are a degree of predictability in the flavour and a little refinement. The second method is delightfully rustic, whereby any half glass, end of bottle or disliked alcohol is added to an ongoing ferment: you add to it when you like, and draw off using a spigot as you want. It is wonderfully unpredictable in outcome, though usually very good; what it lacks in finesse it makes up for in home economy and rustic charm. The cider vinegar recipe (see page 78) is the 'single estate' recipe I use most frequently, and as unpromising as it sounds, you must make banana vinegar (see page 82) – it's quite something.

Homemade single estate vinegar

Choose your booze: a bottle of red or white, a flagon of cider or a can or two of ale. Add it to a large wide-necked jar, along with one sixth of the volume of vinegar with mother. Shake to combine and aerate the liquid. Don't shake the jar again – the transformation into vinegar depends on acetic acid bacteria, which create a mother at the surface of the liquid that may sink and impair fermentation if disturbed.

Cover the opening with muslin and fix in place with an elastic band. Place the jar somewhere dark at normal room temperature and leave to ferment. By all means smell or taste the fermenting booze whenever you like – it should start to smell of vinegar after a few weeks.

After two months or so – depending on the nature of the booze, humidity and temperature – your vinegar should be sour and delicious. If not, leave it a little longer. When you're happy with it, strain through muslin to capture the mother, and bottle the vinegar.

Your vinegar is ready to use, though it will continue to change in character, usually mellowing and developing complexity. If you can bear to, leave a bottle aside for a year to enjoy its changing qualities. The mother can be used to kick-start your next batch of vinegar.

Homemade whatever you got vinegar

Rather than starting with booze, as with the homemade single estate method, this rustic blend starts with a litre of finished vinegar with mother. You can start with less or more, but a substantial volume of vinegar allows you to add a glass or two of booze now and again (remember the conversion to ensure it is no more than 8 per cent ABV) without drowning it.

Because the starting liquid is vinegar and is frequently fed with new sugars in the form of alcohol, microbial activity is lively, and the booze is converted into vinegar more rapidly than with the single estate method.

That said, it is as pleasingly unpredictable as the frequency and volume of the leftover alcohol you add: add little and often and it will be quickly transformed by the greater volume of active vinegar; add a great deluge from an abstemious party and you can expect sour alchemy to take longer. Your tongue is the decision maker; use the vinegar when it tastes as you like.

Verjuice

In a poll undertaken during idle conversation and lacking everything in scientific rigour, it seems most people have a vague idea of what verjuice is, but few have used it. We should put this to rights.

Verjuice is, as most knew, 'somewhere between vinegar and wine'; it means 'green juice', pressed from unripe grapes. It has a long history, certainly from medieval times, though in recent decades the widespread availability of vinegar and lemons, as well as booming wine demand, has seen verjuice become less common than it once was. It inhabits the land between vinegar with its sharp sourness, lemon juice and its delightful sharpness, and wine with its polite, gentle acidity. It's not ordinarily to be found on supermarket shelves, but easy to acquire online from specialist suppliers.

Verjuice is a little more approachable than many vinegars, adding a unique, subtle acidity with a hint of sweetness to anything from salad dressings to cocktails. It's especially good with strawberries and kiwi. And you actually must make the mint and verjuice granita on page 254 if you know what's good for you.

It is a peculiar thing – almost rewarding as a little nip while cooking but just too close to wine not to feel hard done by that it's not. I reach for it where a little finesse is called for, when I'm looking to allude to sourness, or take a fine sandpaper of acidity to a dish rather than a rasp. If you have a really good chicken to roast, pouring 120ml (4fl oz) or so into the pan after a high-temp sizzle makes a beautiful, lightly sour gravy with the roasting juices.

It easy to make your own verjuice if you have access to unripe grapes: de-stem the grapes and whizz them in a blender briefly. Strain through a muslin, applying pressure to encourage as much juice to be released as possible. Depending on the variety of grape and its relative ripeness, this 'green' juice may be gently sour or full-on sharp, so taste and use as you wish. Bottle quickly, as oxidization will cause it to turn brown: work quickly and it'll be light fawn; slowly and it'll resemble malt vinegar. Homemade verjuice will only keep for a week or so: keep it in the fridge and use it swiftly To extend its shelf life by a few days, plunge the grapes into boiling water and then immediately into cold water and drain, before whizzing in the blender; to make it last for another week or two, add citric acid (½ teaspoon to 2kg/4½lb fruit) as it blends. The latter makes the juice a touch sourer, so only do that if you are sure you won't be using it soon.

You can make a less sour version too, using those white supermarket grapes that lean on the sharp side. The juice will be gentler, and you'll need to bear that in mind when making dressings and so on. You can also make one from any sour and/or unripe fruit: blackberries and gooseberries are exceptional, as are unripe tomatoes, strawberries and quince.

A good verjuice is worth paying for – the delicate hand it offers is worth the money. It should be present yet calm, with a bright, fresh acidity that doesn't intrude. It should very obviously remind you of fruit, ideally the one that was its parent. Where you think vinegar's edge might be in danger of taking a recipe beyond where it ought to go, verjuice is often the key.

Shrubs and switchels

A shrub, from the Arabic *shurb* meaning 'to drink', is a delicious interweaving of vinegar, sugar and fruit that is fermented and either drunk as it is, lengthened with water or eased into a cocktail. These drinking vinegars are likely to have originated from the necessity to preserve fruit in an easily digestible, nutritious form that could be taken on long journeys, and became popular in the nineteenth century. They tend to be both sweet and sharp and may be enriched with herbs and spices. The art and pleasure of a good shrub is in exploring combinations of vinegar, sugar source, fruit and herbs that are both characterful and complex.

Switchels are synonymous with the southern States and the Caribbean where they evolved as refreshing drinks (also known as haymaker's punch) for workers. They are similar to shrubs, though unfermented and usually less sweet: in many ways they are to pickled vegetables what shrubs are to fermented vegetables. What switchels lack in probiotic goodness and complexity, they make up for in zing and immediacy – they're typically ready in a few hours rather than weeks – and I can't get enough of them, especially in summer.

Although cider vinegar's agreeable fruitiness is the base I use most for shrubs and switchels, wine vinegars work beautifully too. These easily created drinks are similar to salad dressings, in that as long as you thoughtfully combine ingredients with consideration for the sweet, sharp and aromatic, you can and should play as you like.

Shrubs usually need lengthening either with still or sparkling water, or depending on the shrub's make-up, with something like ginger ale or tonic. One part shrub to five parts diluter is a good ratio to experiment with.

The core shrub recipe is simple: lightly crush your chosen fruit (or vegetable) and combine with sugar and any spices or herb you fancy. Allow to ferment for 24 hours or so at room temperature, before adding vinegar allowing to mature for at least a week, and anything up to a year in the fridge. I tend to leave it 10–14 days, tasting every now and again after a week. My default ratio is 4 parts sugar to 5 of vinegar. As with most things edible, this may occasionally go wrong: if the shrub becomes quite fizzy, cloudy or changes colour more than beyond the subtle, discard it.

Try the couple of recipes on pages 264 and 265, and experiment from there: I have made excellent shrubs using champagne vinegar, apple vinegar and rice wine, with sugar syrup, honey and any number of different sugars. If you use good quality ingredients, it will show in the resulting drink. Preserves can also be turned into shrubs very well: the mojito marmalade (see page 122) combined with extra mint and vinegar to taste is very special. Whether you add white rum and soda water to it is a matter I shall leave to your discretion.

Your finished shrub can be used in so many ways: they tend to work very well in bringing a fruitiness and an aromatic sweet–sour to cocktails and dressings, as a drizzle over roasted fruit, meat or vegetables, or as part of a salad dressing. They're especially fine simmered and reduced to create a gastrique – an excellent French sweet–sour sauce – either on their own, or in the pan that's cooked whatever the sauce is going with.

FERMENTED FRUIT AND VEGETABLES

Humans have spent much of their time on Earth finding ways to hold off the decay of food through drying, salting, burying, smoking and more; fermentation works less aggressively against the natural trajectory of decomposition, by creating favourable conditions that slows the breakdown and harnesses it to our culinary and nutritive benefit.

As with the other souring skills, the process of fermenting fruit and vegetables is remarkably simple. Only salt and (sometimes) water are needed to ferment fruit and vegetables: the rest – the bacteria – are already present, unseen. If your ears close over at the mention of a chemical reaction, it's enough to know that in the absence of oxygen and in the presence of salt, 'good' bacteria change the nature of fruit and vegetables into something altogether more healthy for you. The bacteria produce lactic acid in the process – known as lacto-fermentation – which lends many of these foods their characteristic sourness. That's it. The proportions are important, the temperature and timespan highly influential, but you can proceed direct to the recipes and get going if you prefer.

If you are a little more inquisitive, read on.

When fruit and vegetables are fermented, their building blocks are transformed into more digestible compounds that not only feed us, they nourish us too. Under the right conditions, lactic acid bacteria convert sugars and starches to lactic acid, and (potentially) carbon dioxide and alcohol, in the absence of oxygen. Nutrients, enzymes, vitamins and a wealth of gut-friendly bacteria also result from this partial transformation.

These useful bacteria are present in the air, on the surface of vegetables and other foods, and they can also be introduced either from a fermented food such as yoghurt or a bought culture such as kombucha, a SCOBY or kefir grains.

Whatever their origin, the fermentation process is largely about creating the perfect conditions for encouraging these lactic acid bacteria to thrive – in the case of fruit and vegetables, by using salt and excluding oxygen. The bacteria's action creates an acidic environment which lends sourness, improves nutritional value and preserves the food, while inhibiting redevelopment of harmful bacteria.

That's really it: observe the two rules of using the correct amount of salt and packing the ingredients tightly in order to exclude air – or more specifically, the oxygen on which undesirable organisms depend – and it's quite difficult not to create something delicious and health-giving. Part of getting used to fermenting fruit and vegetables is the idea that it is 'ready' when you like it, rather than at a definite point: once it tastes as you want, moving it to the fridge will dramatically slow its progress.

The principles

You can ferment pretty much any fruit or vegetable you fancy: if it's edible, fermentation is likely to enhance its nutritional value, create new flavours and textures and, with guidance and a little luck, prove delicious.

The crucial ingredients for fermented vegetables and fruit are few, and the conditions under which they combine simple to achieve. A sealable jar, fresh vegetables and/or fruit and salt are what you need. The process is uncomplicated and easily adaptable, the results usually ready within a few days or so.

The vegetables or fruit should be unsprayed, ideally organic; the salt should not include preservatives (they inhibit fermentation); the water should ideally be filtered. If you don't have a water filter, tap water will almost certainly be fine in any event, or you can leave a pan of water open to the air for a few hours to allow the chlorine to evaporate.

Ripe, undamaged fruit and vegetables are best – the fermentation process is driven by the lactic acid bacteria munching their way through the sugar, and underripe ingredients won't give a pleasing balance between sweet and sour, while overripe ingredients can lose their texture entirely. The rule is to rinse the fruit/vegetable and your hands but don't scrub; and sterilize the jar.

While there is much you can experiment with in other aspects of fermenting, the proportion of salt required for fermenting fruit and vegetables is immovably anchored at 2 per cent of the weight of the prepared fruit or vegetable. And by 'prepared', I mean the total weight of whatever you are fermenting once it's been cored, stoned, peeled or whatever you are doing to them first.

So, if you are fermenting cherries (see page 104) you weigh the fruit once the stalks and stones have been removed and calculate the amount of salt as 2 per cent of that weight. For example, if you have 400g (14oz) of de-stalked, stoned cherries, you'll need 8g (¼oz) of salt.

The core method for fermenting vegetables and fruit is typically to chop, grate or slice whatever is to be fermented and combine it with the salt in a bowl. A notable exception is the widespread method for fermenting a whole or half cabbage – I tried it once and the results were underwhelming, but by all means pick up the challenge should you be so minded.

If it is a robust vegetable such as cabbage or carrot, you can rub the salt in a little to encourage moisture to be released, otherwise just stir. Allow the salty fruit/veg to sit for a few minutes or longer, and then stir once more, allowing it a few minutes more in the bowl. Transfer the salty fruit/veg to a Kilner jar, using a rubber spatula or similar to ensure every last drop of saline and every grain of salt is captured. Pack tightly into a jar, excluding air bubbles as much as possible, and add a weight on top to keep the fermenting ingredient submerged in the liquid that forms as the salt draws out its water. I use either a pickle pebble (a glass weight) or a food bag part-filled with water to press down on the fruit/veg to ensure it is kept beneath the surface of the brine. It may take a few hours for the brine to fully appear; so check a little later and top up with a little (ideally filtered) water if needs be.

Set the jar somewhere at reasonable room temperature but away from direct sun, and allow to ferment. Once you have closed the lid on your jar, bacteria present within consume any oxygen in the air bubbles and at the top of the jar. Once complete, conditions are anaerobic (i.e. without oxygen), which is perfect for lactic acid bacteria to dominate. Depending on the temperature, it takes a couple of days or so to reach this point.

The next phase is a little livelier: the lactic acid bacteria accelerate their work, and as well as the characteristic sourness developing, you may see little pockets of carbon dioxide released as a gentle fizz. This phase can last anywhere between five days and a month.

Don't be afraid to taste at this point, and any other that follows: how else will you get to know how the flavour and texture changes over time and be able to decide when it's to your taste? A week is a typical period of time for fermentation to be far enough through its arc to be both delicious and nutritionally enhanced. A delicate white bloom may appear on the surface: fear not, this is a harmless kahm yeast taking its opportunity to flourish before the conditions have become too acidic. Scrape it off with a spoon and discard it.

After 4–6 weeks, the bacteria are likely to have reached their peak. Anywhere on this journey, you have the choice to stop the fermentation when the flavour is as you'd like. The easiest way to do this it to transfer your ferment to the fridge. This drop in temperature arrests the process, and in effect freezes the flavour as it is.

The longer it ferments, the sharper it becomes as the bacteria consume more of the sugar: arresting the process too soon is as bad as leaving it to acidify beyond the palatable, so taste regularly.

At this point, you can either drain the fruit/vegetable, rinse and freeze them for indefinite use, or delve into the jar whenever you fancy. The salty, nutrient-rich fermenting brine is worth saving to use in soups, stews, dressings and wherever else that salty, sour liquid might suit.

It's not uncommon for new fermentistas to err on the cautious side and arrest fermentation at the first hint of sourness: it is perfectly fine to do so, though do allow yourself a little longer each time. As you acquire a taste for the sourer, you'll want to explore the boundaries a little more – generally speaking, the nearer the peak of lactic acid bacteria activity, the greater the digestive benefits, so this is to be encouraged.

Sauerkraut

Occasionally, most often when I'm making sauerkraut, it occurs to me that while this process appears to be me using bacteria to create something delicious in a jar, that perhaps, given that the house in which I live and the tumble of digestive equipment inside me provide the perfect environment in which the bacteria thrive, that it's them farming me. If so, they are most welcome: I shall carry on regardless, the unwitting star in this microbial Truman Show.

Sauerkraut is perhaps the best-known fermented food. Traditionally made with white cabbage and maybe with a little caraway or fennel to enliven it, sauerkraut is created – as with most vegetable and fruit ferments – by introducing salt, which creates an environment favourable to beneficial bacteria and not to those potentially harmful.

There are numerous variations, but the essential elements of it remain constant. So by all means, tweak the recipe as you like – some favour juniper berries or bay in the mix – as long as you keep the proportion of salt at 2 per cent of the weight of the prepared cabbage.

In order to create a special sauerkraut with a consistent texture and level of fermentation, shred the cabbage evenly, pay careful attention to the proportion of salt and taste a little every other day to see how it's progressing, before putting it in the fridge when its sourness suits, to arrest the process.

I think it was Eddie Izzard who observed that once you've written on a banana you never want to write on anything else; similarly, running the sharpest of knives in the tightest of shreds through a squeaky white cabbage makes you wish never to cut anything other again. Happy slicing.

Makes a 1.5 litre (2 ½ pint) Kilner jar

1.4kg (3lb) cone-shaped or round white cabbage, prepared

28g (1oz) fine sea salt

4 tsp caraway seeds

12 juniper berries

Finely shred the cabbage and place in a large bowl. Sprinkle with the salt and massage it through the cabbage. Leave for 30 minutes, during which time the salt will begin to draw out the water from the cabbage. Mix in the spices.

Lift handfuls of the spicy cabbage into the jar, using a pestle or wooden spoon to press down and pound the cabbage after every handful. The slick of moisture clinging to the shredded cabbage will rapidly form a lake as the cabbage gives up more of its moisture and makes its own brine.

It's crucial to keep the cabbage submerged: use a folded cabbage leaf, a glass pebble or a food bag partially filled with water to do the job. Close the lid.

From this moment, your cabbage begins its gentle fermentation. Two days of developing thin beads of fizz at a warmish room temperature will get your cabbage to an enhanced state of nutritional being, but another fortnight of slightly cooler room temperature will allow both the flavour and the beneficials to enhance.

Try a little every couple of days: your kraut will reach the level of sourness you require in anything between 2 days and 6 weeks. When it does, keeping it somewhere cool like a larder slows further fermentation; refrigerating it virtually stops it.

Kimchi

At its simplest, kimchi is sauerkraut taken to the spicy end of the spectrum, but that journey to the hot side turns kimchi into something that is quite a different experience. The transformative process is similar – useful bacteria turn the vegetable or fruit carbohydrates into lactic acid, creating an environment where less interesting bacteria are discouraged and complex flavours generated – but the presence of chilli and fish sauce, and – if you fancy – shrimp paste, creates something quite unique.

To many – especially Koreans – kimchi is their ketchup, their pickle, their coleslaw. As well as being marvellous as a spicy side dish, it embellishes and enhances when added to recipes – try the taco (see page 211) and the kimchi pancake (see page 217). The enlivening hot sourness that kimchi brings makes it quite the seductive accompaniment to pretty much anything from sausages to burgers to fries to grilled fish to soup to noodles. And, if you are making it correctly, don't be surprised if it blows the cobwebs away and the sinuses clear.

Classically, kimchi is made by creating a hot, salty, sometimes fishy, usually garlicky sauce in which to coat vegetables (and sometimes fruit) and allowing the whole to ferment. Chinese cabbage (aka napa cabbage) is perhaps the most commonly kimchi-ed vegetable, its delicate yet substantial leaves are perfect for retaining enough substance through the fermentation process while surrendering sufficiently to the sauce and the acids created. Daikon radishes are another widely popular kimchi favourite. In truth, most vegetables are kimchi-able, though some work better than others, without there being any particular rules as to why. Carrots, leafy greens, cucumber and radishes are very much in the 'yes' gang.

The reference to ketchup is not insignificant; kimchi really is almost a way of life in countries such as Korea rather than simply an occasional accompaniment. While you can buy ready-made kimchi, it is entirely usual for families in its spiritual homeland to make numerous kinds of seasonal kimchi, using the best of what's available; once you have the basic method, you can do the same.

Once you are in the habit of making it, you'll find yourself quietly thanking the kimchi gods time and again. Tired yet hungry? Kimchi and noodles is yours in minutes. Only eggs in the house, and idleness has overtaken? Kimchi pancake (see page 217) saves the day. And so on. Whether pulled pork could do with enlivening, or you have a burger in need of some love, that jar of spicy ferment has the answer.

I have to confess, I am less keen on kimchi made with shrimp paste. It smells like a tram driver's glove. I realize this is exactly the sort of hostage to fortune that will haunt me when I come to write 'The 50 Best Shrimp Paste Kimchis' book in a few years, but still: I'm happier without the degree of fishy funk that comes with shrimp paste. If you like the idea, and many do, add half a teaspoon when adding the fish sauce and see how you get on.

This recipe is a halfway house that uses fish sauce instead of shrimp paste: if you prefer to leave it out by all means do, adding kelp powder for a little salty umami if you fancy.

Fills a 1 litre (1 ¾ pint) jar

2 Chinese cabbages, about 1kg (2lb 4oz), shredded

5 tbsp fine sea salt

2 garlic cloves, finely chopped

5cm (2in) piece of fresh ginger, peeled and finely chopped

2 tbsp Korean chilli flakes

2 tsp fish sauce

2 carrots, grated

5 spring onions, thinly sliced

In a large bowl, rub the salt thoroughly through the cabbage and allow it to soften and form a little brine for an hour or so.

In a small cup, make a paste by combining the garlic, ginger, chilli flakes and fish sauce.

Using a colander, drain the cabbage so that you retain some of the brine in a bowl. Combine the carrot and spring onions with the cabbage, and stir through the hot fishy sauce. By all means add a little of the brine if you need to loosen the mix. Spoon the kimchi into a jar, pressing down well to exclude air bubbles. Use a freezer bag part-filled with water to keep the vegetables submerged and seal the jar. Allow the kimchi to ferment for 5 days at room temperature. Taste it: it should be pleasingly sour and lovely, yet not what you'd call fizzy. If so, transfer it to the fridge to slow fermentation dramatically; leave it another few days (or weeks!) if you prefer it sourer.

FERMENTED DRINKS

I was weaned on dandelion and burdock, and limeade, which served as the gateways for sparkling Ribena and in turn those bottles of elderflower pressé that once emptied some plant a candle in, inadvertently signifying both middle-class aspirations and working-class origins. I have a long and close relationship with pop that requires a great deal to be unfaithful to, yet I promise you, kombucha, tepache, water kefir and their infused, embellished and second-fermented children will call you, as they have I, into a torrid affair.

You might hesitate at that first fermented sip of the unknown but that first draught will suck you in to an easy world of delicious, nourishing tipples.

The main difference between fermented foods and drinks, is that the fermentation of most drinks needs oxygen, and in many cases calls on you to add a colony of bacteria to stimulate the process. With kombucha – a fermented tea drink – a specific SCOBY (symbiotic culture of bacteria and yeast) in the form of a rubbery disc floats on the surface, busily creating good things; with kefir, a clutch of 'grains' resembling miniature white ball bearings enriches water (or milk), and so on.

Each drink has its own spectrum of flavours but all share a marvellous sour tone, as mild or strong as you like, along with a good dose of the bacteria that can do so much to promote health and vitality. Sugar is the bribe that the bacteria require to get to work, converting it into acids and carbon dioxide and feeding a thriving community of organisms, ready to infect your gut with goodness.

Why make fermented drinks

I've found that unconsciously my days have now evolved so as to be punctuated with kombucha, water kefir, or with a tepache or two – if my daughter hasn't finished them first. I worry those bottles of fermented liquid as I once did my childhood, dimple-necked bottles of cherryade.

I notice its absence when I'm away or the brewing batch isn't quite ready to take over where the last one ended and, unscientific as it may be, I feel a notch down on the energy levels without it, missing a bit of pep.

Fermented drinks have similar benefits to fermented foods: aside from the pleasure of drinking them – and really, these are special – the dose of beneficial bacteria boosts your gut's ability to digest food more effectively. Many report they feel their immune system is stronger, dietary intolerances are reduced and their general sense of wellbeing and health is improved.

I also found fermented drinks to be the way that most people overcome any hesitancy with fermented foods. An inch of kombucha with breakfast, a small glass of raspberry and hibiscus kefir with a meal, or a measure of tepache with rum, mint and ice, are easy to accommodate in your day. They build trust for anyone hesitant, using the best bribe of all: pleasure.

Kombucha

If there was a way of disguising that kombucha was fermented tea, I would. It doesn't sound appealing. A dark, stewed, foaming gravy appears in the mind's eye, yet the reality is delightfully different. Originating in China, kombucha has become more widely popular in recent years; thankfully, it is simple and cheap to make, and is endlessly adaptable to the flavours you fancy.

Rather than relying on airborne bacteria and those already in the ingredients as sourdough and many other ferments do, a 'starter' colony (known as a SCOBY) is introduced to a jar of sweetened tea, by way of a gelatinous disc. I know, it's not getting any sexier; stay with me. In the presence of air, this miraculous community of organisms works its way through the sugars to convert them into lactic acid, transforming the deeply unappealing cold, strong tea into a light, bright drink that's somehow full of uplift in both flavour and effect. Genuinely, it is as delicious as the process sounds not.

If you remain unconvinced, shell out on one of those uncompetitively priced bottles you can now find anywhere from supermarket shelves to high-street café chains; they are easily good enough to convince most that kombucha is a fine thing. Well, homemade is a different league.

As with most ferments, when you stop, the process is entirely down to your preference for the flavour: do go beyond your usual boundaries once in a while, as the sourer end of things makes a refreshing change and carries with it a greater wealth of probiotic goodness.

You can also use kombucha as a gently acidic ingredient in cooking, my favourite way being in mayonnaise (see page 119) where its subtlety is really something special. By all means allow your kombucha to ferment a little longer if you are looking for more of a vinegar-like kick; a few more days or even weeks of fermentation will bring a steady increase in sharpness.

The method is almost as simple as letting tea go cold. Order a SCOBY plus a little starter kombucha (see page 282 for sources) and you are away.

As with the first pancake in the pan, for reasons unknown but likely to be everything (including you) settling down into the process, your first batch or two might be just okay rather than extraordinary; you might get lucky, but if not, stay with it and you'll soon be making incredible kombucha.

One variation you absolutely must try is to use white tea and honey; it is extraordinary.

Makes 2 litres (3 ½ pints)
2 litres (3 ½ pints) water, ideally filtered, as chlorine can inhibit fermentation
1 heaped tbsp tea of your choosing (green, black, white etc)
160g (5 ½ oz) sugar
1 SCOBY
2 tbsp starter kombucha

Boil the water and pour over the tea, leaving it to brew for 15 minutes or so (less or more will affect the flavour so experiment to your taste).

Clean a large 2.5 litre (4 ¼ pint) jar with boiling water rather than antibacterial products as they can affect the fermentation process. Once clean, pour the tea into the jar straining out the tea leaves. Add the sugar and stir until dissolved. Leave to cool completely before adding the SCOBY and starter kombucha.

Cover the top of the jar with a muslin or clean tea towel and fix with an elastic band, leaving in a light place, but not direct sunlight, for about 10 days. The amount of time is dependent on how warm your room is and how sour you like the kombucha so keep tasting to find the right point. I find that two weeks is about right for us and I usually make this batch once a week so we have a constant supply. Decant the kombucha into two 1 litre (1 ¾ pint) ceramic flip-top bottles.

At this point you can drink it or do a second fermentation to add more fizz and flavour. You will need something sweet to feed the fermentation process alongside any other ingredients such as herbs and spices; this can be juice or whatever fruit you fancy. A reasonable ratio of kombucha to juice/fruit is around 6:1. My favourite ingredients for second fermentation are raspberries, mulberries, apple, pear and quince, with herbs such as lemon verbena, star anise, fresh ginger or turmeric. Most commonly, I add a handful of raspberries and a broken up sheriff's badge of star anise to the bottled kombucha and allow it to ferment for two or three more days. Pop the top to release some of the gas that is produced as the gentle fizz develops. Refrigerate to chill the kombucha and all but stop the fermentation process.

Water Kefir

Like kombucha, water kefir is a fermented drink teeming with beneficial bacteria. If made with just kefir grains, water and sugar, it tastes like a mild, gently fizzy lemonade: it's almost impossible not to like. That said, it is improvable with any number of embellishments.

I'm not suggesting you drink water kefir because it's good for you: drink it because it's delicious, remarkably easy to make, the perfect substitute for high-street fizzy drinks, virtually free and because it's good for you. Like kombucha, water kefir is made using a SCOBY (symbiotic culture of bacteria and yeast) that feeds on the sugar in a weak syrup, turning it into beneficial acids, numerous B vitamins and enzymes, but most importantly it is a truly fine drink. And it indulges my love of pop.

The SCOBY takes the form of water kefir 'grains' – raisin-sized, squidgy, translucent globules of beneficial bacteria, yeast and polysaccharide (a substance produced by one of the bacteria, *Lactobacillus higarii*). You may be reassured to know that water kefir grains have been used for centuries, with Mexico or Tibet as possible origins though so widespread in their use that it's impossible to be certain.

These bacteria metabolize sugars into lactic acid, a small amount of ethanol and carbon dioxide, which means you get a lightly sour drink with a gentle fizz that is enriched with a whole range of probiotic goodness. The alcohol produced is almost negligible – around 0.5 per cent ABV is usual; less than the Top Deck shandy of my youth.

The grains multiply slowly; when you have more than you need, pass them on.

Don't use water kefir grains for making milk kefir (see page 42), or vice versa – the bacterial composition of the grains is particular to each.

Making water kefir is a simple process of fermentation, to which you can hitch another carriage should you wish. The initial fermentation takes around three days, after which you can add a little extra fruit or sugar to reinvigorate microbial action and generate more fizz, should you wish. Sometimes I do, sometimes not.

Follow the instructions that come with your kefir grains if you like; my default method is below. Do this a few times and you'll find it a pretty flexible undertaking: you might let it ferment for a week, you'll realize you no longer measure the ingredients any more, and that rather than always planning what's next, the solo kiwi in the fridge or those slightly over-the-top raspberries may well dictate the flavour of the next batch.

The choice of sugar makes a big difference to the flavour. I almost always use white cane sugar as I prefer the flavour of the results, but it's fair to say that unrefined, raw sugars provide a greater range of minerals for the kefir to operate in, so do try them. If you like that slightly treacly taste that flits across your tongue right when you think it's not going to, then use an unrefined sugar as the kefir will be more mineral-rich. If using other fruit, you can omit the raisins.

60g (2¼oz) sugar
handful of raisins
a little under 1 litre (1¾ pints) filtered water
3–4 tbsp water kefir grains

Add the sugar and raisins to a 1 litre (1¾ pint) jar along with around a quarter of the water. Swirl the water in the jar to part dissolve the sugar, then add the water kefir grains and enough water to leave 2cm (¾in) or so space at the top.

Cover the top with muslin and secure with an elastic band, then leave somewhere warm for 72 hours or so. An airing cupboard will result in a quick ferment, a cool room may need longer. When the water kefir is ready, it will be a little cloudy, almost chalky looking, slightly tart, possibly with an easy fizz. The surface of the liquid may look a little rubbery. This is all normal.

Strain the contents of the jar through a plastic sieve into a jug, and pour into a flip-top bottle. At this point, the kefir is perfectly delightful to drink – if it has had a short fermentation, it is likely to be sweetish, a little bland even, with a soft fizz. You can allow it to develop further in the bottle – the more it ferments, the more sugars are transformed into acids and the sourer it becomes. If you keep it out of the fridge this will happen more quickly.

You can also activate a second fermentation by adding another source of sugar for the bacteria to feed on and convert in the bottle. A teaspoon of sugar, a few slices of ginger, kiwi or banana, or some hibiscus flowers are just a few possibilities to get you going. After a day or two the flavours will intensify and the fizz will become more pronounced following a second fermentation. Again, this happens more quickly out of the fridge. Do 'burp' the bottle by releasing the top a couple of times a day.

Your kefir is ready when you like the taste of it. That's really the only rule there is, although I shall introduce another: by all means have favourites, but try different flavours, and leave timings a little longer sometimes to see how the final drink is different. You never know, you might discover something you prefer.

As long as you keep them active, the grains can be used indefinitely. As soon as they are strained out of the fermented drink, they should be submerged into another batch. If you are going on holiday or have enough water kefir to be going on with, prepare a batch as normal, then keep it in the fridge – this ensures the grains have something to feed on but greatly reduces the rate of fermentation. They can be kept for a few weeks in this state, before using again.

Your strained water kefir will keep for 3–4 days out of, and for up to a month in, the fridge.

SMALL THINGS

SODA BREAD

If you are the unconfident sort in the kitchen, make soda bread. It convinces even the terminally incompetent that Nigella lives within them. This is the easiest of loaves, moving from lightbulb moment to breakfast, lunch or snack in only an hour or so. The flavour and texture is somewhere between a classic loaf and a scone, making it equally happy with sweet or savoury, sharp or salt.

Soda bread is not really so sour, but aside from the ghost of sharpness that balances the whole, it is the sourness within – buttermilk, usually – that enlivens the bicarbonate of soda into action.

This is not a recipe to fuss over; make it like you're nonchalantly trying to convince someone you know what you're doing – move quickly, shape it as you like – in order to get it in the oven before the bicarb loses its mojo.

The ratio of buttermilk to milk isn't crucial – I chose it because commercially available buttermilk tends to come in that size pot, and that split actually makes a perfect loaf – but you can use all buttermilk, or sour milk, or whole milk with a tablespoon of lemon juice to curdle it. Do try the vinegar version, below too.

Makes 1 medium-sized loaf

225g (8oz) plain white flour, plus more for dusting

225g (8oz) coarse wholemeal flour

50g (2oz) rolled oats

1½ tsp salt

1 tsp bicarbonate of soda

1 tbsp honey

280ml (9½fl oz) buttermilk (or sour milk, or milk with 1 tbsp lemon juice)

170ml (6fl oz) whole milk

Preheat the oven to 200°C/400°F/gas mark 6 and dust a baking sheet lightly with flour.

Put the dry ingredients into a large bowl and stir to combine. Pour in the honey, buttermilk and milk and mix together with your hand to form a tacky dough.

Shape into a dome on the baking sheet and slice a deep cross into the surface. Bake for 40–45 minutes; the crust should be golden and the loaf sound hollow when tapped on the bottom.

Cool on a wire rack if you prefer a hard crust (I so do), or wrap in a clean tea towel if you are the sort of heathen who prefers a soft crust.

Vinegar soda bread

Soda bread can also be made with vinegared water in the absence of dairy, using the same other ingredients as above, and is the work of 3 minutes plus 26 minutes in the oven. This is proper 'there's nothing in the house to eat and I can't be arsed/am too hungover/it's too late to go out' food. Stir 1 teaspoon of salt (less if you fancy, but I like it salty) and ½ teaspoon of bicarb into 270g (9½oz) plain flour. Whisk an egg (optional, but crustier if used) and 2 teaspoons of vinegar (your choice) into 150ml (5fl oz) water. Make a well in the dry mixed ingredients and pour in, stirring like you mean it. Bring it all together sharpish, using more flour to make a slightly tacky but not sticky dough and plonk in a not-overly-finessed mound on a parchment-lined baking sheet. Slash an X in the top and bake at 210°C/410°F/gas mark 7 for 25 or so minutes. A smasher.

SOURDOUGH PANCAKES

I suspect my daughter loves these pancakes more than she loves her father; if you add maple syrup, no wisp of doubt remains. All you need to add for the perfect Sunday morning is good coffee, the papers and the prospect of a good lunch cooked by someone else.

Allowing the batter to ferment overnight gives a pleasingly robust texture even to thin pancakes, and it rounds out the flavour beautifully – even an hour of fermenting makes a difference. There are, of course, some Sundays when you wake ready to eat a telephone directory or in need of something of heft to counteract last night's overindulgence: in which case, make and use the batter immediately. It still tastes delicious.

Of the many toppings that work, figs with honey and yoghurt, maple syrup and banana, rhubarb and yoghurt, bacon and blueberries (honest) and, of course, lemon and sugar, are a few great combinations to get you started.

They also make great wraps: a generous sprinkle of chaat (see page 96) on the uncooked surface of the pancake before you flip it gives them a wonderful, deep, gently sour, spiciness. Leftover summer rojak with either halloumi or leftover chicken and plenty of sambal oelek dressing (see page 113) make a fine filling.

Makes around 12 pancakes

240ml (8fl oz) milk

160g (5 ½oz) sourdough starter (see page 30)

140g (4 ½oz) plain white or spelt flour

pinch of salt

4 eggs

30g (1oz) melted butter or vegetable oil, plus more to cook the pancakes

Whisk the milk, sourdough starter, flour and salt to a smooth batter in a large bowl. Leave to ferment in the fridge overnight, or for an hour at room temperature.

When you are ready to cook, whisk in the eggs, along with the melted butter or oil.

Wipe a large frying pan with just a little butter or oil and place over a medium heat. Add a ladleful of the batter at a time, swirling to create a thinnish pancake, around 20cm (8in) wide. Cook for 1 minute until golden brown, then flip and cook on the other side until golden and cooked through. Repeat with the remaining batter.

Ideally, a loved one will be cooking these pancakes for you, serving them straight from pan to plate: otherwise, keep them warm under foil in a warm oven.

SOURDOUGH PASTA

You don't have to be poor as Blackadder's church mouse 'that's just had an enormous tax bill on the very day his wife ran off with another mouse, taking all the cheese' to make your own pasta; nor is it just for those kicking around in a sea of time and tenners looking for something to do. It's a proper pleasure in the doing and the eating: simple, quick and as good a use for sourdough starter (that would otherwise form a slurry in the food recycling bag) as I know.

This works best for tagliatelle-style ribbons and simple shapes rather than for filled pasta. It freezes very well, although freeze the pasta in a single layer on a tray before tipping into a freezer bag. And bear in mind that due to the moisture content of the starter, ribbons are a bit brittle for storing, so use them within a day tor two.

Makes enough for four

240g (8½oz) sourdough starter (see page 30)

360g (12½oz) pasta flour (I use ⅓ 'oo' and ⅔ fine semolina), plus a little more semolina for rolling

4 egg yolks

a large pinch of salt

In a large bowl, mix all of the ingredients well and knead until really smooth and supple, adding a bit more flour if the dough seems too wet.

Cover with a damp tea towel or clingfilm and (depending on your day) allow it to prove for either an hour at room temperature or 3–4 hours in the fridge, until it has increased in volume by about a third.

If you've proved the dough at room temperature then chill it for an hour to make it easier to shape.

To shape, cut the dough into 2cm (¾in) squares. Dust well with extra semolina and use your finger or a palette knife to scrape across the work surface to create a soft curl – imagine you are stroking a very small cat.

Place in a single layer on a tray while you shape the remainder of the dough. Freeze or use immediately. Cooking in plenty of salted, simmering water for 1–2 minutes from fresh, or 3–4 minutes from frozen.

GOOSEBERRY AND SAGE FOCACCIA

Twenty years ago, I took a train to Corsica. On the way, I stayed for a few days on the Ligurian coast, where the olive oil is good and buttery. I did little other than walk, sit by the waves and eat focaccia, listening to the crazy frogs croaking the last of the light down the hill to the sea.

I left to spend a couple of weeks with the scent of *maquis* – Corsica's take on the wild aromatic scrubland that coats much of the Mediterranean coastline – in my nose, and the ghost of that incredible bread still in my mouth. I am now ruined for all but excellent focaccia; thankfully this is one such.

At first glance, making focaccia looks a palaver, but it requires only a few minutes of your time here and there. This is quite a wet dough: don't be tempted to dry it up by adding more flour. If you have my unquenchable appetite for focaccia yet a propensity for midriff expansion, make this when there are people coming to share it with.

Makes one large loaf

400ml (14fl oz) warm water

10g (¼oz) active dry yeast

250g (9oz) bread flour

250g (9oz) 'oo' pasta flour

1 tsp fine salt

10 tbsp extra virgin olive oil, plus more for brushing and serving

around 35 small sage leaves, half finely chopped and half left whole

300g (10oz) gooseberries, topped and tailed

2 tsp coarse or flaky sea salt

2 tbsp sugar

Stir together the water and yeast in a large bowl and let it sit for 5 minutes until foamy.

Add both flours, the fine sea salt and 2 tablespoons of the olive oil to the yeasty water and mix well for about 10 minutes, either by hand or using the dough hook on a mixer, until it becomes a bit less sticky. Add the finely chopped sage towards the end. Brush a large bowl with 1 tablespoon of olive oil, tip the dough in, cover with a tea towel and let it rise in a warm place until it doubles in size, about 1–1½ hours.

Brush a large baking tray – or two smaller ones – with 1 tablespoon of olive oil. Tip the dough on to the tray and use your fingertips to flatten the dough. Brush the top with more olive oil. Cover with a tea towel and leave for 20 minutes.

Dip your fingers in olive oil and press and stretch the dough into a large rectangle, leaving dimples from your fingers in the dough and pressing the whole sage leaves into some of the dimples. Cover again with the towel and let it rise for about 40 minutes.

Preheat the oven to 230°C/450°F/gas mark 8.

Brush the top with 1 tablespoon of olive oil and scatter the gooseberries and coarse sea salt evenly over the dough, nudging the gooseberries into the dough a little. Bake for 25 minutes until the crust is golden brown and puffed around the edges, sprinkling the surface with the sugar 5 minutes before the end. Generously anoint with the remaining oil.

Try and allow it to cool for at least 10 minutes, before serving warm or at room temperature.

CIDER VINEGAR

The marvellous transformation of apples to juice to cider to vinegar is really one of patience and a gentle guiding hand. By all means, start where you wish on that journey; at my age, it's with cider. There are so many recipes for making cider vinegar and they vary wildly in process and timing; most work, but in my search for something more predictable than 'pour cider into a wide-necked jar and wait', I've settled on (and tweaked) Harry Rosenblum's readily repeatable process from *Vinegar Revival* for turning alcohol into vinegar.

You won't be the only one who's dedicated time to stopping that exact process occurring through expedient consumption, but once you've fallen in love with vinegars – and if you haven't already, you shall – you'll be doing all you can to hurry it along.

Most cider is below 8 per cent alcohol (our homemade cider is 7 per cent) and if it's cider you're using, it won't need diluting. If you are following this process with wine, strong ale or by some coincidence, using the same cider we had for our wedding party from a local cider circle (it was 13 per cent!), then dilute appropriately (see page 50). Wine that is 16 per cent should be diluted with the same volume of water; to 12 per cent wine, add half the volume of water, etc.

Makes 1.1 litres (2 pints)
1 litre (1¾ pints) cider
125ml (4fl oz) raw vinegar with mother (see page 49)

Pour the cider into a 1.5 litre (2½ pint) Kilner jar along with the raw vinegar. Cover with a piece of muslin, secure with an elastic band and place the jar somewhere cool and dark to ferment.

By all means check it regularly, but don't stir: after a month, the mother should start to appear on the surface. You may smell vinegar at this point. By all means taste too: it's good to experience the transformation of flavours.

After two months, carefully sneak a spoon beneath the mother and taste the vinegar. It should be delightfully sour, with more than a little evidence that it is the child of apples. This transformation may occur more quickly, it may take a little longer, depending on temperature and the particularities of your home. Let your taste guide you.

When it's how you fancy it, decant into bottles, saving the mother for the next batch of vinegar, instead of using the raw vinegar. You can use your vinegar immediately or allow it to mature and become more complex. Both are marvellous.

ROSEHIP VINEGAR

My wife is a plant botherer, delving deep into their medicinal and other beneficial qualities. It is not unusual for me to find a new mini collection of jars and bottles by the kettle, and find my enquiries regarding their culinary promise not always met in the affirmative: 'No: poultice.' 'I wouldn't; it protects against athlete's foot.' 'It's for the dog's breath, so...'

Once in a while, there will be something met with almost a dare: 'Try it', and I do. And this is one of the best: a rich, lightly floral, bright vinegar.

There is little point in me giving exact weights and volumes as the method is simple and depends entirely on how much you find. The best rosehips for this should be whole and fresh, from dog rose (*Rosa canina*) or Japanese rose (*Rosa rugosa*), picked just as they have reached their deepest colour and are starting to soften to the touch.

Although you can use wine vinegar, I like this made with cider vinegar, unpasteurized and with mother for preference (see opposite).

Put the whole rosehips in a lidded glass jar and just cover with cider vinegar. You can speed up the infusion by slitting the rosehip's skin, but be careful not to open the hip up or you will release the many tiny hairs, which are best reserved for use as itching powder, down the collar of an irritating child or spouse.

Leave on a sunny windowsill for 3 or 4 weeks and then filter through a sieve and bottle. It makes an excellent dressing and a pleasant change to straight cider vinegar in the switchel (see page 267).

TARRAGON VINEGAR

Tarragon is really the Bob Dylan of herbs: so very wrong a lot of the time, but when its right, right doesn't get much better. Chicken, broad beans, tomatoes, cream, green beans, leeks and potatoes are all so much better for its smoky aniseed loveliness. And eggs, how did I forget eggs? And hollandaise with tarragon's excellence becomes béarnaise – even my dog's collar would taste good slathered in béarnaise. Here, a few sprigs left to infuse in vinegar becomes a kitchen essential, awaiting deployment in dressings, sauces, mayo and more, and it's a piece of cake to make.

By all means use cider vinegar for this; I just prefer white wine vinegar. I know some people add a few spices here and there; that way lies madness, smothering too much of the subtle end of tarragon's flavour and scent. A few Szechuan peppercorns is all I'll allow, if you insist.

Makes (surprise surprise) about 500ml (18fl oz)

500ml (18fl oz) white wine vinegar

6 large sprigs of French tarragon

Pour the vinegar into a tall jar or bottle, add the tarragon, seal and allow to infuse for a fortnight or so. Taste it after a week – it may be as you like. Pull out the tarragon (or decant and discard if easier) – this is important as it can get a little woody and stale-tasting if left too long. Store in a cupboard – somewhere cool and away from light.

BANANA VINEGAR

Life is too short for many things: sorting out the cupboard under the stairs and Formula 1 for starters. You may, not unreasonably, wish to add 'making banana vinegar' to that list, but as Asimov said, you'd be wronger than wrong.

Firstly, both these methods take just a few minutes of your life, and secondly, the vinegar that results is peculiarly extraordinary. Making your own vinegar allows you to taste it regularly, to get to know it as it develops – it will be floral, fruity and sharp in varying proportions as it matures. It's ready when your mind starts to turn to it for everything from a salad dressing to ceviche.

Makes 200ml (7fl oz)

5 bananas

Banana vinegar 1

Although this is quite the tribute to fawn, the results are marvellous and quick to arrive. Use very ripe, brown bananas for the best results.

Peel the bananas and mash them thoroughly in a bowl. Spoon the pulp into a jar – it shouldn't be more than two-thirds full – close the lid and leave it somewhere cool and dark.

After a week, a delightfully unattractive banana fudge will rise to the top and liquid will form beneath. Over the next fortnight or so, the liquid ferments into vinegar. Leave it longer and the flavour will become more sour.

When it has the flavour you like, spoon out the fudge (don't worry about a few surface moulds), pour the remainder through a fine sieve into a jug, and then into a sterilized bottle.

Makes 1 litre (1 ¾ pints)

200g (7oz) unrefined granulated sugar

200ml (7fl oz) maple syrup

2 tbsp cider vinegar with mother

1 litre (1 ¾ pints) water

skins of 9 very ripe (ideally black), preferably organic bananas

Banana vinegar 2

Add the sugar, syrup and vinegar to a sterilized, wide-necked 1.5 litre (2 ½ pint) jar, along with a third of the water, stirring to dissolve the sugar. Add the skins and as much water as needed to leave an inch or so of air at the neck. Cover with a piece of muslin, secure with an elastic band and store somewhere cool and dark.

A little white yeast may appear on the surface; lift it off with a spoon if so. Over the weeks, a thin opaque film may appear on the surface – this is a SCOBY (see page 60) and is exactly as it should be. The skins may rise to the surface, in which case you can either use a fermenting stone or a food bag of water to keep them down, or just push them below the surface from time to time to reduce the chance of mould.

In 2–3 months you'll have a litre of wonderful vinegar. Taste it after 8 weeks. You'll probably like it but fancy a little more acidity, so check weekly.

PASSION FRUIT CHILLI SAUCE (AJI DE MARACUYA)

I was once suspicious of passion fruit: the seedy soup within its wrinkly egg looks more like something you'd have left over once you'd eaten it, than the actual fruit itself. It looks alien, how I'd imagine octopus spawn or the eggs of Madagascar's deadliest spider to be – and yet it has become one of my favourite fruit.

That heady, aromatic, sweet/sharpness now sits on more pavlovas and fools than are good for me, sharpens up my favourite ceviche (see page 182) and helps make this chilli sauce so extraordinary. Aji (chilli) de maracuyas (passion fruits) hails from Chile, and in that way perhaps only food can, the scent, colour and flavour of this hot, aromatic and sour sauce disproportionately informs my sensory picture of a place I've yet to visit. One day.

Make this once and it will become a go-to for everything from roast chicken to avocado salad. By all means add finely chopped coriander if you fancy.

Makes enough for four

1 yellow pepper, roughly chopped

3 passion fruits – squeezed and strained of seeds

2 tbsp vegetable oil

1–2 hot yellow chillies, deseeded

juice from ½ juicy lime

sea salt and freshly ground black pepper

sugar, to taste

Boil the yellow pepper in a pan of salted water for about 10 minutes until just softened. Drain and refresh under cold water, then drain again.

In a blender, combine the passion fruit juice, yellow pepper, vegetable oil, chillies, lime juice and a big pinch of salt and some pepper and blitz until smooth. Check the seasoning, adding more salt and maybe some sugar (depending on the sweetness of the passion fruit) to taste. Use quickly as it only keeps for a day or two in the fridge.

PICCALILLI

Of the many ways in which my father was peculiar, allowing certain delicious foods into the house only for a fortnight over Christmas may have taken the festive biscuit. Walnuts, After Eights, ginger cordial, dates, and – sadly – piccalilli, were no more likely to be in the house in February, August or November than Elvis. I refuse to bring any child of mine up in such appalling conditions.

There are few things to which this delightful preserve doesn't add a welcome sharp jolt: I've enjoyed it with pork pies, ham, cheese, a roast dinner; I'm not above dunking crisps into it. It is the last pickle I would be without, and homemade piccalilli is an extraordinary upgrade on the perfectly agreeable jars in the shops.

The basic method here owes much to Pam Corbin – whose preserving advice has been generously dispensed over the years from just a few miles along the road – though it evolves with every new batch I make. I made piccalilli once without onion and have preferred it like so ever since. I want crunch and bite, so I go for the ingredients below, but if you are the sort of heathen who thinks it better to include cucumbers, tomatoes, peppers and other unsuitables, be my guest.

Makes approx 1 x 1.5 litre (2½ pint) jar (or 3 x 500ml/18fl oz jars)

1kg (2lb 4oz) washed vegetables, cut into pieces no larger than 2cm (¾in) – I go for equal amounts of sugar snaps, mini courgettes (or usual size cut into quarters lengthways and sliced), cauliflower and carrots

50g (2oz) fine salt

600ml (1 pint) cider vinegar

80g (3oz) honey

120g (4oz) granulated sugar

25g (1oz) cornflour

4 tsp ground turmeric

4 tsp English mustard powder

3 tsp celery seeds

3 tsp fenugreek seeds

3 tsp yellow mustard seeds

1 tsp cumin seeds

1 tbsp crushed coriander seeds (or 1½ tbsp harissa for harissa piccalilli)

Ensure the vegetables are relatively dry. Place them in a large bowl and sprinkle with the salt. Turn the vegetables over to distribute the salt thoroughly, then cover and leave somewhere cool for 24 hours.

Rinse with cold water and drain well.

Put 550ml (19fl oz) of the vinegar in a pan with the honey and sugar and bring to the boil. While that is happening, stir the cornflour in a bowl to ensure it is lump free, add the spices and combine well. Add a little of the remaining vinegar to the bowl and stir into the spicy cornflour to create a paste. Gradually add the remaining vinegar to thin the paste a little.

Once the pan of sweetened vinegar has reached the boil, reduce the heat a little and add the paste a little at a time, stirring constantly. Boil for a few minutes to thicken the sauce, stirring occasionally.

Turn off the heat, put the vegetables in sterilized jar(s), pour the spicy vinegar over and seal immediately. To be honest, I tend to start eating this within a day or two, but some prefer the more mellow flavours that develop over the weeks and months.

PICKLED QUINCE

Harder than a goat's knee and sharper than an ostrich's toenail when raw, give a quince what we all crave – some warmth and perhaps a little booze – and they transform into one of the things that makes me long for short, dark days. And the scent, my god! Like the perfume of a lost lover.

Almost always, I am happy to say goodbye to the end of each of the tightly seasonal foods – asparagus isn't right outside April/May, give me forced rhubarb only in the year's first quarter – but with quince it's different: I want to enjoy its uniqueness for as much of the year as possible, and this (along with quince gin) is the best way I know how. Expect your consumption of ham and cheese to increase exponentially.

Makes approx 1 litre (1 ¾ pints)
600ml (1 pint) cider vinegar
400g (14oz) caster sugar
8 cloves
8 juniper berries
8 black peppercorns
1 star anise (optional)
1kg (2lb 4oz) quinces

Put all but the quinces in a large non-reactive pan and bring to a simmer, stirring to dissolve the sugar. Leave over a low heat.

One quince at time (they discolour quickly), peel, then cut into eight and remove the core from each segment. Add the quince to the sweetened vinegar, cooking until tender, 20–30 minutes is usual but this may vary a little.

Use a slotted spoon to transfer the quinces into a sterilized jar. Turn the heat up on the vinegar and boil until it has reduced to 500ml (18fl oz) or so, then pour over the fruit and seal the jar immediately.

QUICK PICKLED RED ONIONS

Every time I make this, I want to peel two onions as one surely can't make much, or even enough: but it does. However, you can always make double quantities, if you are similarly afflicted.

I love a quick pickle. A couple of minutes of minimal effort and you have something that you'll use in everything from sandwiches to salads, tacos (see page 211) to burgers. These quick pickled onions are perhaps my favourite. Once you get the taste for them, by all means embellish: change the citrus with the seasons, add chilli flakes, black pepper or oregano, and use a white onion – though I choose red onions as they turn a fabulous pink. If your onion is approaching cricket ball size, up the quantities of salt and juice by half. There are few things with which this will not go, especially where you might reach for a pickle or relish.

1 red onion, very thinly sliced

2 tbsp salt

juice of ½ Seville orange (or 1 lime and 1 lemon, or half and half)

Rub the salt into the onion slices between your hands; the same action you might make to keep your hands warm. Lay them on a plate for the salt to draw out the moisture and soften the onions.

Rinse the onions off in a sieve. Return the slices to the bowl, add the citrus juice and leave to stand for about 30 minutes.

If you are in even more of a dash, you can make this by just pouring boiling water over the onions and leaving them for a few minutes before draining through a sieve, adding the citrus and a pinch of salt, and cutting the time the onions are in the salty citrus down to 10 minutes at a push.

RHUBARB AND CARDAMOM RELISH

Of the many small annoyances that litter the life of a middle-aged man, few rile more than the jumble of half-full jars clogging up the fridge – that strawberry jam brought back from France, a grainy mustard long since separated, those woody capers behind the cauliflower in front of which sits a newer jar – but this relish is worth its space. For a start, it won't be there for long. Ham, cheese, chicken, roasted vegetables and more are much improved by its sweet and sour marvellousness.

Makes about 750ml (1¼ pints)

220g (8oz) caster sugar

200ml (7fl oz) cider vinegar

80g (3oz) honey

1 star anise

3 cloves

1 tsp Aleppo pepper

1 onion, very thinly sliced

3cm (1¼ in) piece of fresh ginger, peeled and finely chopped

400g (14oz) rhubarb

Put the sugar and vinegar into a pan and place over a medium heat, stirring occasionally until the sugar dissolves. Add the honey and spices and simmer for 10 minutes. Add the onion and simmer for 7 minutes, then add the ginger and simmer for a further 3 minutes. The mixture will have thickened a little.

Slice the rhubarb as you like – sometimes I go for as fine as I can get it, or in chunks of 2cm (¾in). Add the rhubarb to the spicy vinegar and cook for 1 minute for very thinly sliced or up to 5 minutes for chunks, until just tender. Beware of overcooking, as you will lose texture and colour. Allow to cool just a little, then spoon into sterilized jars.

GOOSEBERRY SALSA

The magnificent gooseberry, 'tart as any kindergarten martinet' as Amy Clampitt put it, makes me as happy as any strawberry can. Much as I love the sweeter late gooseberries, where the sun has had chance to get under their skin, I still crave the glorious wince of the first raw gooseberry of the year most. This sweet/sour salsa may need a tweak in the sugar if the gooseberries are on the sweeter side: as ever, taste and taste again. Try this with oily fish, smoked anything, cheese; it's even pretty special with vanilla ice cream.

Serves 4

4 tbsp caster sugar

3 tbsp white wine vinegar

150g (5oz) gooseberries, topped and tailed

3 shallots, thinly sliced

zest and juice of 1 small lime

20–25 mint leaves, finely shredded

small handful of chives, chopped

2 lovage leaves, very finely chopped

sea salt and freshly ground black pepper

In a small pan, stir the sugar into the vinegar with a generous pinch of salt and a good grinding of pepper and bring it slowly to a simmer.

Add the gooseberries and cook gently, stirring often, to soften the fruit just a little – this may take only a few minutes. Remove from the heat.

Once cool, stir in the shallots, lime zest and juice and herbs. Refrigerate for at least a couple of hours before serving. Use within a week or so.

PICKLED CELERIAC

This is my core full-on, high-vinegar, pickling recipe, from which I embellish, tweak and otherwise fanny about: fennel, allspice, cinnamon, Szechuan pepper, juniper and many other aromatics might make their appearance. If I might suggest, don't go large on cloves and cinnamon: this should smell like the nights are drawing in rather than a night on the mulled wine.

Makes 500ml (18fl oz)

500ml (18fl oz) white wine vinegar

½ star anise

1½ tsp sea salt

3 strips of orange zest

1 tsp caraway seeds

1 tsp coriander seeds

1 clove

12 black peppercorns

1 celeriac, about 600g (1lb 5oz) unpeeled

Bring everything but the celeriac to a simmer in a medium pan over a medium heat. While that's getting to temperature, peel and halve the celeriac and thinly slice into half-circles, then slice each of these into three strips.

Place the celeriac strips in a sterilized 500ml (18fl oz) jar – I drop a handful in vertically and jiggle the jar to enable them to settle, then add the rest. Pour in the spicy vinegar and seal. Once cool, place on a cool, dark shelf; once open, keep in the fridge or in a cold larder. The longest I've taken to finish the jar is three months, so it should keep at least that long.

PICKLED JERUSALEM ARTICHOKES

As much as I love the wakey-wakey sourness you get with the pickled celeriac (see above), a gentler hand is sometimes called for. With so much water to vinegar, there's no element of preserving here: in truth, it's as much of a two-gins flirt with an 'a la Greque' – where the vegetable is cooked in a diluted liquor of vinegar/lemon juice and wine – as a pickle. Rather than slap you around the cheeks with sourness, this method just sharpens the artichokes a little, making them stand to attention, keeping their texture, colour and flavour bright and tight.

I love this with seafood, crab especially (see page 200). It doesn't keep as long, but if you're after a light pickle to eat today or tomorrow, you can turn this to whatever vegetable appeals: salsify and turnips are superb.

Makes 500ml (18fl oz)

80ml (2fl oz) white wine vinegar

50ml (2½ fl oz) water

1 tsp black peppercorns

2 sprigs of thyme

50ml (2fl oz) extra virgin olive oil

300g (10oz) Jerusalem artichokes, scrubbed, unpeeled

Put the vinegar, water, peppercorns, thyme and olive oil in a pan and bring to a simmer. Remove from the heat and allow to infuse for 5 minutes.

Slice the Jerusalem artichokes to about 5mm (¼in) thick and add to the spicy liquid immediately, to prevent them discolouring. Bring back to a simmer for 3 minutes, then remove from the heat until you're ready to serve. Refrigerate if not using on the day.

LEMON AND LIME PICKLE

As a kid, few things thrilled like the promise of a visit to the local Chinese. It happened once, maybe twice, a year. Everything jangled the senses. I walked through the doors to be filled with the scent of Everywhere I'd Never Been. The wallpaper – loud, beyond bright – as exotic as mine (with its repeated pastel moonlanding motif) was calm. I'd be smiling all the way on the bus.

I wanted three things: fried rice, pineapple fritters in a sea of syrup, and what to my mind were huge crisps – poppadoms and the small silver bowls of accompaniments. This was one of a handful of Indian specialities that were incorporated into the menu: the peculiarness of this strikes me only now.

Eight-year-old me couldn't work out whether he loved the hottest pickle: the first hint of flavour promised a spicy marmalade sweetness that never arrived, but I kind of liked what did. In the years since, my love has deepened, and although I still nurse a tiny resentment that it never delivers on its sweet promise, I think I love it all the more for it.

This hot and sour pickle must be lively, so don't hold back on the chilli; time and the other spices will ensure it also has a full, deep flavour. This is traditionally made entirely with limes, but as often as not I use lemons too.

Makes approx 3 x 250ml (9fl oz) jars

8 unwaxed limes

5 unwaxed lemons

3 tsp ground turmeric

2 tsp ground fenugreek

10 garlic cloves, thinly sliced

25g (1oz) fresh ginger, peeled and finely chopped

1 tbsp, plus 1 tsp Aleppo pepper

2 medium-heat Thai chillies, deseeded and finely chopped

2 tsp asafoetida

30g (1oz) sea salt

40g (1½oz) caster sugar

3 tbsp vegetable oil

15 curry leaves, dried or fresh

1 tsp nigella seeds

2 tsp mustard seeds

1 tsp fenugreek seeds

Cut 6 limes in half through the poles (rather than the equator), and thinly slice each half into thin semicircles. Cut 4 lemons in half through the poles, turn each half cut side down, cut in half again through the poles and then thinly slice into quarter-circles. Juice the other 2 limes and 1 lemon, and place the citrus slices and juice into a non-reactive bowl: I use glass.

Add the turmeric, ground fenugreek, garlic, ginger, 1 tablespoon of Aleppo pepper, chillies, asafoetida, salt and sugar to the citrus and combine well.

Warm the oil in a small frying pan over a medium heat. Add the curry leaves, nigella seeds, remaining teaspoon of Aleppo pepper, mustard and fenugreek seeds; as they begin to pop and crackle, take the pan off the heat.

Combine the oily spices with the citrus and spoon into sterilized jars. Invert the jars once in a while for a fortnight to incorporate the spices well. The pickle will be good after a fortnight, but become even finer with time.

PICKLED CHERRIES

Man, these are good. This may seem an expensive cul-de-sac in which to park pricey cherries, but I promise you'll be glad you did. Even the hardest of unsatisfactory supermarket cherries will improve immeasurably under the spices' spell.

Pickled cherries are really good with rich meats – venison and duck especially – as well as scallops, of all things. Once the cherries are consumed, don't waste the colourful vinegar – it makes an excellent dressing.

Makes approx 800ml (1½ pints), enough to almost fill a 1 litre jar (1¾ pint)

500ml (18fl oz) white wine vinegar

50g (2oz) sugar

1 tsp fennel seeds

1 star anise

6 peppercorns

1 bay leaf (2 if using dried)

350g (12oz) cherries

In a medium pan, bring all but the cherries to the hint of a simmer over a medium heat. While that's getting up to temperature, stone and halve the cherries over the sterilized jar you intend to use, to catch every drop of their juice.

Pour the aromatic vinegar, spices and all, over the cherries and seal. Give the cherries a fortnight at minimum to develop, ideally a month or two.

PICKLED CUCUMBERS

As fine as they are in their raw state in summer, cucumbers were made for pickling; clothed in vinegar and spices they come alive. By all means experiment with the spices, but try with those here as they work really well. Yes, you can salt the cucumber slices for a couple of hours first, but mostly I don't, and I find the difference negligible.

Enough to almost fill a 500ml (18fl oz) white wine vinegar

120g (4oz) caster sugar

2 tbsp sea salt

350g (12oz) cucumber, cut into 3mm (⅛ in) slices

1 garlic clove, thinly sliced

1 Thai chilli, split lengthways, deseeded and stalk end removed

18 Szechuan peppercorns

4 slices of fresh ginger

Bring the vinegar, sugar and salt to a gentle boil, stirring to dissolve the sugar, then simmer very gently for 10 minutes or so.

Place the cucumber, garlic and spices into a sterilized 1 litre (1¾ pint) jar, pour the vinegar into the jar and seal. Allow to cool and refrigerate once cool. You can eat this as soon as it's cool and it should be good for a week or so, after which the texture of the cucumbers gets a little sludgy.

CHAAT MASALA

There are only a few places in this book where I'm inclined to give you a direct order, and here is one: you must make chaat. It is one of those go-tos that can quietly change how you eat. This Indian spice blend, where the sourness of amchur (dried mango powder) mixed with cumin, coriander, salt, asafoetida and chilli helps create an extraordinary spiral of sweet, sour and earthy. Chaat is anything but subtle, and yet used sensitively it can bring intensity, depth, heat and a bright sourness to curries, dals, salads (see page 133), and it has a particular affinity with eggs and tomatoes. It is most commonly used in vegetable dishes, but having been put on to the pleasure of using it with pork chops by Nik Sharma, I'd recommend you try it with meat too. As with vinegar, add a little chaat late when making soup and you'll find those flavours accentuated, clarified and made more distinct. Try it with the rojak (see page 150) in place of the sambal oelek dressing too.

You can buy chaat masala relatively easily from Indian supermarkets or online, but making your own is easy and has quite the edge.

There are endless variations on chaat, with two constants: amchur and salt. Black rock salt is traditionally used – Asian supermarkets and online suppliers are your best bets for this and ajwain – but good sea salt works well too.

Makes approx 80g (3oz)

2 tbsp cumin seeds

1 tbsp coriander seeds

1 tbsp fennel seeds

½ tsp asafoetida

2 whole cloves or
½ tsp ground cloves

1 tbsp amchur

1 tbsp sea salt

1 tbsp Kashmiri red
chilli powder

¼ tsp ground ginger

1 tbsp dried mint (optional)

1½ tbsp ajwain

Toast the cumin, coriander and fennel seeds in a dry frying pan over a medium heat until their scent is released, stirring regularly to avoid burning. Add the asafoetida and allow a minute or two more toasting, then allow to cool slightly. I use a small coffee grinder to reduce the spices and the cloves to a powder; a pestle and mortar will be fine if you don't have one. Add the rest of the ingredients and pulse/pound to a powder.

Store in an airtight container, ideally in a cool dark cupboard. Use enthusiastically on everything.

SWEET AND SOUR APRICOTS

Everyone needs a simple, repeatable, adaptable sweet and sour recipe: here is mine. It's so good, I find all the excuses to eat it often: with pork chops, sumac duck (see page 166), in upside down cake (see page 247) and with porridge for breakfast – I kid you not.

This owes a good deal to Diana Henry's method of cooking everything in a roasting tray – I used to chop the apricots and slowly develop this in a pan and it was good, but this is so much better at ensuring the flavours remain just a little more distinct, plus it's easy as hell. And by all means try this with plums, nectarines or peaches instead of apricots.

Makes enough for 4, to serve with yoghurt

320g (11oz) apricots (about 8 whole apricots), halved and stoned

4 tbsp cider vinegar

4 tbsp medium-dry cider

50g (2oz) soft light brown sugar

20g (¾oz) soft dark brown sugar

good pinch of ground coriander

good pinch of Aleppo pepper (or other mild chilli flakes)

½ tsp yellow mustard seeds

1 star anise, broken into its spokes

3 cardamom pods, seeds only

few sprigs of lemon thyme

3 tbsp honey

Preheat the oven to 170°C/340°F/gas mark 3.

Place the apricot halves in a single layer on a roasting tray and shower with the vinegar, cider and sugars. Scatter the coriander, Aleppo pepper, mustard seeds, star anise pieces and cardamom seeds over, lay the thyme sprigs on top and drizzle with the honey.

Roast for 1½ hours, carefully basting the fruit occasionally, and checking halfway through to taste (by all means add a little sugar or vinegar if needed). The apricots should have surrendered their vigour but not so much as to have fallen to pieces. Serve warm or at room temperature.

SAMBAL OELEK

I fell in love with sambal oelek the day we met. A jar added late to a spice order helped me across the 'free delivery' threshold, and two days later I was staring out of the window with a teaspoon pecking at the jar, daydreaming about our new life together.

At its simplest, a sambal is a lively blend of chilli, vinegar and salt, hugely popular in Malaysia and neighbouring countries. Herbs and spices, vegetables and fruit (see page 116 for strawberry sambal) may embellish but at its heart it must have a kick of heat and acidity.

As fine as this chilli sauce is from a jar, it is simple to make yourself and tastes even better. You can make this in smaller amounts using the same proportions if you have just a few chillies to hand, which will be easier to do using a pestle and mortar.

Makes approx 250g (9oz)

250g (9oz) red Thai chillies

25ml (1fl oz) lime juice or rice wine vinegar

1 tsp sea salt

Remove the stems and seeds from the chillies. Add all the ingredients to a processor and blitz to a smoothish paste. If you want a thinner sauce, you can let it down a little with a tablespoon or two of water.

If using a pestle and mortar, roughly chop the chillies and then gently work them into a thick paste with the salt. Add the lime juice or vinegar and incorporate well.

POKEY PINK SAUERKRAUT

This is, as Stevie said, hotter than July. And perhaps my favourite of all sauerkrauts too. What starts bright and pokey mellows into something altogether more approachable, yet don't be lulled into an easy sense of security: it carries a punch that never goes away.

Fills a 1.5 litre jar (2 ½ pint) jar

1.3kg (2lb 14oz) red cabbage (about 1 large cabbage)

1 tbsp unrefined sea salt

5 garlic cloves, thinly sliced

4 medium jalapeño chillies, thinly sliced

Halve, core and finely shred the cabbage. Sprinkle with the salt and massage it into the cabbage for a few minutes. Allow to rest for a few minutes, and then repeat the massaging. Tumble the cabbage, garlic and chillies together with your hands or a spoon. Massage for a few minutes more, then allow to rest.

Place the mix into a sterilized 1.5 litre (2 ½ pint) Kilner jar, pressing down firmly to encourage the air out and more water to be released. Use your fist to press down and twist to encourage the release of yet more liquid. Pack the vegetables down as tightly as you can – the water should rise slightly above the cabbage. If not, leave it to release more for six hours or so. If you have to, add just a little water to raise the level. Use a pickle pebble or a food bag of water to ensure the vegetables stay submerged.

Leave to ferment at room temperature, out of direct sunlight. The sauerkraut will be nicely sour after two or three weeks, but by all means try it along the way to see how it changes. I usually let sauerkraut ferment for considerably longer, now that I have developed a taste for it, and while I'd encourage you to experiment beyond your usual date, where you stop the ferment by placing the jar in the fridge is entirely your choice. It will keep for at least six months in the fridge.

FERMENTED CUCUMBERS

Delicious as they are, pickles made with vinegar lack the microbial benefits that result from fermentation. The process here is simple – the cucumbers ferment in a spiced brine for anything from a week to a month, depending on your taste – resulting in a salty, sour delight that enriches your gut microbiome. By all means ease off a little on the salt if you like – keep it at 25g or above – but I confess a weakness for it as below; it must've been all those salt and vinegar crisps as a child.

These spices work so well with cucumbers, and are the same as in the pickled cucumber recipe on page 95; try making both on the same day and compare the results. You'll also notice that fermented cucumbers (on the right in the image) usually retain their bright colour a little more than pickled.

Fills a 1 litre (1 ¾ pint) jar

35g (1 ¼ oz) fine sea salt

700ml (1 ¼ pints) water

400g (14oz) cucumber, cut into 3mm (⅛ in) slices

1 garlic clove, thinly sliced

1 Thai chilli, split lengthways, deseeded and stalk end removed

18 Szechuan peppercorns

4 slices of fresh ginger

Make a brine in a sterilized 1 litre (1 ¾ pint) jar by stirring the salt into half the water. Add all the ingredients to the brine and stir, then add the rest of the water.

Use a food bag part-filled with water to keep the cucumbers submerged. Seal the jar. Allow the cucumbers to ferment for a week, removing any harmless white scum that may appear on the surface. Taste after a few days to familiarize yourself with how the flavour changes. After a week, it should be just right to eat, but if you like it after 6 days, or want to leave it a few days longer for a little extra sourness, that's all good. Pop the jar in the fridge when it's as you'd like it, as this all but halts the process. I'd suggest eating this within a few weeks – they'll be fine for longer, but the texture of the cucumbers becomes softer than I like after a fortnight or so.

FERMENTED CHERRIES

The first taste of fermented cherries may seem peculiar – you have a brain with a lifetime of hardwiring to expect a cherry to taste like a cherry – but keep nibbling. It is quite the glorious crossover of sweet, sour and salt, and goes with everything from poultry of all persuasions to using instead of the gooseberries in the focaccia (see page 75) to the clafoutis (see page 224).

You can use this method with any fruit you fancy, though make sure you cut larger fruit such as plums into half-cherry-sized pieces. Whatever weight of fruit you use, the 2 per cent ratio of salt to fruit is crucial as it impedes the development of harmful bacteria and creates conditions that encourage beneficial lactic acid bacteria to thrive.

Once you try them, you'll find any number of uses for fermented cherries, but do try them in salsas, with rich meats and in cherry clafoutis.

For clarity, 400g (14oz) is the weight of the cherries after they've been halved and pitted.

400g (14oz) halved and pitted cherries

8g (¼oz) salt

Place the cherries in a bowl with the salt and combine well. Allow them 15 minutes to form a little brine, then transfer to a sterilized jar using a rubber spatula to capture as much of the salty liquid as possible.

Use a pickle pebble or freezer bag part-filled with water to keep the cherries beneath the brine that is created. Seal the jar.

Allow the cherries to ferment at room temperature, checking them on day 4 to taste: they should be lightly but definitely sour. I usually find day 6 or 7 is when they have a great balance of sweet, sour and salty, though by all means taste them earlier to see how they develop. To all but halt the fermentation process, transfer the jar to the fridge. Use within a fortnight or so to enjoy the cherries with a firm texture.

FRUIT KIMCHI

There are a handful of people who inspire immediate love, and Hans and Gaby Wieland from Neantóg, Ireland, and fermentistas supreme, are two such, exuding as they do an open warmth that makes you truly believe that everything is, after all, all right. Hans is imperfect, believing as he does that Bob trumps Joni, but our shared love of Yahtzee (so much more pleasingly named Kniffle in his native German) and his generous introduction of their fruit kimchi to me means I will overlook his peculiarnesses. I hope he will be suitably affronted that I have tweaked their recipe.

Made without the usual cabbage and fish sauce, this kimchi is a revelation of fruit, sour, salt and sweet. It is more liquid than some kimchi, and I prefer to eat it relatively young and crisp: after a couple of months the fruit becomes considerably softer.

Makes 1 litre (1 ¾ pints)

½ pineapple (about 570g/1 ¼ lb), to give 320g (11oz) peeled and cored

4 plums, halved and stoned

2 pears, halved and cored

1 apple, halved and cored

1 medium bunch of seedless grapes (about 250g/9oz), halved

1 ½ tsp sea salt

juice of 1 lemon (optional)

1 fresh jalapeño chilli, finely chopped

1 yellow pepper

1 medium onion, thinly sliced

2 plump garlic cloves, finely chopped

3 tbsp grated ginger

1 ½ tsp Korean red pepper powder

Peel and chop the pineapple, plums, pears and apple into 1cm (½ in) pieces, add to a bowl with the remaining ingredients and mix well.

Spoon into a sterilized 1 litre (1 ¾ pint) Kilner jar and press down with your fingers until a brine rises and covers the mix – add fruit juice or water if necessary. Weigh down with a pickle pebble, or sealed bag of water. Cover loosely with a lid.

Leave to ferment for at least 2 days, ideally for one week. After this, store in the fridge. I prefer to eat this within about a month or so, as the texture gets a little too soft after that.

RED GRAPEFRUIT AND RADISH KIMCHI

If you've ever made blackberry whisky – and if not, stand in the corner and have a think about what you've (not) done – you'll know that however glorious it may be, it's impossible to tell from a sip that its parents are blackberry and whisky: so too, this magnificent kimchi. What you have here is a wildly vivid pink/orange/red kimchi, with a hot sourness that shuffles the senses like a new deck. By all means up the grapefruit to radish ratio, or vice versa.

Fills a 1 litre (1¾ pint) jar

800g (1lb 12oz) radishes

2 tbsp fine sea salt

5 spring onions, thinly sliced

4cm (1½in) piece of fresh ginger, peeled (a spoon is best for this) and finely chopped or grated

3 garlic cloves, finely chopped

40g (1½oz) Korean chilli powder

1 red grapefruit

Slice the radishes; it's easiest and creates least waste if you cut off the base and hold the leaf end. Place the sliced radishes in a large bowl and combine with the salt, mixing well.

Add the spring onions, ginger and garlic and combine, along with the Korean chilli powder.

Top and tail the grapefruit, and then slice off the rest of the peel and white pith, from pole to pole is easiest. Segment the grapefruit by carefully slicing each free from the membrane that separates them from their neighbour. Squeeze the handful of membrane over the bowl to relieve it of as much juice as you can. Slice each grapefruit segment into three and carefully stir into the spicy radish.

Spoon the mixture into a sterilized 1 litre (1¾ pint) Kilner jar, pressing down carefully to squeeze out any air bubbles. The brine may be quite thick and the vegetables and fruit should stay beneath the surface, but you can use a pickle pebble to keep them submerged if you like. Seal the jar.

Allow the kimchi to ferment for 2 weeks, burping the jar every day or two. Taste it after a few days and then every couple of days to become familiar with how the flavour develops – I'd give it at least a fortnight of fermenting. Transfer the jar to the fridge when it has the flavour and sourness you like, where it will keep for at least six months, and very possibly much longer.

SUMMER SALSA

Often, the difference between a good meal and a special one is all in the dots that join. This salsa makes finer friends of a freshly grilled mackerel and any neighbouring leaves, a few slices of ham and a green bean salad, and – well, you get the point.

A regular salsa is easy enough to make and perfectly marvellous, but fermentation takes some of the best of summer and creates a salsa that's somehow brighter, yet deeper. This is an eminently substitutable recipe: plums for nectarines, apple for pepper, etc; adapt the recipe to make it anytime you have a few of this and one of those.

Fills a 750ml (1¼ pint) jar

2 nectarines, stoned and cut into 6–7mm (¼in) dice

10 cherry tomatoes, halved, with each half sliced into 6

1 red pepper, deseeded and cut into 6–7mm (¼in) dice

½ red onion, cut into 5mm (¼in) dice

2 garlic cloves, finely chopped

sea salt

juice of 1 lime

Combine the fruit, vegetables and garlic in a medium bowl. You need to add 2 per cent salt; to calculate this, multiply the weight of the fruit, vegetables and garlic by 0.02: if the ingredients weigh 600g (1lb 5oz), you will need 12g (½ oz) salt. Add the salt and gently but thoroughly stir through. Add the lime juice.

Spoon the mix into a sterilized glass jar, using a spatula to transfer as much of the salt and juice as possible. Keep the ingredients beneath the liquid that forms, using a pickle pebble or part-filled freezer bag, and seal.

Allow the salsa to ferment at room temperature for about 5 days, after which point it will be perfect to eat. Refrigerate (unless you'd like it sourer) and use when you fancy. It will keep for a couple of months, after which the texture declines past where I like it.

UMEBOSHI GOOSEBERRIES

I have a friend who now lives in Tokyo, and to my shame I have yet to visit him. Of the many things I hope to experience when I do, the best umeboshi plums rank high. Made with green, sour ume plums that are salted, fermented and dried, umeboshi are supposed to cure everything from hangovers to anaemia. As they are rare here in the UK, I've adapted the method to common plums as well as apricots: both are excellent, but these gooseberries are just extraordinary. Their size makes the process both reliable and quick, and their sour intensity is perfect for the further souring of fermentation.

As with quince, the flavour of good gooseberries registers in the nose as much as the tongue. Salty, bright and doubly sour from the fruit itself and acidity of fermentation, these are anything but subtle, but what pleasure. While umeboshi plums are fermented for a few weeks, before being dried in the sun, gooseberries are pleasingly quick: 7–10 days in the brine they create from being salted, followed by 10 hours in a low oven or dehydrator and they are ready. If you are fortunate enough to live in a climate where three days of proper sunshine and breeze can be guaranteed, by all means dry them outside. Dry them further or eat them undried if you prefer: I like them best as what the French call 'mi cuit', half dried.

I love these as no-reason nibbles, in place of the redcurrants with the asparagus on page 134, and as a variation on the regular gooseberries in the focaccia on page 75 – just ease back on the salt sprinkled on the top of the dough.

Don't discard the liquid: the pink brine that leaches from the fruit is known as umeboshi vinegar, and mighty fine it is too. This recipe should give you 140ml or so, depending on the juiciness of the gooseberries. it makes a superb salad dressing (with olive oil, mustard and honey in quantities to taste).

750g gooseberries
60g fine sea salt

Top and tail the gooseberries using a truly sharp knife: I find this easiest on a chopping board, as it avoids squeezing the berries too hard - you need them unsplit.

Add the berries to a jar and sprinkle the salt over. Place a weight on top to gently apply pressure to the salted berries: a couple of pickle pebbles or a small feedbag part-filled with water will do the job. Over the next day or so, you'll notice the salt forming a brine from moisture drawn out of the fruit: within a day or two more the brine's tide will have risen over the berries and the serious business of fermentation will be underway.

After 10 days, try a gooseberry: it should be intense, salty, sour and bright. Drain the fruit and place on kitchen roll to soak in what liquid clings to the skin. Lay on a tray and either set on a dehydrator on low-medium for 10 hours or place in the oven overnight on the lowest setting.

SOUR CREAM DRESSING

The doubling up of sours here is pretty special. The cream and lemon combine with the garlic to create a punch that I love. Feel free to let it down a little with olive oil or water should a gentler hand be in order, or add a teaspoon or two of Dijon mustard and a little sherry vinegar if you fancy. Try this with the leeks 'vinaigrette' on page 204, with steamed sprouting broccoli, or pretty much anywhere its garlicky sour bite might work.

Makes comfortably enough for a salad for 4

200ml (7fl oz) sour cream

juice of ½ lemon

1 garlic clove, finely chopped

½ tsp hot smoked paprika (optional)

sea salt and freshly ground black pepper

Whisk together all the ingredients in a cup. Taste and adjust the seasoning, adding a dash more lemon juice and/or salt and pepper if required.

RED GRAPEFRUIT AND ELDERFLOWER DRESSING

Happy accident is a fine thing. This came about from playing with variations on the ceviche on page 182 and wondering how I might use the scraps of grapefruit left. A bottle of elderflower cordial was on the side by the bits of grapefruit, and here we are. This works so well with pink and the familiar white grapefruit too, but the gentle floral acidity of red has the edge for me. It makes a really special dressing for salad leaves, steamed greens and is perfect in the chicory recipe on page 138.

Makes comfortably enough for a salad for 4

2 tbsp red grapefruit juice

4 tbsp elderflower cordial

1 tbsp wholegrain mustard

2 tbsp extra virgin olive oil

sea salt and freshly ground black pepper

Whisk the grapefruit juice, cordial, mustard, a good pinch of salt and a generous peppering together in a glass. Add the oil, whisking to create an emulsion. Taste and add a little more salt and pepper if needed.

SAMBAL OELEK DRESSING

I've been returning to the fridge a little too frequently this evening. The last four visits have each been to steal a piece of my daughter's fudge (a swingeing Dad Tax) and to dip my finger in this leftover dressing for a cheeky taste. I confess, that on the last visit I even dipped the fudge in the dressing. It was truly, truly good.

Full of zing and punch from the three sours, this dressing is for when a proper wakey-wakey is in order, with sambal's vinegar, the lime and tamarind ensuring it is brightly refreshing. Try this to dress the rojak (see page 150), as a dip for chips or flatbreads, or as a late night dip for your finger.

Makes comfortably enough for a salad for 4

juice of 1 lime

1 tbsp runny honey

2 tsp sambal oelek (see page 113, or use shop-bought)

2 tsp tamarind paste (see page 18)

½ tsp sea salt

3 tbsp extra virgin olive oil

Whisk together all the ingredients, apart from the oil. Then add the oil and whisk thoroughly until completely combined, adding a tweak of salt if needed.

TAHINI AND LIME DRESSING

Dressings are exactly that: clothes that other ingredients dress up in, so choose well. A classic vinaigrette is your little black dress that's rarely out of place, but sometimes you fancy a bit more pizzazz – what an old pal used to call 'a showing-out shirt' – and this is one to consider. I've had it on the plainest of single lettuce salads and the prawn waldorf on page 141 and it was superb on both. Don't be scared to thin this out with water to a consistency you fancy; tahini can vary in viscosity between emulsion and cement.

Makes comfortably enough for a salad for 4

2½ tbsp tahini

1 tsp soy sauce

juice of 1 lime

1 tbsp runny honey

1 tbsp toasted sesame oil

1 garlic clove, finely chopped

sea salt and freshly ground black pepper

Whisk all the ingredients together in a bowl. Taste and adjust the seasoning, adding a little more soy sauce and/or lime juice to balance if required. If the dressing is still a little too thick, add a little water – though it should definitely dollop rather than run freely.

SPICY TAMARIND DRESSING

My friend Max's mother was a lovely woman, who once delivered the most withering of gentle demolitions of a person she saw as having questionable taste: 'Oh Maxwell, she's the sort who thinks geese are swans.' I think of that every time I use tamarind paste from a jar rather than making my own from a tamarind block (see page 18); it's a goose, but on a wet Wednesday in March when all you want to do is have a good meal and put your feet up, sometimes a goose will do.

Whenever you can manage it, use the tamarind block that comes with seed and all: it really is a swan. This dressing requires such a small amount but it is SO worth it, but if you're in too much of a dash bringing everything together to fanny around using tamarind block for a dressing, paste from a jar will be fine.

Try this with the halloumi, mango, shallot and rocket salad (see page 137), on a crisp lettuce or even steamed sprouts: make it once and it'll become a staple.

Makes comfortably enough for a salad for 4

1 large garlic clove, finely chopped

2cm (¾in) piece of fresh ginger, peeled and finely chopped

1 tsp Aleppo pepper

a good pinch of ground coriander

4 tsp tamarind paste

juice of ½ lemon

4 tbsp extra virgin olive oil

4 tsp honey or jaggery (optional)

sea salt and freshly ground black pepper

Pound the garlic and ginger in a pestle and mortar with a little salt until it becomes a smoothish paste. Add the Aleppo pepper, coriander, tamarind paste and lemon juice and a little black pepper and stir well to combine. Add the oil and whisk into an emulsion. Taste and adjust the seasoning if needed, and depending on what you are serving it with, whisk in the jaggery or honey if you'd like it a little sweeter.

QUINCE BUTTERMILK DRESSING

My good friend Liz Knight is a forager apart, and it is to her that I owe this combination. Inventive and insightful in the kitchen, she is the best company for learning about how to make the best of wild food as much as identifying and locating it. I think even a little foraging – and who doesn't love late summer blackberrying or picking early spring wild garlic at least – is not only good for the soul and the diet, it alters your sensitivities to flavour combinations; when you have a handful of something like clove root – similar in scent and flavour to clove and yet more besides – you have to think a little harder in the absence of recipe books telling you what to try it with, allowing creative culinary leaps to occur. I'm convinced that this so-delicate coming together wouldn't have been on the radar of many without a forager's inquisitive palate. You should look Liz up and go on foraging with her: it is a life-enriching pleasure.

Rarely have a perfume and a flavour been so closely bound as with quince; their shared subtleties are easily lost in the company of strong flavours, and yet you have to roast or poach the bone-hard fruit into delicious submission in a sea of sweet booze. As wonderful as cooked quince is, there is a sense that some of its magic is distilled and lost to the steam. This dressing, gentle as snow, captures at least some of that magic.

I love this dressing just as it is, to sip or on a leafy salad. That said, its adaptability increases if whisked into a quarter of its volume of groundnut oil, creating an emulsion that coats leaves more obsessively. By all means add a little pepper, a squeeze of lemon if you must (it's not a wildly sour dressing, though the buttermilk gave me the excuse to include it), but please, an easy hand: you want to retain all the delicacy of the quince juice. Try this with a plain butterhead lettuce, with just-steamed asparagus or sprouting broccoli, or a salad of bitter leaves, manchego and blackberries.

There are no measurements for this: quinces vary hugely in their size and juiciness, and you only find out mid-recipe: so see what happens. It will keep in the fridge.

2 or 3 aromatic quinces
buttermilk
salt

Wash the quinces, removing any of the charming down that can patchily cover the skin. Finely grate – ideally using a microplane – the quince into a bowl lined with a fine muslin. It may start to discolour but it's not a bad thing here.

Lift the muslin and twist it so that the grated quince is forced to release its juice through the material into the bowl. Whisk this with an equal volume of buttermilk, a good pinch of salt, and marvel at the gentle, aromatic perfection of a sip of it.

STRAWBERRY SAMBAL

I used to share a house with a fine man by the name of Jumbo. I once asked him why he drank Stella: 'I'm not sure. It comes over all lovely when you're drinking it, and then all of a sudden your legs stop working.' And so too, this sambal – all strawberry summer charm until the chilli slides around on you a third of a second after the strawberry. It's very good.

This sambal is best with the sort of half-ripe strawberries my dad would've buried in sugar and Ideal milk; if using riper fruit, ease back on the sugar. This would be very good with kiwi or mango in place of strawberries too. You could certainly try this using lemon juice, tamarind or cider vinegar as the sour should you wish: I just like the light zing of the rice vinegar and lime together.

Makes about 200ml (7fl oz)

400g (14oz) strawberries, hulled

3cm (1¼in) piece of fresh ginger, peeled and chopped

4 garlic cloves, chopped

4 Thai chillies, deseeded and chopped

80g (3oz) sugar

3 tbsp rice vinegar

1½ tbsp lime juice

sea salt and freshly ground black pepper

Place a third of the strawberries in a blender, add the ginger, garlic and chillies and blitz on high until a smooth paste forms. Add a little of the sugar if you need, to help 'bite' on the mix and get it relatively smooth – a little texture is fine. Add the rest of the strawberries and the rice vinegar and blitz again.

Pour the purée into a non-reactive pan and simmer over a medium heat, stirring regularly. As the liquid reduces, you'll think it's gone far enough but stir and if you see liquid miraculously release, allow it a little longer to cook. Once it reaches a jammy state, add the lime juice and simmer just long enough for it to recover its jamminess. Taste and adjust with sugar, lime, salt and pepper as you like – it should have a sweetness that's balanced by a late acidity on the tongue.

Funnel into a sterilized jar and once cool, refrigerate and use as you like. It's good with the rojak (page 150), or as a sort-of chutney, with cheese. Lasts at least two months.

HOLLANDAISE SAUCE (*AND BÉARNAISE*)

Hollandaise makes everything ok. Barely cooked asparagus, poached eggs, chips, a spicy sausage, the end of my finger. Its offspring, the gently aniseed béarnaise, is equally loveable, and once in a while – with steak and chips, for one – it has the edge. Do try the pink eggs Benedict on page 221.

Italics are for béarnaise only.

Makes enough for 4 as a dip or sauce

1 small shallot, very finely chopped

200ml (7fl oz) white wine vinegar or cider vinegar or tarragon vinegar (see page 81)

1 tsp black peppercorns

bunch of tarragon, leaves separated from the stalks

2 large egg yolks

150g (5oz) unsalted butter, melted

sea salt and freshly ground black pepper

Put the chopped shallot, vinegar, peppercorns *and chopped tarragon stalks* into a small pan over a medium-high heat and reduce to about a quarter of its original volume.

Set a large metal bowl over a pan of simmering water, making sure the base of the bowl doesn't touch the water. Strain the shallot vinegar reduction into the bowl, add the egg yolks and whisk for 2–3 minutes until thick. Very gradually, and leaving as much of the white milk solids behind as you can, whisk in the melted butter in a thin stream until thick and creamy, another 4–5 minutes. Season with salt and pepper to taste. *Stir in the chopped tarragon leaves*. If the sauce is too thick, add a little hot water. You can add a tiny bit more vinegar if you'd like it sharper.

Keep the sauce warm in the bowl over hot water, stirring occasionally, while you prepare whatever else you are having with it.

KOMBUCHA MAYONNAISE

If you are intimidated by the idea of making your own mayo, step in – it really isn't tricky providing you heed the words 'constantly' and 'very' in the instructions. I know ready-made mayo can be perfectly good, but homemade is really something else; the difference is like that between squash and juice. So, do try this at least once: the minimal faff is worth it at least for the special times, which might just mean you're enjoying a day without Other People.

Kombucha vinegar makes such a delicately flavoured mayonnaise – it's really so special – but the method works perfectly well with white wine and cider vinegars too.

Makes enough for 4 as a dip

1 egg yolk

1 tbsp Dijon mustard

1 tbsp kombucha (or other) vinegar

130ml (4½ fl oz) light olive or sunflower oil

sea salt and freshly ground black pepper

Combine the egg yolk, mustard and vinegar with some salt and pepper. Using a teaspoon and whisking constantly, add 2 tablespoons of the olive oil to the yolk mixture a few drops at a time until you have an emulsion. Carefully add the remaining oil in a very slow, thin stream, whisking constantly, until the mayonnaise is thick. Make immediate plans for chips.

ANCHOVY BUTTER

I met Matt Williamson and Claire Thomson's food before I met them. Their marvellous Bristol restaurant, Flinty Red, made me repeatedly happy, and never more so than when eating their anchovy butter. This is a tweak of their recipe. It makes quite a lot, which is good as you'll end up putting it on everything: try it smeared on lamb chops, blobbed on pizzas, as a dip for bright, hot radishes and with steamed broccoli. And (I kid you not) smothered on just-toasted hot cross buns, it is extraordinary. As much as the anchovies are the lead, it is the vinegared shallots that dance on the tongue. You can chop really finely and incorporate everything into a smooth amalgamation, but I prefer to leave the anchovies and shallots rough and the flavours semi-distinct: the islands of salt and sour in the sea of silky butter satisfy beyond words. Apparently, it keeps well for a week or so.

Makes about 250g (9oz)

3 shallots, very finely chopped

about 100ml (3 ½ fl oz) white wine vinegar

200g (7oz) unsalted butter, cut into cubes and allowed to soften

1 small tin of anchovies (50g/2oz), drained and roughly chopped

1–2 tsp thyme leaves, roughly chopped

chilli flakes, to taste

sea salt and freshly ground black pepper

Put the shallots into a small pan and just cover them with white wine vinegar. Bring to the boil and simmer until almost all the liquid has evaporated to leave a syrup coating the shallots. Allow to completely cool.

Once the shallots are cool beat them into the butter along with the anchovies. Add the thyme and chilli, salt and pepper to taste; mix well. Roll up in a cylinder of greaseproof paper or put in a bowl and keep in the fridge.

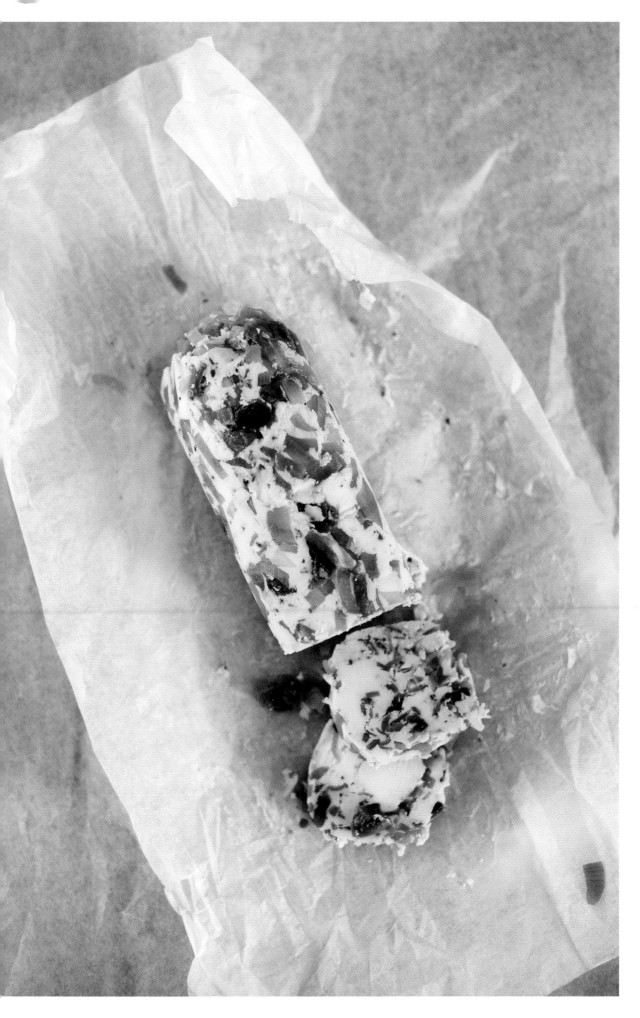

MOJITO MARMALADE

Sometimes you can chase an idea for a recipe around the houses, into town, behind the bike sheds and back, thinking you have it cornered down a cul-de-sac, and yet it escapes time and again until, if you are lucky, you finally wrestle the thing to the floor. Once in a blessed blue moon, the reverse. I woke – like McCartney did with 'Yesterday' – with this, front of brain: I made it once as a test, and boom, there it was. And here it is, untweaked.

Makes approx 2 x 500g (1lb 2oz) jars

12 unwaxed limes

1.7 litres (3 pints) water

about 1kg (2lb 4oz) sugar

50ml (2fl oz) white rum

32 mint leaves, very thinly sliced

Place the limes in a large bowl and cover with boiling water. Leave for 3 minutes, then dry well with a tea towel.

Cut each in half through the equator and juice into a jug.

Turn each half inside out, and working from the centre, scrape the pith and membranes from the skin with a knife. Tie the pith and membranes into a muslin bag – they are high in pectin and will help make the marmalade set.

Cut each lime skin in half again (so that the slices aren't too long for the marmalade) and slice very thinly. Add the lime juice, sliced skins, the muslin bag and water to a preserving pan and leave overnight – the skins will soften considerably, shortening the cook time.

Bring the pan to the boil and gently simmer for about 2 hours – you are looking for the skin to break in two when pinched between finger and thumb. It can vary with the freshness of the limes and thickness of their skin, so test after 1 hour and 40 minutes.

Pour into a large measuring jug, and squeeze the muslin bag to extract as much liquid as you can. If you have the patience of a saint, you can set the muslin bag over a colander to drip its liquid into the jug, thereby perhaps resulting in a cloudless marmalade, but for me, life's too short.

Return everything but the muslin bag to the pan along with the equivalent weight of sugar, so for 900g (2lb) limey liquid, add 900g (2lb) sugar.

Bring the pan to a slow simmer, stirring constantly to dissolve the sugar. Increase the heat and boil until the temperature reaches 104°C/220°F on a kitchen thermometer. Turn off the heat, make a cup of tea and relax for 12–15 minutes – this allows the marmalade to thicken a little, which will help the lime and mint stay suspended when you transfer it to jars.

Add the rum and the mint and stir thoroughly, before spooning into sterilized jars. Eat as soon as is cool, or any time over the next year or two. Refrigerate once open.

SEVILLE ORANGE CURD

This is the most fabulously silky and crazily simple curd to make. I owe a negroni or six to Thane Prince, who suggested using cream rather than butter when making curd: butter is perfectly excellent here, but cream brings silk. If you are going to make this direct over the hob, success is entirely down to patience: keep the temperature low and stir frequently. And of course, this is similarly sweet–sourly wonderful with limes, lemons or gooseberries in place of the Sevilles.

Makes about 600ml (1 pint)

120ml (4fl oz) double cream

finely grated zest of 6 Seville oranges

200ml (7fl oz) Seville orange juice (about 6 oranges)

270g (9½oz) granulated sugar

2 large eggs, plus 2 egg yolks

If you have a responsive induction hob, you can make the curd in a pan directly on the top over a low heat in a heavy-based pan; otherwise, set a heatproof bowl over a pan of gently simmering water such that the base of the bowl doesn't touch the water.

Add the cream, zest, juice and sugar to the pan (or bowl) and incorporate well – don't worry about splitting, it'll come back together. Warm through over a low-medium heat, stirring frequently with a whisk.

Gradually add the eggs and egg yolks to the pan, using a balloon whisk to thoroughly incorporate them. Cook for about 10 minutes, whisking every minute or so and scraping down the sides if necessary. Use a kitchen thermometer to check the temperature – when it reaches 82°C/180°F, remove the bowl from the heat.

Pour into warm sterilized jars and seal immediately. The curd will keep in a cool place for about a month. Keep in the fridge once opened: my oldest jar is 10 months old; it may keep much longer.

SIDES, SALADS AND SOUPS

SOURDOUGH SOUP

If you are not familiar with Donald O'Connor's genius, stop reading and google 'Make 'Em Laugh'. If you are familiar with Donald O'Connor's genius, stop reading and google 'Make 'Em Laugh'. There is not much better that you could be doing. One of the other characters in *Singin' in the Rain*, Lina Lamont, played by Jean Hagan, has all the looks for cinema but when she opens her mouth: gah. This soup is, most definitely, the reverse.

Truly delicious, yet only likely to be instagrammed by those in search of few followers, it also happens to be about the best use for sourdough starter when you discard some in the process of refreshing it. It adds silk and a little punch of probiotic goodness, even if most is lost to the heat. Warming, sustaining and nutritious. Just what you need if you are about to dance with a mannequin on a sofa and run up a wall.

Serves 4

2–3 tbsp extra virgin olive oil, plus more to serve

1 onion, finely chopped

4 celery sticks, finely chopped

1 leek, finely chopped, washed and drained

2 carrots, peeled and finely chopped

4 garlic cloves, peeled but left whole

200g (7oz) Savoy cabbage, spring greens or kale, stalks removed and leaves shredded

400g (14oz) tin plum tomatoes

1 tbsp tomato purée

small bunch of rosemary or sage (about 3 big sprigs), leaves chopped

2 bay leaves

250g (9oz) sourdough starter

1 litre (1¾ pints) chicken or vegetable stock or water

400g (14oz) tin borlotti or cannellini beans, drained and rinsed

sea salt and freshly ground black pepper

small bunch of flat-leaf parsley, roughly chopped

Heat the oil in a large pan over a medium heat and fry the onion, celery, leek, carrot and garlic until completely soft, stirring occasionally – this may take 20 minutes or so.

Meanwhile simmer the greens in a pan of salted water for about 5 minutes until completely tender, then drain.

Add the plum tomatoes, tomato purée, rosemary or sage and bay leaves to the cooked vegetables, breaking the tomatoes up with a wooden spoon, and cook for a further 5 minutes until the tomato is rich and thick. Meanwhile put the sourdough starter in a large bowl.

Add the stock to the tomatoey vegetables and bring to a simmer, then add a couple of ladlefuls to the sourdough starter and mix well.

Add the sourdough mix back to the soup pan and stir occasionally while cooking over a medium heat for about 10 minutes until thickened.

Check the seasoning of the soup, amending if necessary, and adding a little more hot stock or water if it has become too thick. Remove the bay leaves.

Blend around a quarter of the soup until smooth, return to the pan, add the drained beans and cooked greens and gently heat through. Serve immediately, scattered with parsley and drizzled with olive oil.

SQUASH SOUP WITH DOUBLE LIME

When October comes and the world and his wife gets busy turning squash into soup, it fills me with anti-hunger. So often, it is as if all the leftover puddings in a 1950s rest home have been liquidized for your pleasure.

What squash needs, is a little sharp attention. As with gin and tonic, its delights are all the better for being complemented while diluted – here the lentils settle squash's sweetness down and add a little cotton to the silk. The sour comes in waves, with the lime zest adding depth from getting in there early, and the last-minute juice adding brightness and zing.

I often add coriander leaf at the end: it joins hands with the sour cream and lime in a wave of exotica that reminds me of a warm sea island I've yet to visit.

You can approach this in one of two ways: peel and dice the squash and simmer in the water for 15–20 minutes until cooked, or, as I usually do, roast the squash in segments if you have the oven on for something else, and once cooled, scoop the flesh from the skin for this soup.

Serves 4

3 tbsp olive oil

3 red onions, thinly sliced

3 celery sticks, chopped

5 garlic cloves, chopped

2 tbsp ground cumin

1 tbsp ground coriander

about 700g (1½lb) squash, peeled and diced (to give 300g/10oz prepared weight)

3 bay leaves

pared zest of 1 lime

1.2 litres (2¼ pints) water

250g (9oz) red lentils

200g (7oz) sour cream

½ tsp Aleppo pepper

2 limes, halved

sea salt and freshly ground black pepper

Heat the oil in a large pan, and gently cook the onions and celery until softened, about 15–25 minutes. Add the garlic, cumin and coriander, and a little salt and pepper, and cook for a few minutes.

Add the squash, bay leaves, lime zest and water, turn the heat up and bring to a simmer. Add the lentils and simmer for 15 minutes. If you are using cooked squash, add it after 10 minutes of simmering so that it heats through.

Use a spoon to lift out and discard the bay leaves and lime zest. Blitz the soup in a blender until smooth, then return to the pan and warm through a little over a medium heat. Season to taste with salt and pepper. Ladle into bowls, swirl each with sour cream, scatter with Aleppo pepper and serve each bowl with a lime half to squeeze over.

TURKISH YOGHURT SOUP

I first ate yoghurt soup in Istanbul many years ago while recovering my breath after being chased by two men through the streets near the Grand Bazaar. I still have no idea why they were after me, but when you hear heavy, quick paces and you are the only person ahead of them it's best to give it toes and wonder later at your leisure. The clever money is on them being rightly offended by my ludicrous hair of the time.

The soup was both restorative and a surprise: I mean, just how good can a soup made primarily of yoghurt be? Very, it turns out.

This is especially fine when a climatic or emotional winter has been around just a little too long. You can add cooked chickpeas (and use the liquid as the stock) or leftover cooked chicken if you like. A rubble of toasted pine nuts or almonds makes a fine topping too.

Serves 4

1 litre (1 ¾ pints) chicken stock (or use vegetable/chickpea liquid)

150g (5oz) white rice

1 tbsp plain flour

1 egg

500g (1lb 2oz) full-fat natural yoghurt

30g (1oz) butter

2 tsp dried mint

2 tsp chilli flakes (preferably Turkish), or more to taste

salt

Pour the stock into a large pan, add the rice and place over a medium heat. Cook the rice in the stock for about 25 minutes, giving a good stir every now and then so it doesn't stick, until the rice is fully cooked. Remove from the heat.

Whisk the flour, ½ teaspoon of salt and the egg into the yoghurt.

Whisk the yoghurt mixture into the rice and mix well, then gently simmer for 10 minutes until the soup has a creamy consistency. Check the seasoning, adding salt to taste.

While the soup is simmering, heat the butter in a small pan and when it foams add the dried mint and chilli flakes and immediately remove from the heat.

Pour the butter over the soup and serve, and life will feel that little bit better.

WHITE GAZPACHO

I have never been to Andalusia – it is, like the West Highland Way and contract bridge, set aside for when I can dedicate proper time to it. If it is half as wondrous as this soup from that region – also known as ajo blanco – leads me to imagine, I shall be happy.

In all fairness, I have no idea why garlic (ajo) enjoys lead billing here: this is a soup where almonds are king and sherry vinegar is queen. At a pinch, you can swap sherry vinegar for another, but this is one where a good sherry vinegar shines. You can get away with ground almonds if you're too idle to get to the shops for blanched, but the texture will suffer a little: the freshness and oils released by the blanched almonds makes such a difference. If you fancy, lightly toast the almonds in a dry pan first – it wafts a ghost of smoke across the soup. By all means, use green grapes, slices of a good sharp apple, chives, cucumber or peach instead of the cherries if you fancy.

Serves 4

200g (7oz) crustless stale white bread

150g (5oz) blanched almonds

3 garlic cloves, roughly chopped

600ml (1 pint) ice-cold water

150ml (5fl oz) extra virgin olive oil, plus a little more to garnish

2 tbsp good-quality sherry vinegar

salt

To serve

16 cherries, pitted and halved

few basil leaves

Soak the bread in cold water for 10 minutes, then strain and squeeze dry.

Use a food processor to grind the almonds to a fine powder, then add the garlic, bread and a pinch of salt and blend until smooth, adding a splash or two of the water if required. Taste to get a feel for the garlickiness, adding more if you like.

With the motor running, slowly add the rest of the water, followed by the oil and finally the vinegar. Blend until smooth, then season to taste with salt. Chill for at least 1 hour.

Serve topped with the cherries, drizzled with olive oil and a couple of basil leaves – this may be frowned upon in Andalusia but it works.

HOT AND SOUR SOUP (TOM YAM)

I have to admit, I'm not wildly keen on thin soups and broths: this is a happy exception. The chilli makes this as lively as Bonfire night, with the limes' sourness brightening the whole perfectly.

    If you use whole prawns, the heads and shells add depth of flavour, but use peeled if that's what you have. I usually make this with water but chicken stock will give a deeper flavour if that's what you fancy. Bird's-eye chillies can be exceptionally hot, and while tom yam should have plenty of chilli bite, you should certainly adjust the amounts to your taste.

Serves 4

1 tbsp vegetable oil

16 whole prawns, heads and shells removed and reserved, prawns de-veined

1 litre (1 ¾ pints) chicken stock (or use water)

4 lime leaves, torn in half

3 lemongrass stalks, each cut into 3

3 bird's-eye chillies (red or green), ½ thinly sliced, ½ left whole

2 slices of fresh galangal (or use fresh ginger)

½ small bunch (about 6 stalks) coriander, leaves and stalks separated

2 tomatoes, roughly chopped (underripe is quite good here)

100g (3 ½ oz) enoki or oyster mushrooms, roughly chopped

juice of 2 limes

2 tbsp fish sauce, plus more to taste

Heat the vegetable oil in a large pan and fry the prawn heads and shells (if you have them) for 3 minutes until pink, then add the stock or water and bring to the boil. Cook for 5 minutes, then strain out the shells and return the pan to the heat with the stock – if you don't use the heads and shells just heat the stock.

Bruise the lime leaves, lemongrass, whole chillies, galangal and coriander stalks in a pestle and mortar, or use a bowl and the end of a rolling pin, then add these along with the chopped tomato to the stock and allow to infuse at a gentle simmer for 5 minutes.

Add the prawns and the mushrooms and simmer for 2–3 minutes until just cooked.

Remove from the heat, remove the lime leaves and lemongrass and immediately add the sliced chillies, lime juice, fish sauce and coriander leaves, adjusting to your taste, and serve straight away.

CHANA CHAAT SALAD

So many cultures have a version of cucumber-tomato-onion-herb salad, a combination that captures the sun so perfectly. This classic Indian street food brings both refreshment and sustenance, and is endlessly adaptable – using potato (aloo) in place of chickpeas makes it aloo chaat, and so on. The key is striking the right balance, keeping sour a step forward in the mix. Whether you use this combination of lemon, yoghurt, pomegranate seeds and chaat masala, or substitute with (for example) lime, quick pickled red onions (see page 88) and crème fraîche is entirely up to you.

Chaat masala is a mesmerizing blend of spices led by amchur – a powder made of dried sour mango – bringing a gentle yet deep sourness. You can make your own (see page 20), but it is available in Indian supermarkets and online.

Serves 4 as a side

400g (14oz) tin chickpeas, drained and rinsed

1 cucumber, peeled, deseeded and finely chopped

1 small red onion, very finely chopped

3 ripe tomatoes, finely chopped

seeds from ½ pomegranate

small bunch of coriander, roughly chopped

juice of ½ lemon

115g (4oz) natural yoghurt

1 green chilli, finely chopped (optional) 50g (2oz) Bombay mix, sev or peanuts

2 tsp chaat masala (see page 96)

sea salt and freshly ground black pepper

Stir the chickpeas into the cucumber, onion, tomato, pomegranate seeds, coriander and lemon juice in a large bowl, then season to taste with salt and pepper.

Put on individual plates or a large platter and top with the yoghurt, chilli (if using) and the Bombay mix. Finish by sprinkling over the chaat masala.

ASPARAGUS, REDCURRANTS AND TAPENADE

Many years ago, I had the most vivid of dreams: I was living in a rooftop flat high above the streets of the French capital, the dream interwoven with half-remembered glimpses down streets, through shop windows and from café tables. It felt utterly real. I was (in) An American in Paris, it was spring and I was in love. Since discovering his blog, I suspect David Lebovitz to be living my my dream life: his updates fuelling my ever-expanding envy. His excellent fig and olive tapenade became a springboard for many of my own, including this punchy fellow. Sometimes I use just enough to provide a scant dressing here, other times it almost acts as a vegetable itself. It will keep for a week or three in the fridge.

A word of warning: this combination is full on. The coming together of bitter, sweet and salt is slapped about the head by the uncompromising lemon. I encourage you to dive in, to revel in the wince. If it's too much for you, reduce the amount of lemon and the size of the pieces, you big Jessie.

Serves 4 as a starter

400g (14oz) asparagus

2 lemons

a generous handful of redcurrants (frozen is fine)

small handful of mint leaves, very thinly sliced

sea salt

For the tapenade

100g (3½oz) plums, stoned and cooked

130g (4½oz) black olives, pitted

2 tbsp lemon juice

1 tbsp mustard (I like English for this)

1 garlic clove, peeled but left whole

1 tbsp capers

1 tbsp chopped thyme (ideally lemon thyme)

160ml (5½fl oz) extra virgin olive oil

freshly ground black pepper

First make the tapenade. In a blender, briefly blitz all the tapenade ingredients except the oil and pepper into a thick, coarse paste. Use a spatula to scrape the tapenade into a bowl and stir though 120ml (4fl oz) of the olive oil to create a loose, glossy sauce. Depending on the juiciness of the plums and olives, you may need to add a little more. Season with black pepper, if necessary.

Bring a pan of water large enough to comfortably accommodate the asparagus to a steady simmer. Add enough salt to make you wonder whether a fish might survive in it. Add the asparagus and simmer for 3–7 minutes, depending on the thickness of the asparagus – it should just resist while surrendering to the bite. While the asparagus is simmering, top and tail each lemon, peel and using a very sharp knife, slice either side of each membrane to release each segment of lemon. Drain the asparagus into a colander, then submerge briefly in cold water to hold its colour while not chilling it completely.

Toss the asparagus in half the tapenade, and either on a serving plate or individual plates, add as much extra tapenade as you fancy. Adorn with lemon segments, cast over the redcurrants and mint leaves and serve immediately.

HALLOUMI, MANGO, SHALLOT AND ROCKET SALAD WITH SPICY TAMARIND DRESSING

When the idea for this popped into my head, I could almost taste it. It's such a fine tumble of contrasting flavours and textures, and the sourness comes from the mango or the tamarind: you can never be sure of a mango until you taste it, so hold fire on finishing the dressing until you've tried the mango – add a little honey if it is unripe and sour; leave it alone if it is edging towards sweet.

This is great with pea shoots in place of rocket, coriander rather than mint, a red onion instead of the shallot, and by all means cast pomegranate seeds over the top. Play with it as you like.

Serves 2 as a lunch

2 tbsp olive oil

125g (4½oz) halloumi, sliced 5–7mm (¼in) thick

70g (2½oz) rocket

1 medium mango, peeled, stoned and cut into wedges

1 eschalot or other long shallot, halved lengthways and thinly sliced

12 mint leaves, very thinly sliced

pinch of Aleppo pepper

sea salt and freshly ground black pepper

spicy tamarind dressing (see page 114)

Heat the olive oil in a frying pan over a medium heat. Once shimmering, add the halloumi slices and fry until mottled golden on both sides. Lift out on to kitchen paper to drain.

Arrange the rocket in a large serving dish, lay the mango slices around fairly evenly spaced, and – tearing each slice in two as you go – dot the halloumi over the dish. Break the shallot slices into individual arcs and scatter them over the top. Use the tips of your fingers to agitate and gently disturb everything – you're aiming to combine a little but mostly just introduce a degree of pleasing dishevelment.

Sprinkle both the shredded mint and pinch of Aleppo pepper over the top, and grind a little salt and pepper across the ensemble.

Finally, having tasted a little of the mango for ripeness, make up the spicy tamarind dressing, adding the honey if the mango is sour, or leaving it out if the mango is sweet. Dot the dressing over the dish and serve.

CHICORY, RED GRAPEFRUIT, OLIVE, AVOCADO, TOASTED PINE NUT AND DILL SALAD WITH A RED GRAPEFRUIT AND ELDERFLOWER DRESSING

This is one of those salads that is as much of a split carrier bag of ingredients as it is a recipe. Its magic lies in the contrast of sweet, sour, bitter and salt – and while you can (and should) alter this to your heart's content, don't hold back on any of those flavours. Here, boldness rewards.

I use half red and half green chicory for looks, keeping the smallest leaves whole.

Serves 4

50g (2oz) pine nuts

1 red grapefruit

4 small-medium heads of chicory, leaves separated and sliced

130g (4½oz) black olives, pitted

1 avocado, peeled, stoned and sliced

small handful of dill, chopped

red grapefruit and elderflower dressing (see page 112)

Toast the pine nuts in a dry frying pan over a medium heat for a few minutes, agitating the pan frequently to prevent the nuts from burning.

Top and tail the grapefruit and then peel off the skin and membrane with a sharp knife – do this over a bowl so you can catch the juice, which you'll need to make the dressing. You can either slice the fruit thinly parallel to its equator, or slice either side of each membrane to release the segments.

Tumble the pine nuts, grapefruit, chicory, olives and avocado together with as much/little care and flair as you wish, serve on a large platter or individual plates, sprinkle with dill and splatter with the sweet/sharp dressing.

PRAWN WALDORF WITH SOUR CREAM DRESSING

This is exactly the sort of food that wouldn't have interested me in my twenties, with its clash of flavours and the hand of celery at large. Now, I find it brightens my mood on cold days or warm.

Thankfully, it is the work of just a few minutes and takes as well to being considerately composed for guests as it does to being tumbled into a lunchbox for a healthy lunch. A word to the wise: prepare the apple last; the cut sides darken quicker than my mood when United score late.

Serves 4

100g (3½oz) shelled pistachios

1 romaine lettuce, finely shredded

1 celery heart, shredded

2 sharp eating apples

300g (10oz) cooked peeled king prawns, deveined if necessary

130g (4½oz) seedless grapes, halved

sour cream dressing (see page 112)

Toast the pistachios in a dry frying pan over a medium heat for 2–3 minutes to stir up their flavour a little.

Combine the lettuce leaves with the celery. Core the apples and cut into wedges, then combine/arrange them over the leaves, along with the prawns and grapes. Spoon over the dressing and combine as little or as much as you fancy.

MANGO SALAD

If ever I tire of the home-worker's high-carb, quick-grab lunches and crave a
cold shower of freshness, this is one I turn to. It's a waltz, a cha cha cha and a
tango in the mouth, all at once. I tend to leave the herbs large-leaved and barely
shredded, to give a big hit of independent flavour from each, and I use red
(rather than green) chillies for looks, but the recipe is really a blueprint to play
with as you like. The mango should be unripe and sour, but if yours has
sweetened, consider upping the lime for balance. And, if you can find them,
small green mangoes are perfect here.

Serves 4

2 bird's-eye chillies,
deseeded and finely
chopped

1 garlic clove, finely
chopped

juice of 2 limes

50ml (2fl oz) fish sauce

2 tbsp sesame oil

2–3 tsp soft light brown
sugar

1 unripe mango, peeled and
julienned

2–3 shallots, thinly sliced

60g (2¼oz) unsalted
peanuts, roughly chopped

small handful of coriander
leaves, barely chopped

small handful of mint
leaves, barely chopped

3 tbsp toasted sesame seeds

sea salt and freshly ground
black pepper

Stir together the chillies, garlic, lime juice, fish sauce, sesame oil, sugar and
plenty of black pepper – this dressing should be a jumble of flavours more
than a complete amalgamation.

Combine the mango, shallots, two-thirds of the peanuts, coriander, mint,
sesame seeds and the dressing in a large bowl, season with salt to taste and
serve immediately with more nuts to the side and a cold beer.

ROAST PLUMS, GOAT'S LABNEH, TOASTED HAZELNUTS AND HONEY

This is little more than a simple invitation to bring a number of edible pals together, with each of their flavours, textures and scents bringing out the best in the others just by sitting next to them. An oven can coax flavour out of even the hardest of plums, but sour or not, don't add sugar – allow the honey to do its work against the sourness of the fruit and labneh.

The plums can be warm or at room temperature, and if you have ginger rosemary or orange thyme, use either instead of regular rosemary. The earthy acidity of the goat's labneh works particularly well in stitching the hazelnuts to the plums and the honey, but cow's milk labneh or even yoghurt are grand here too.

Serves 4

500g (1lb 2oz) plums, halved and stoned

1–2 sprigs of rosemary

1 star anise, broken into segments

150g (5oz) shelled hazelnuts

300g (10oz) goat's labneh

generous drizzle of honey

sea salt and freshly ground black pepper

Preheat the oven to 190°C/375°F/gas mark 5.

Place the plums in a small roasting dish, scatter with the rosemary and star anise and roast for 20–30 minutes until the fruit is cooked but before it has collapsed. If you do overcook them, it's not the end of the world.

While they're cooking, toast the hazelnuts in a dry frying pan over a lively heat, shaking the pan regularly to prevent burning – you are after only a little colour and your nose filling with their divine scent.

Bring this together however you like – I tend to start with a lifeboat of labneh to which the plums and hazelnuts cling, then slightly over-generously drizzle with a good, dark, strong honey and finish with a hint of salt and pepper.

RHUBARB AND RADISH SALAD

Young people take a moment to listen: there was once a dry, dark time when you rang a building in the hope that the person you wanted to speak to was in it. These were the Days Before The Internet, when you relied on the back of a book, the paragraphs before a recipe's ingredients, and word of mouth to guide you from recipe to recipe, from idea to inspiration. The pleasure of this culinary relay may have been slow, but it was no less rewarding for it. This cracking salad began when reading about radishes in *Jane Grigson's Vegetable Book* many years ago; she pointed me in the direction of Claudia Roden's Moroccan orange and radish salad, and from there, via a few side streets, I arrived here.

This salad owes everything to the freshness of the radish and rhubarb and your touch with the acidity. You can use lemon, orange or lime juice (or, like Claudia R, a combination of the first two), but to my mind this is the place for an excellent, characterful vinegar – I've used Burren Balsamics blood orange and cardamom vinegar and Cult Vinegar's Rose Vine Verde to great effect. The rose water sets everything off and encourages the radish and rhubarb to sit a little closer together while retaining their independence.

I haven't included amounts as they are yours to play with, though I like this with equal amounts of radish and rhubarb. With the blue cheese this has just enough about it to see you right for lunch; without, it makes a great side with oily and/or smoked fish, and is wonderful with tortilla and other egg-heavy recipes. A Zorro of pomegranate molasses over the top works well if you fancy extra zing.

Do keep the vinegar at the table – a few drops here and there might be just what you fancy.

rhubarb, very thinly sliced

rose water

radishes, very thinly sliced

vinegar

caster sugar

blue cheese, broken into nuggets

a little dill, barely chopped, to resemble the feathers of a small bird

sea salt and freshly ground black pepper

Sprinkle the rhubarb lightly with the rose water, and the radishes with the vinegar and the very merest hint of caster sugar, and allow both to infuse for a few minutes.

Lay the slices on a platter with as much/little artistic licence and your nature/hunger allows, dot with cheese, sprinkle with dill, salt and a little more pepper than you think would be right.

BRAISED SWEETCORN WITH CHILLI AND LIME

This is really an indoor compromise of a combination of Cuban street food and perfect outdoor barbecue fair; the combination is even better when the sweetcorn is barbecued; wood smoke being a great ingredient in itself. This also demonstrates the importance of adding sourness, and how well two sours can work together: the contrasting impact of the early, warming depth of the lime zest and the late refresher of the juice is just perfect here.

Serves 4 as a side or snack

70g (2½oz) butter

3 tbsp olive oil

4 corn cobs, cut in half

zest (ideally microplaned, for fineness) and juice of 1 lime

100ml (3½fl oz) boiling water

Aleppo pepper, or other dried chilli flakes

sea salt and freshly ground black pepper

Warm the butter and oil in a large pan over a medium heat. Carefully add the corn and cook for a couple of minutes, shaking the pan once in a while to ensure as much of the sweetcorn gets a few moments of the heat from the base of the pan. Add the lime zest and boiling water. Cover and braise for 8 minutes, shaking the pan to stir up the sweetcorn once in a while.

Turn off the heat, and remove the lid. Add the lime juice, a good few pinches of salt, a twist of pepper and a nice confetti-ing of Aleppo pepper. Agitate the pan to combine the spices with the citrusy, buttery oil. Serve immediately and eat with whatever slippery-chinned decorum you can muster.

SPROUTS, ALEPPO PEPPER AND CARAWAY

When life reaches a certain point, its primary goals – perhaps a great deal of outstanding sex, global travel and happiness – commute rapidly into the promise of a quick midweek tea. This – with a bit of leftover chicken, a slice or two of ham, or as it is (perhaps add a little bacon) – fits the bill perfectly and is one of my favourite ways with Brussels. Throw in a teaspoon of black mustard seeds, poppy seeds, fennel, or whatever spices take your fancy. I often stir in a generous splash of double cream at the end.

Serves 4 as a side

several good glugs of extra virgin olive oil

600g (1lb 5oz) Brussels sprouts, peeled and shredded into pound-coin thickness

4 tbsp cider vinegar

2 tsp caraway seeds

1 tbsp Aleppo pepper

Pour a good slick of oil into a large frying pan over a medium heat. Once it starts to ripple, add the sprouts and leave them for a minute: you want the sprouts to catch just a little, enough to smell vaguely of a day-after bonfire. Swish a little more oil over the back of the sprout slices, and flip them over to cook on the other side. Up the heat a little if progress seems slow. Once they're starting to soften nicely, add the vinegar. It should soak in to a degree while leaving a very shallow, bubbling gloss in the pan – add another tablespoon or two if not. Stir the sprouts and once there is no vinegar visible in the pan, stir through the caraway. Sprinkle over the Aleppo pepper and serve.

NEW POTATOES, BROAD BEANS, LEMON AND MINT

I love New Year. I wake up unbearably enlivened by possibility. The clean slate. The new dawn. The better me. In my mind, New Year's Day is always still, bright, crisp: suitable to my mood. I crave the sea and a lunchtime pint. It feels like it must be spring. This recipe is a breath of April at least – it's so fresh and bright, with the lemon melting into the oily butter. If I could have this on the first day of the year with fresh broad beans, everything would be ok: sadly, I must wait a few months, but when the first beans arrive, I eat this on a still, bright, cold, somewhat late New Year's Day of sorts.

Serves 4 as a side

500g (1lb 2oz) early salad potatoes

3 tbsp olive oil

few sprigs of lemon thyme (optional)

1 lemon

250g (9oz) podded broad beans

large handful of mint leaves, finely shredded

25g (1oz) butter

sea salt and freshly ground black pepper

Preheat the oven to 180°C/350°F/gas mark 4.

Halve any potatoes that aren't small and place them all in the centre of a piece of foil on a baking tray. Drizzle with olive oil, add the lemon thyme (if using) and season with a good few pinches of salt and twists of pepper. Make a parcel of the foil, crimping the edges together like a silver pasty. Cook for 30 minutes or so.

Meanwhile, remove the peel and pith of the lemon by slicing off the ends and then slicing from cut end to cut end. Cut the lemon in half through the equator and, over a bowl to catch the juice, release each half segment from its membranes. Squeeze the membranes of their juice, into the bowl.

Simmer the broad beans in a large pan of boiling water for 3–5 minutes, depending on their size. Drain and refresh under cold water.

Open the parcel, add the beans, lemon segments, mint leaves and butter, reseal and cook for a further 15 minutes or so until the potatoes are perfectly cooked. Serve with roast lamb, grilled fish, or with a leafy salad.

SUMMER ROJAK

Comfort food needn't be heavy and slow-cooked: rojaks are South East Asian salads, full of fruit, leaves, sprouts and crunch; a festival of sweet, sour and hot that's both restorative and quietly energizing. Every mouthful feels like a celebration of life and sunshine.

The dressing is all-important: don't be shy with the heat or sourness of the sambal oelek dressing as it's what makes everything else work.

You can use this as a template to make a quick, midweek supper with whatever is sitting in the fridge in otherwise unpromising quantities, but when you have the time and inclination, try this as is: it's beyond refreshing. Be organized: make the dressing first, so you can serve quickly once the peeling and chopping are done.

And whatever you think of pineapple, indulge me here. I spent most childhood summers in Lancashire with the cousins, discovering sticklebacks, dandelion and burdock, and Kendal mint cake, and, being a terrible taker-oner of accents, I would come back speaking like George Formby; give me a two-mile cab ride through London and I'll see the driver off with a 'Stay lucky, treacle'. Pineapple is my fruit equivalent – sweet as your nan, but stand it next to anything even slightly acidic and it lets out a glorious roar of sourness, and that's what joins the dots between everything here.

Serves 4
½ large ripe mango, peeled
½ ripe papaya, deseeded and peeled
8 good-sized radishes, sliced
½ cucumber, peeled
½ ripe pineapple, peeled
280g (9¾oz) firm tofu
4 tbsp extra virgin olive oil
50g (2oz) shelled pistachios
150g (5oz) beansprouts
90g (3¼oz) lamb's lettuce
sambal oelek dressing (see page 113)

Chop the fruit and vegetables into smallish pieces. Cut the tofu into 2cm (¾in) cubes. Warm the olive oil in a large frying pan over a medium heat. Add the tofu and fry, turning the cubes regularly, until golden on all sides, this should take 10 minutes or so. Drain the tofu on kitchen paper.

Toast the pistachios in a dry frying pan over a medium heat, agitating the pan occasionally to prevent them from burning; you want to smell the scent of the nuts rising, not see it.

You can assemble this either as a glorious tumble of everything in a large bowl, with the dressing coating everything, or with more consideration on a platter, with hot red splashes of dressing heat across it, with more dressing in a jug.

SPICED AUBERGINE

This is really quite something. Make it with year-old spices from the supermarket and it will be truly delicious; if you use the freshest of spices from a specialist, it's off the scale. I ought to talk at length about amchur – the dried mango powder that brings such a special sour flavour to this spiced aubergine (aka *baingan bharta*), curries, soups, desserts and pretty much anything you want to bring a bit of zing to – but the actual secret here is the much underused asafoetida. A little bitter, oniony and pungent, asafoetida not only lays a base against which the sweet onion and garlic, the spices and the sour amchur work, it acts as a harmonizer, an accentuator and a catalyzer to everything around it. It is that excellent host who makes the party fly, everyone relaxed and inter-woven. I find asafoetida works best with warmth rather than heat, so don't serve this fully hot, as the herbs and spices can get a little lost in a single wave of flavour; allowing it to cool and relax a little allows the distinctiveness of each ingredient to come through. This is one to repeatedly taste as it cooks – aubergine can be a salt-hungry little devil, so you may want to season regularly as you go.

You can, of course, char the aubergines over a naked flame, and if you have anything going into the oven for an hour or more and you have an aubergine or two in danger of becoming as baggy as a tapir's nose, pop them in and freeze the peeled flesh for using in this later.

Serves 4 as a side or snack, perhaps with flatbreads

2 medium aubergines (about 600g/1lb 5oz)

3 tbsp vegetable oil

1 onion, finely chopped

1 tsp finely chopped ginger

2 garlic cloves, finely chopped

½ tsp asafoetida

½ tsp ground turmeric

½ x 400g (14oz) tin chopped tomatoes

1 tsp garam masala

1 tsp ground cumin

2 tsp ground coriander

¼ tsp red chilli flakes

½ tsp amchur

salt

small handful of coriander leaves, roughly chopped

Preheat the oven to 200°C/400°F/gas mark 6. Wrap each aubergine in foil, place in the oven and roast for about an hour. It should feel like its structure collapses on a gentle squeeze. Allow to cool wrapped in foil, then peel and discard the skin.

Heat the oil in a medium frying pan and cook the onion slowly until soft, stirring occasionally. Add the ginger and garlic and cook for a few minutes before stirring in the asafoetida and turmeric and cooking for a few minutes longer. Add the tomatoes and simmer for a couple of minutes, stirring occasionally. Add the garam masala, cumin, coriander, chilli flakes and amchur.

Roughly chop the aubergines and add to the pan, along with a generous pinch of salt. Simmer for 10–12 minutes, stirring occasionally and using the back of a wooden spoon to encourage the aubergines to break up a little. Bring quickly to a boil and immediately remove from the heat. Taste and add a little more salt if needed.

Allow to rest a little before serving sprinkled with a good amount of chopped coriander.

CHAAT ROASTED CABBAGE

Few weeks pass when I don't make this. Four waves of the knife (five if you're the sort to take a sliver off the base), a bit of drizzling and dusting and you have the quickest, cheapest of delicious side dishes to anything you might be roasting. I love this with lamb, roasted vegetables or sausages in particular, but it's so easy and good it gets eaten with almost anything.

It is eminently tweakable too: try caraway or fennel for star anise; anardana or ras al hanout for the chaat.

This is not one to over-fuss: if you are cooking something on 20°C above or below, it will be just fine – just adjust the timing. What you are looking for is a good degree of charring without the full towering inferno: the sweetness in the green and bitterness in the black go with the sour chaat just perfectly.

Serves 4 as a side
1 pointed green cabbage
2 tbsp olive oil
1 star anise
4 tbsp chaat masala
(see page 96)
juice of ½ lemon (optional)
sea salt and ground black pepper

Preheat the oven to 200°C/400°F/gas mark 6.

Quarter the cabbage, from top to tail. Lay the wedges on a tray and drizzle with olive oil, turning each quarter so its cut side is uppermost to encourage oil into the folds. Salt and pepper generously.

Zap the star anise in a coffee or spice grinder until it is fairly fine. Sprinkle this on each cut edge, then sprinkle each with chaat.

Roast in the oven for 15 minutes or so. Check after about 12 minutes: it's ready when it looks like it's found its way home from the pub with its tie to one side having had a couple after work. Serve with a squeeze of lemon juice for an extra dash of brightness.

MAIN COURSES

CHICKEN ADOBO

My wife calls this 'chicken in Marmite', which isn't entirely accurate, but then she's not completely off aim either. The wildly salty, sour sauce will have your fingers going back for more even when you're full. It's up to you as to how viscous you make the sauce: I like it to cling to the chicken like my auntie's perfume to my cheek when she administered an unwelcome kiss when I was 6, so I simmer it if needed.

Serves 4

8 bone-in, skin-on chicken thighs

1 head of garlic, broken into cloves, and peeled

180ml (6fl oz) white wine vinegar

120ml (4fl oz) soy sauce

4 dried bay leaves, torn up

1 medium-sized, moderately hot, green chilli, finely chopped

1 tbsp soft dark brown sugar

2 tbsp olive oil

freshly ground black pepper

Preheat the oven to 200°C/400°F/gas mark 6.

Place the chicken pieces in a roasting dish of a size that accommodates the pieces in a single layer. Add all the ingredients except the oil and tumble the chicken pieces through to coat them well. Leave to marinate for half an hour, turning the chicken through the ingredients once after 15 minutes.

Turn the chicken pieces so they are skin side up, brush with olive oil and season with black pepper.

Roast for 15 minutes, then turn the temperature down to 170°C/340°F/gas mark 3 and cook for another 35 minutes. I usually find that the sauce is perfect as is, but as with most things, it can vary and be a little thinner than usual from time to time. In which case, pour into a pan and simmer until reduced, keeping the chicken warm in the dish while you do.

I like this with smashed new potatoes, plain rice or chips. And a touch of greenery, if forced.

CHICKEN AU VINAIGRE

Sherry vinegar, mustard and double cream: I suspect my shoes would make a fine supper simmered in that trio; with chicken it is extraordinary, the sour vinegars and wine bringing the complex best from the tomatoes and shallots. You can make this with chicken thighs, jointed chicken or as here, a whole bird in a pot. Any leftovers make a weirdly special pasta sauce. Serve with over-buttered white-peppered mash, and sprouting broccoli.

Serves 4

4 tbsp olive oil

1.3kg (2lb 14oz) free-range chicken

3 tomatoes

3 tbsp butter

4 shallots, cut in half lengthways and very thinly sliced

8 garlic cloves, finely chopped

1 tbsp tomato purée

2 tbsp sherry vinegar

3 tbsp white wine vinegar

350ml (12fl oz) white wine

1 tbsp Dijon mustard

100ml (3½fl oz) double cream

3 tbsp tarragon leaves, finely chopped

salt and freshly ground black pepper

Preheat the oven to 180°C/350°F/gas mark 4.

Heat the oil in a large casserole and fry the chicken – adding salt and pepper to the skin as you go, until golden on all sides. Remove the chicken from the pan, on to a plate.

While that's happening, place the tomatoes in a bowl and pour boiling water over; after 2 minutes pour off the water – the skins should come off easily. Remove the tough scar from the stalk, and finely chop the tomatoes.

Melt the butter in the casserole and gently cook the shallots until soft and glossy, 10–15 minutes. Add the garlic and chopped tomato and cook for 2 minutes. Stir in the tomato purée and cook for a couple of minutes.

Add both vinegars and cook until the sauce is glossy and the vinegar largely taken up. Pour in the wine and cook until it has reduced by about a third.

Place the chicken in the casserole and pop it into the oven. Cook for 50 minutes, then check to see if it is cooked – I usually cut between leg and body; if the juices run clear, it is done. Allow another 10 minutes if not, and/or the chicken is a little bigger, longer if needed.

Lift the chicken out on to a plate. Stir the mustard into the pan, add the cream and bring to a gentle simmer. Season with salt and pepper, turn off the heat and stir in the tarragon. Slice or joint the chicken as you like, and either spoon over the sauce, or add the chicken back to the pan and serve from there.

WINTER TABBOULEH

This is a dish to please both your slovenly and inventive sides: to make either with great consideration and finesse, or for those times when you have one or half of everything in the fridge and want to create a quick, incredible meal. Here, the pomegranate molasses dressing and pomegranate seeds ring sour punctuation without dominating.

Prepare the vegetables that turn brown first (in this case, just the pears), and stir them in a bowl with the lemon juice to prevent them discolouring.

Serves 4

150g (5oz) coarse bulgur wheat

2 pears, peeled, cored and sliced

1 large parsnip, peeled, core removed and coarsely chopped

½ small cauliflower, trimmed of leaves and shaved into tiny florets

½ fennel bulb or celery heart, trimmed and finely chopped

200g (7oz) curly kale or ¼ savoy cabbage, stalks removed and leaves thinly sliced

1 large chicory or radicchio, thinly sliced

1 tsp sumac (optional)

juice of 1 lemon

small bunch of mint or dill, roughly chopped

small bunch of flat-leaf parsley, roughly chopped

seeds from 1 large pomegranate

80g (3oz) walnuts or almonds, roughly chopped

sea salt and freshly ground black pepper

For the dressing

zest and juice of ½ lemon

80ml (3fl oz) olive oil

50ml (2fl oz) pomegranate molasses (or use fresh pomegranate juice mixed with honey)

1 small garlic clove, crushed

½ tsp ground cinnamon

Put the bulgur wheat into a bowl, cover with 5cm (2in) of warm water and soak 15 minutes, then drain well in a sieve.

Put all the salad ingredients into a large bowl, reserving some pomegranate seeds and nuts to sprinkle over the top.

Mix all of the dressing ingredients together and season to taste, then mix into the salad ingredients along with the drained bulgur; check the seasoning. I sometimes serve the dressing in a jug as it dulls the bright colours of the salad. Scatter over the reserved pomegranate seeds and nuts and serve.

BUTTERMILK FRIED CHICKEN

Growing up in the late seventies and early eighties, there were few things you wished for more than a bucket of fried chicken. It had arrived from the States along with *The Dukes of Hazzard*, Harleys and Pepsi in a wave of wild exotica: everything from the States seemed better than what we were used to. Well, it's payback time. This blows socks off the high-street fried chicken, with the buttermilk tenderizing the chicken beautifully.

Serves 4

800g (1lb 12oz) boneless skinless chicken thighs, cut into 2 through the joint

300ml (10fl oz) buttermilk

2 garlic cloves, crushed

1 tsp Tabasco (optional) or Sambal oelek (see page 113)

1 tbsp chopped rosemary or thyme leaves (or use both)

300g (10oz) polenta

100g (3½oz) cornflour

100g (3½oz) self-raising flour (or use 400g/14oz panko or other dry breadcrumbs instead of the polenta, cornflour and self-raising flour mix)

sea salt and freshly ground black pepper

vegetable oil, for frying

Mix the chicken with the buttermilk, garlic, 1½ teaspoons each of salt and pepper and the Tabasco or Sambal oelek (if using). Refrigerate for 8–24 hours.

Remove the chicken from the fridge 1 hour before you want to start frying. Combine the polenta and both flours (or the breadcrumbs) with ½ teaspoon salt.

Carefully heat a large, deep pan with enough vegetable oil to fully submerge the chicken. Add a thin slice of onion; when it starts to brown it will be ready to fry.

Remove the chicken from the marinade and dredge the chicken directly into the flour mix or breadcrumbs, coating each piece well, and fry in batches of about 3 pieces, so you don't crowd the pan, for about 3–4 minutes until cooked through and golden brown.

Drain on kitchen paper and repeat with the remaining chicken pieces. Serve immediately.

LIME PICKLE CHICKEN WITH KOSAMBARI SLAW

When I made my first batch of lemon and lime pickle (see page 94), my brain ran around searching for excuses to eat it. After a few interesting experiments with marinades, this resulted: by all means serve it with rice and raita, greens or leaves, but I love it with this simple kosambari slaw. Classically, kosambari is an Indian salad including pulses, but here the warming signature mustard seed and curry leaf spicing works beautifully with cabbage, carrot and lemon-onion slaw. A handful of crushed cashews scattered over just before serving works well if you are in the mood.

And no, you don't have to shred the chicken: feel free to serve the pieces whole.

Serves 4

4 tbsp lemon and lime pickle (see page 94), or use shop-bought lime pickle

2 garlic cloves, finely chopped

1 tsp ground turmeric

1 fresh green chilli, finely chopped (plus 1 more to serve if you like)

3 tbsp yoghurt

1 small onion, finely chopped

8 small (or 4 large) bone-in, skin-on, chicken thighs

1 lemon

1 small pointed cabbage, thinly sliced

1 large carrot, coarsely grated

1 tsp mustard seeds

3 tbsp sunflower oil

4 curry leaves (optional)

small bunch of coriander, roughly chopped

small bunch of mint, roughly chopped

sea salt and freshly ground black pepper

In a blender, blitz the pickle, garlic, turmeric, green chilli, yoghurt and half the chopped onion to a smooth purée. Smear over the chicken and allow it to marinate in the fridge for at least 1 hour and for up to 8 hours. If marinating for a good while, remove the chicken from the fridge 1 hour before cooking to allow it to reach room temperature.

Sprinkle the remaining onion with salt and leave for 1 minute, then rinse and drain. Squeeze over the juice of half the lemon and put to one side.

Preheat the oven to 180°C/350°F/gas mark 4.

Season the chicken with salt and pepper, then place in a single layer in a snug baking tray, spooning over any excess marinade. Add 50ml (2fl oz) water and roast for 40–45 minutes, basting three or four times, until the chicken is cooked through and just beginning to char.

While the chicken is roasting, mix the cabbage, carrot and lemon-marinated onion, then season with salt and pepper to taste. Fry the mustard seeds in the oil until they start spluttering, add the curry leaves, then pour over the cabbage and toss well. Spoon on to plates or platters.

Remove the chicken from the oven, allow to rest for 10 minutes before cutting or tearing into large shreds, removing bones.

Serve the chicken on top of the slaw, sprinkle over the coriander and mint and serve.

SUMAC DUCK, CHICORY, CELERIAC AND POMEGRANATE

In Iran and neighbouring countries, it is perfectly usual for sumac to be on the table, alongside salt and pepper, to use as you wish: I greatly encourage you to do the same. A dusting of its bright citrusy excellence on chips or hummus should convince you.

Sumac works very well with chicken, and perhaps even more happily with duck, as here. This has so much good going on: salt, sweet, bitter and the glorious layering of sours, with sumac on the duck, chicory cooked in verjuice, pomegranate seeds and a final swizzle of pomegranate molasses to serve.

If you fancy a salad of rocket, mizuna or watercress to go with, you'd be a good person.

Serves 4

300g (10oz) celeriac, peeled and chopped into 3cm (1¼in) pieces

600ml (1 pint) whole milk

60g (2¼oz) butter

2 heads of chicory, halved lengthways

4 tsp caster sugar

100ml (3½fl oz) verjuice (or pomegranate juice)

4 duck breasts

3 tsp sumac

a little pomegranate molasses (optional)

seeds from 1 pomegranate

sea salt and freshly ground black pepper

Preheat the oven to 200°C/400°F/gas mark 6.

Simmer the celeriac in the milk with ½ teaspoon of salt for 15–20 minutes until the celeriac is tender. Drain the celeriac, reserving the milk. Blend the celeriac until smooth, using a little of the milk to help achieve a spoonable consistency.

Fry half the butter until it is a light nut-brown colour, then remove from the heat and stir into the celeriac purée. Cover and leave to one side.

Melt the remaining butter in the same pan, add the chicory cut side down in a single layer and season with salt and pepper. Fry for 2 minutes, then use a spatula to turn the chicory, sprinkling each half with the sugar. Cook for a further 2 minutes.

Pour in the verjuice and cook for another 6–8 minutes (you want to keep the chicory slightly resistant to the bite).

Season the duck on both sides with salt and pepper and half the sumac.

Place skin side down in a dry, cold ovenproof frying pan. Place over a medium-high heat and cook for 5 minutes without moving, or until the skin is golden brown and caramelized in places. Turn the duck breasts and transfer to the oven, skin side up, for 5 minutes for pink, or until cooked to your liking. Remove from the oven and leave to rest for 5 minutes.

Warm the celeriac and chicory and slice the duck. Arrange on plates or a platter topped with the remaining sumac, a scant drizzle of pomegranate molasses (if using) and the pomegranate seeds.

PHEASANT, BLACKBERRIES, WATERCRESS AND PEAR

I was born autumnal. Give me nine months of food like this, an unnecessary open fire and Nick Drake on repeat and I'd be content. The coming together of the fruit with the pheasant and the kick of watercress is really special, and the three sours – blackberries, vinegar and anardana (see page 19) – create a bright backdrop against which everything is projected.

If the temperature outside drops enough for the fire to be on, try this with the shredded sprouts (see page 148) in place of the watercress, and/or the celeriac purée (see page 166). A scattering of bacon lardons on serving is entirely excellent too, if not strictly necessary.

Serves 4

30g (1oz) melted butter

3 tbsp olive oil

2 firm but ripe pears, each sliced into 6

4 x 150g (5oz) pheasant breasts, preferably with skin on

3 tbsp anardana (optional)

1 shallot, finely chopped

2 tbsp red wine vinegar or sherry vinegar

1 tbsp nut oil (walnut or hazelnut if you have it, olive oil if not)

½ small bunch of chives, finely chopped (about 3 tbsp)

150g (5oz) blackberries

1 bunch of watercress, stalks trimmed

sea salt and freshly ground black pepper

Warm half the butter and 1 tablespoon of the olive oil in a frying pan over a medium heat, add the pear slices and fry for 2–3 minutes until golden brown. Remove from the pan and keep warm.

Brush the pheasant on both sides with the remaining butter and season with half the anardana (if using) and salt and pepper.

Sear the pheasant in a hot pan, starting skin side down, for 2–3 minutes each side until golden brown. Reduce the heat a little, cover and cook gently for 3–4 minutes on each side until just cooked through. Place on a plate, cover and leave to rest for 5 minutes.

Fry the shallot in the same pan for about 30 seconds until slightly softened, then add the vinegar to deglaze the pan, scraping up the snaggly brown bits.

Remove from the heat and mix in the nut oil, remaining olive oil, chives, blackberries and salt and pepper to taste.

Slice the pheasant breasts thinly.

Place the watercress on to four plates or a big platter. Add the pheasant and pear, then drizzle with the warm blackberry dressing, dust with the rest of the anardana and serve immediately.

TAMARIND PORK RIBS

It's 8.07am and I'm writing about tamarind ribs and now all I want for second breakfast is tamarind ribs. And all I'll want for lunch and dinner is tamarind ribs. They may take a while in the oven, but the only attention you need to pay here is in softening the onions slowly: after that, you just have to come back in a couple of hours with an appetite.

The sauce is hugely adaptable: when I couldn't get good pork ribs, I tried it with a rack of lamb – cooked hard at 200°C/400°F/gas mark 6 for 15 minutes, before being slathered on the sauce and cooked for another 25 minutes at 160°C/325°F/gas mark 3 – and it was extraordinary.

Serves 2–3 (or just me watching a game)

4 tbsp olive oil

2 onions, finely diced

10 garlic cloves, thinly sliced

15g (½oz) fresh ginger, peeled and finely chopped

1½ tsp fennel seeds

1 star anise

1½ tsp Aleppo pepper

5 tbsp dark soy sauce

3 tbsp tomato ketchup

3 tbsp maple syrup

60g (2¼oz) soft dark brown sugar

5 tbsp tamarind paste (ideally made from tamarind block, see page 18)

1kg (2lb 4oz) pork ribs

sea salt and freshly ground black pepper

Preheat the oven to 150°C/300°F/gas mark 2.

Warm the oil in a frying pan over low-medium heat, add the onions and fry slowly, stirring often – we are after sweet softness, without burning, so expect it to take 15–25 minutes. Add the garlic and ginger and cook for a few minutes more. Add the spices, stir and cook for a couple of minutes. Add the soy sauce, ketchup, maple syrup, sugar and tamarind paste and stir to incorporate thoroughly. Season with salt and pepper. Cook just for a minute or two.

Place the ribs into a roasting tray large enough to accommodate them in a single layer, close-ish but not jammed in. Spoon the spicy paste over the ribs.

Cover the tray in foil and cook for 2 hours. Turn the heat up to 180°C/350°F/gas mark 4. Uncover the ribs and taste the paste, seasoning more if needed. Spoon some of the paste from the tin over the ribs. Replace the foil, and return to the oven for 20 minutes more – be careful; you are after dark and sweet–sour gooey rather than black and burnt.

Remove from the oven and allow the ribs to cool a little, before serving with pea shoots and a sharp dressing, or just a cold beer.

PORK VINDALOO

If you are the sort of excellent person who likes to look forward to what you'll eat later in the week, you can make this well ahead. Marinate overnight, and then allow another 24 hours once everything is cooked to allow the flavours to develop. Warm through slowly and thoroughly.

Vindaloo is defined more by its acidity than the infamous heat. The Portuguese, who used vinegar to preserve meat on long journeys, introduced its acidity to India around 600 years ago. The word 'vindaloo' originates from the Portuguese *carne de vinha d'alhos*; meat in vinegar and garlic. Neither of those ingredients is used sparingly here, and the tamarind adds more fruity sourness.

Serves 4 generously

800g (1lb 12oz) pork shoulder, cut into 3cm (1¼in) chunks

4 tbsp coconut oil or vegetable oil

500g (1lb 2oz) onions (about 4 medium onions), thinly sliced

75g (2½oz) tamarind block or 5 tbsp paste from a jar

12 garlic cloves, thinly sliced

6cm (2½in) piece of fresh ginger, peeled and finely chopped

4 medium-hot chillies, deseeded and finely chopped

400g (14oz) tin chopped tomatoes

16 curry leaves

3 tsp black mustard seeds

1 tsp salt

For the masala paste

2 tbsp Kashmiri red chilli powder or hot paprika

10 green cardamom pods, seeds only

1 tsp black peppercorns

6 cloves

1 tbsp cumin seeds

1 tbsp coriander seeds

1 tbsp ground turmeric

6cm (2½in) cinnamon stick

80ml (3fl oz) banana vinegar (see page 82) or cider vinegar

Using a pestle and mortar or coffee grinder, reduce the masala spices to a rough powder. Stir in the vinegar to create a loose paste and tumble the pork through. Leave to marinate for 3 hours minimum, ideally overnight.

Heat the oil in a large pan over a medium heat and fry the onions until soft, 12–15 minutes at least, stirring regularly. While they are cooking, break up the tamarind block (if using) and stir into twice its weight of boiling water – if you love tamarind as much as I do, it's useful to prepare more than you need for this recipe, so that you have more to use in dressings, cocktails and so on.

Add the garlic, ginger and chillies to the onions, and cook for 5 minutes or so, stirring frequently. Add the tomatoes and curry leaves and use the back of a wooden spoon to encourage the tomato pieces to break down and soften into the sauce.

Add the pork, mustard seeds, salt and tamarind and bring back to a lively boil before lowering the heat to the laziest of simmers. Cover and cook for an hour or so, stirring once in a while.

Uncover and cook until the meat is really tender and the sauce has thickened nicely – this should take 30–45 minutes. Serve with basmati rice and/or flatbreads.

HAM CHOUCROUTE

This is almost worth being ill for: I know of no finer restorative. If you can lay your hands on a ham hock (ideally smoked) for this, then happy days, but it is almost as magnificent with gammon. There is a bit of flexibility on the spices/aromatics so don't worry if you are missing the odd one. You could certainly increase to two hocks or a larger gammon if you're feeding meat fiends. There will be ham stock left over for soups and so on, too.

Serves 4 generously

1 smoked ham hock or 400g (14oz) gammon

2 large onions, 1 left whole and 1 finely chopped

2 large carrots, 1 left whole and 1 finely chopped

2 garlic cloves, 1 left whole and 1 finely chopped

2 celery sticks, 1 left whole and 1 finely chopped

2 bay leaves

1 star anise

2 tsp coriander seeds, lightly crushed

1 tsp juniper berries, lightly crushed

1 tsp black peppercorns

2 tbsp butter or oil

100g (3½oz) smoked streaky bacon, finely chopped

500g (1lb 2oz) sauerkraut (see page 56)

1 glass of dry white wine, such as Alsace (optional)

4 tbsp crème fraîche (optional)

2 tbsp finely chopped flat-leaf parsley

sea salt and freshly ground white or black pepper

If using a ham hock, place it into a large pan, cover with cold water and bring to the boil. Drain and discard the water. (If using gammon, you don't need to do this.)

Return the hock/place the gammon into a pan and cover with fresh cold water. Add the whole onion, carrot, garlic and celery and bring to the boil.

Give a quick skim to remove any foamy scum, then add 1 bay leaf, the star anise, half the coriander seeds, half the juniper berries and half the peppercorns.

Reduce the heat, partially lid the pot and cook at a gentle simmer for 2–3 hours for the hock, and 50 minutes or so for the gammon (add 20 minutes for each additional 400g/14oz). When cooked the hock should easily pull away from the bone with a skewer or fork.

Leave to cool in the liquid until cool enough to handle. Remove from the stock and pull off the meat in large chunks, discarding excess fat and the bone if using a ham hock. Strain the stock and reserve.

Heat the butter in a pan, add the bacon and gently sauté until very lightly coloured. Add the finely chopped vegetables, the remaining spices and bay leaf and cook for 10 minutes until soft and sweet. Add the sauerkraut and the wine (if using) and stir well.

Add the reserved stock and gently bring to the boil while you cut a circle of greaseproof paper to fit the pan. Nestle the meat into the choucroute. Wet the greaseproof paper and scrunch up, then unfold and use to cover the choucroute and meat snugly.

Gently braise the choucroute for about 45 minutes until the liquid has just about completely evaporated. Finish by checking the seasoning, adding salt and pepper, removing as many of the whole spices as you can.

To serve, stir in the crème fraîche (if using) and parsley and serve piping hot.

SAUERBRATEN

My wife accuses me of thinking about what's for tomorrow's tea while enjoying today's breakfast. She's not always wrong. Occasionally, as with sauerbraten, I'm even thinking another day ahead, as the beef sits in a joyous marinade for a couple days, tenderizing the meat and deepening its flavour.

Sauerbraten is usually made with red wine and red wine vinegar, but red wine can give me a fluorescent migraine, and I prefer the blend of a hoppy ale with apple cider vinegar. Traditionally, the vegetables and spices are not used for the sauce and it is thickened not with flour but with ginger biscuits, but I rather like blending all those marinated vegetables and most of the spices in the sauce, and saving the biscuit crumb later for flavour and contrast.

Serves 6

500ml (18fl oz) bottle of hoppy ale

200ml (7fl oz) cider vinegar

3 carrots, chopped

3 celery sticks, chopped

3 onions, thinly sliced

4 garlic cloves, thinly sliced

1 tbsp whole black peppercorns

1 tbsp juniper berries

1 tbsp yellow mustard seeds

3 cloves

4 bay leaves, torn in half

handful of fresh thyme sprigs

1kg (2lb 4oz) beef silverside

2 tbsp vegetable oil

6 ginger biscuits, crushed to a crumble

generous handful of flat-leaf parsley, chopped

sea salt and freshly ground black pepper

Add the ale, cider vinegar, carrot, celery, onion, garlic and all the spices and herbs to a medium pan and bring to the boil.

Meanwhile, sprinkle salt over the beef on all sides and place it in a high-sided container that will accommodate the beef and marinade. Once the pan has reached a boil, remove it from the heat and set aside to cool. When it is completely cool pour over the beef. Cover and refrigerate, turning once a day, for two days.

Preheat the oven to 170°C/340°F/gas mark 3.

Lift the beef from the marinade, removing as much of the herbs and spices from its surface as you can. Heat the oil in a pan over a medium heat and brown the beef on all sides.

Place the beef in a cast-iron pan with a lid (or similar) and pour the marinade over. Cover and cook in the oven for around 2 hours 45 minutes, at which point the beef should be very tender.

Lift the beef from the pan and while it rests, spend 5 minutes removing and then discarding as many of the juniper berries and peppercorns as you can be bothered to. Blitz the liquid, spices and vegetables in a blender until it becomes a smooth sauce. Slice the beef and either serve on a platter or individual plates, spooning the sauce over and adding some of the ginger biscuit crumb and a good sprinkling of chopped parsley.

SIRKA GOSHT

Having spent the first 13 years of his life in Sri Lanka, my dad had a healthy fondness for spicy food that was sadly unmatched by culinary inquisitiveness. I now suspect life's disappointments made him lean towards the familiar: we ate the same blindingly hot curry often. In fairness, it banished any potential colds that might be lurking and flushed the tear ducts effectively. Were he alive, I would make this curry for us all to eat together; I have a feeling he would have liked it, lively as it is and with malt vinegar (his favourite vinegar) at its heart. And eating with his granddaughter across the table might have eased those disappointments a little too.

This is hugely rich, so go easy on the portions. It is fairly adaptable too, as long as you use some kind of vinegar (sirka) and lamb (gosht). Reduce the cooking time by an hour or so if using diced lamb. And if you can, use the outstanding malt vinegar from The Old Nuclear Bunker, Coverack, Cornwall (see page 282); it makes a real difference.

Serves 4

1 tbsp finely grated fresh ginger

3 garlic cloves, crushed

1 onion, thinly sliced

2 tsp ground cumin

2 tsp chilli powder

1 tsp salt

100ml (3 ½ fl oz) malt vinegar

half shoulder of lamb (about 800g/1lb 12 oz)

2 tbsp ghee or vegetable oil

1 cinnamon stick

5 cloves

2 black cardamom pods

4 green cardamom pods

150ml (5fl oz) double cream

2 tsp garam masala

mint leaves and pomegranate seeds, to serve

In a blender, whizz the ginger, garlic, half the onion, cumin, chilli powder, salt and vinegar to a smooth sauce. Rub this into the lamb and leave for at least 2 hours, ideally overnight, to marinate.

Preheat the oven to 180°C/350°F/gas mark 4.

In a good-sized heavy-based lidded casserole, fry the remaining onion in the ghee or vegetable oil for 10–15 minutes until soft, then add the whole spices and then the lamb. Add enough water to just cover the meat. Cover and place in the oven for 3–4 hours until the meat is completely tender.

Remove from the oven, and take the meat out of the liquid with a slotted spoon, putting it to one side on a plate and covering with foil. Place the pan over a high heat to bring up to a good simmer and reduce the sauce by about half, stirring often.

Add the cream and simmer for a further 10 minutes until the sauce is rich and coats the back of a wooden spoon. Check the seasoning and return the meat to the pan, along with any juices on the plate. Warm through, then sprinkle over the garam masala and top with pomegranate seeds and mint leaves. Serve with rice and/or flatbreads.

RHUBARB KHORESH WITH CAULIFLOWER AND YOGHURT

I do like an Iranian stew. Often, it is simplicity that makes them so very good: the few ingredients all leave their impression rather than getting lost in a more complex festival of flavours. All you have to do is take time to do the few things well – don't rush the onion, don't cook the rhubarb too long: let the gently sour pomegranate molasses and rhubarb sing. By all means, eat this with rice or flatbreads instead of cauliflower if you prefer. And if there's any left over, it makes a fine breakfast, on toast.

Serves 4

6 tbsp vegetable or olive oil

1 onion, finely chopped

600g (1lb 5oz) diced lamb shoulder

½ tsp ground turmeric

1 cinnamon stick

¼ nutmeg, freshly grated

50ml (2fl oz) pomegranate molasses

400ml (14fl oz) water or chicken stock

3 sticks of rhubarb, sliced on the angle

1 tbsp honey (or brown sugar)

1 cauliflower, cut into chunks

sea salt and freshly ground black pepper

To serve

yoghurt

4 sprigs of fresh mint, leaves only, thinly sliced

Aleppo pepper (optional)

Fry the onion in 2 tablespoons of the oil in a large heavy-based pan or casserole over a low-medium heat until soft, stirring occasionally – this may take 20–25 minutes so make a cup of tea. Season the lamb with salt and pepper, then add to the onions with the spices and cook for 5 minutes, stirring to coat the meat in the spices.

Add the pomegranate molasses and the water or stock. Bring to a bare simmer and cook, uncovered, over a low heat for about 1 ½ hours until the meat is completely tender and the sauce is thick. If it threatens to dry out add a splash of water and cover. Add ⅔ of the rhubarb and cook for 15 minutes – leave uncovered if the sauce seems too thin, adding a splash of water if it's too thick.

While the lamb is cooking, poach the remaining rhubarb in just enough water that it's almost covered, and the honey for around 4 minutes - until just-tender.

Check the seasoning of the meat, adding more salt, pepper or pomegranate molasses to taste. Take off the heat.

Whizz the cauliflower in a food processor just until it becomes rubble. Heat the remaining olive oil in a large frying pan over a medium-high heat, spoon the cauliflower into the pan and season generously. Stir the cauliflower regularly – you want it to cook quickly but not stick. It should be done in 5–6 minutes.

Spoon the cauli into bowls, top with the khoresh and a generous spot or two of yoghurt. Sprinkle the whole with the poached rhubarb, mint leaves a little Aleppo pepper if you fancy.

SORREL BUTTERED LAMB CHOPS WITH NEW POTATOES

Sorrel is a salad leaf that dresses up like a herb, and one for those who'd reach for the lemon before the basil. It even takes its name from the French *surele*, from *sur*, meaning 'sour'. These delightfully sharp leaves – collapsible as spinach, are a proper lemony wakey-wakey to oily fish, eggs and salad potatoes.

The leaves are full of oxalic acid – hence the tartness – which reacts with aluminium or cast-iron pans and affects the flavour, so avoid using them. Sadly, you should expect the delightful vibrant leaves to turn that khaki of the parka worn by the only Mod in the class.

If you find yourself with chops, sorrel and sunshine in May, this is incredible cooked on the barbecue too, when wood smoke and char become ingredients of their own. By all means, flatten the chops out between clingfilm to about 1cm (½in) with a rolling pin if you fancy. This also works beautifully with anchovy butter (see page 120). Yes, you could serve this with a bowl of rocket, pea shoots or another fairly direct salad leaf, but I usually prefer to wallow in the slippery pleasure without.

Serves 4

2 garlic cloves, finely chopped

big handful of sorrel, washed, dried and thinly sliced

100g (3½oz) softened butter

12 lamb chops or cutlets

600g (1lb 5oz) Cornish earlies, Jersey Royals or other small new potato, unpeeled but scrubbed well

sea salt and freshly ground black pepper

Beat the garlic and a quarter of the sorrel into 60g (2¼oz) of the butter. Season the chops with salt and pepper. Spread the butter on both sides of the chops and pop them in the fridge for at least 30 minutes.

When ready to eat boil the potatoes in salted water until just cooked – about 10–12 minutes if not too large. Drain well, stir through the remaining butter and keep them warm while you cook the chops.

Heat a large frying pan or griddle pan until very hot and cook the lamb chops, in batches to avoid crowding them; cook them briefly on one side and flip them over to cook on the other side. The cooking time should be anywhere between 2–5 minutes on each side depending on the heat and how you like them cooked.

Allow the chops to rest on a warm plate for a few minutes while you stir the remaining sorrel leaves through the potatoes and season again with salt and pepper, tossing them in a hot pan if they need a bit of reheating.

Serve the chops with the sorrel potatoes and a few napkins for those fine folk who must eat chops with their hands.

PRAWN CEVICHE

This is pretty much the perfect thing on a sunny day, when you want something special and you want it in the time it takes to listen to a couple of songs while you bring it together. And there are three points of pleasure here: you get to pour yourself a dram of the lager in which the prawns have been cooked (it's incredible); the final dish is as fresh and bright as a mid-morning mojito; and you get a dash of ice-cold lager left in the bottle to enjoy while you bring it all together.

This is great with the passion fruit chilli sauce on page 83 or the sambal oelek on page 113.

Serves 4

330ml (11½floz) lager or light ale

1 garlic clove, thinly sliced

400g (14oz) raw peeled prawns

1 small red onion, very thinly sliced

juice of 1 lime

juice of 1 small orange

juice of 1 small lemon

200g (7oz) ripe cherry tomatoes or mango, finely chopped

1 avocado, peeled, stoned and finely chopped

10g bunch of coriander, roughly chopped

sea salt and freshly ground black pepper

chilli flakes, to serve

In a small pan, bring the lager to a gentle simmer. Add the garlic, a pinch of salt and the prawns, then simmer until the prawns are just cooked through aorund 3–4 minutes, no longer. Drain the prawns, reserving about 50ml of the cooking liquid, and allow to cool; pour the rest into a glass, and when cool, down it in all its garlicky deliciousness.

Cover the sliced onion with boiling water, leave for 1 minute, then drain and add half the lime juice and a pinch of salt. Allow to cool.

Mix the prawns with the remaining citrus juice, the tomatoes or the mango, avocado, pickled onion, coriander and reserved prawn cooking liquid and add salt and pepper to taste.

Allow to macerate for about 10 minutes before serving in bowls with plenty of the delicious juice, a generous dusting of chilli flakes and whichever sauce you prefer.

PASSION FRUIT, GRAPEFRUIT AND POMEGRANATE CEVICHE

I once accidentally walked 30 miles of the South Downs Way in a day, carrying two rucksacks (thanks to my companion's just-tweaked back), a misread bus timetable and the need to reach civilization before dark. A friend (Max, he of the wooden Peter Lorre, see page 190) lived a few hundred yards from the end of the path in Winchester, and as dusk descended, he opened the door to us and wordlessly showed me to his fridge where four stone-cold beers impersonated Battersea Power Station. I drank two without pause as they wept condensation on my grateful hands. They remain my benchmark of ultimate refreshment; this ceviche is the only thing that runs it close.

To my mind, ceviche needs at least two citrus at play. I've used lemon here as lime would drive a bus through the grapefruit; orange would work differently, but equally well. I prefer the passion fruit seeds left in here – crunch is deeply important to me, but by all means remove them if you wish/are mad. Diced mango works beautifully in place of the pomegranate seeds too.

Serves 4

500g (1lb 2oz) fresh white fish, cut into 2cm (¾in) squares

juice of ½ lemon

juice of ½ grapefruit

juice and pulp of 2 passion fruits, with seeds

1½ grapefruits, peeled and white pith removed

½ small red onion, finely chopped

1 Thai or other small, medium-hot, chilli, thinly sliced

a good handful of chopped coriander

a good handful of pomegranate seeds

sea salt

Place the fish in a bowl and pour the lemon and grapefruit juices over the top. Add the passion fruit juice (and seeds) and allow to rest for 15 minutes.

Using a sharp knife, free each grapefruit segment from its membranes and slice each into three. Stir the grapefruit pieces, chopped onion and sliced chilli into the fish, add a pinch of salt and the coriander and pomegranate seeds. Serve immediately.

MACKEREL ESCABECHE

My perfect evening might well involve being bathed in the salt spray of my native Devon coastline, casting a line in hope rather than expectation, while worrying a bottle of hoppy ale as the sun slips behind the cliffs. The first few fish (should fortune shine) would be cooked over a driftwood fire, and any spare would likely be for this, a day later. There are as many variations on this wonderful vinegar-infused stew as there are fish, but in my eyes mackerel makes the best. I hope you think so too.

Serves 4

8 mackerel fillets, pin bones removed

2 tbsp plain flour

3 tbsp olive oil

pared zest and juice of 1 orange

sea salt and freshly ground black pepper

For the escabeche

1 carrot, peeled and very thinly sliced

1 onion, very thinly sliced

1 small fennel bulb, trimmed and thinly sliced

3 garlic cloves, thinly sliced

200ml (7fl oz) white wine

200ml (7fl oz) water

1 tsp coriander seeds

½ tsp fennel seeds

2 bay leaves

big sprig of thyme

1 dried red chilli (or use chilli flakes)

3 tbsp olive oil

80ml (3fl oz) red wine vinegar (or use either white wine or cider vinegars if you prefer)

To make the escabeche, mix together all the ingredients in a wide pan. Bring to the boil, then lower the heat and leave the mixture to cook over a very gentle heat for 10 minutes. Season to taste with salt and pepper and leave to one side.

Season the mackerel fillets with a little salt and pepper, then dust them in the flour. Heat the olive oil in a frying pan and fry the fillets over a medium heat for 2 minutes each side until cooked through (you may need to do this in batches), then place in a non-reactive dish.

Bring the escabeche back to a simmer, then pour over the fish along with all the flavourings. Stir in the strips of orange zest and the juice and leave to cool, then chill in the fridge for 2 hours. The longer the mackerel sits in the escabeche with the vegetables, the more the flavour develops.

Serve the fish along with some of the dressing and vegetables and some excellent bread, if you fancy.

PAD THAI

Somehow pad thai seems to easily sit astride the fence that apparently separates perfectly rough and ready street food with poised and refined restaurant food. To many, it is Thai food: the equivalent of the paella of Spain, the coq au vin of France, the fried chicken of the southern States. Get it right and pad thai is as happy-making as food gets, and making it is mostly a matter of timing and the balance of sour and heat.

Prep everything first and it's all ready to eat in just a few minutes. And if you haven't made your own kimchi, a good brand of ready-made is fine here.

Serves 4

200g (7oz) flat rice noodles (dried weight), or use 600g (1lb 5oz) ready-cooked flat rice noodles

1 tbsp tamarind paste (ideally from block, see page 18)

3 tbsp fish sauce (or use soy sauce for vegetarian)

1 tsp sugar

1–2 tsp chilli flakes (or use fresh chilli)

2 tbsp vegetable oil

300g (10oz) diced chicken or tofu or prawns

1 onion, thinly sliced

2 garlic cloves, finely chopped

2 eggs, lightly beaten

40g (1½oz) cashews or peanuts, roughly chopped

bunch of spring onions, thinly sliced

150g (5oz) kimchi

200g (7oz) beansprouts

To serve

small bunch of mint, leaves roughly chopped

small bunch of basil (ideally Thai basil, but not essential), leaves roughly chopped

more fish sauce, to taste

more chilli flakes or chilli sauce, to taste

1 lime, cut into wedges

If using dried noodles cook them according to the packet instructions, then drain and toss in a little oil so they don't glue together.

Make the sauce by combining the tamarind, fish sauce and sugar in a small pan; bring to the boil to dissolve the sugar. Add the chilli flakes or fresh chilli to taste and put to one side.

In large pan, ideally a wok, heat the vegetable oil over high heat. Add the chicken (or prawns/tofu) and the onion and stir-fry for 8 minutes until coloured and just about cooked through. Add the garlic and beaten egg to the pan for the final 2 minutes of stir-frying time.

Add the noodles and stir-fry for a further 3 minutes, making sure that the chicken is cooked through. Add half the nuts, the spring onions, kimchi and beansprouts and fry for a minute to combine.

Stir through the sauce and cook for a minute longer before removing from the heat. Sprinkle with the remaining nuts and all the herbs. Add a splash more fish sauce and/or chilli if you fancy and serve with the lime wedges.

SQUID WITH HOT, SWEET AND SOUR DIPPING SAUCE

My fine friend Max has an old, life-size wooden cut-out of Peter Lorre, he of
Casablanca and *The Maltese Falcon*, that I imagine stood outside a cinema for
a premiere a lifetime ago: I have rarely coveted an item so completely. Every
time I eat this, I am reminded both of a giant squid and that I have yet to prise
wooden Peter from Max's grip. One day.

Prepare one of the dipping sauces (see below) by whisking together the
ingredients in a bowl (or use the passion fruit chilli sauce on page 83) before
proceeding with the squid.

Serves 4

500g (1lb 2oz) cleaned squid

vegetable oil, for
deep-frying

100g (3½oz) plain flour

100g (3½oz) cornflour

sea salt and freshly ground
black pepper

**For the tamarind
dipping sauce**

150g (5oz) tamarind
chutney (see page 216)

1 bird's-eye chilli, finely
chopped (or another red
fresh chilli)

1 garlic clove, very finely
chopped

2 tbsp fish sauce

sugar, to taste

**For the sweet and sour
dipping sauce**

100ml (3½fl oz) rice wine
vinegar or cider vinegar

1–2 bird's-eye chilli, finely
chopped (or another red
fresh chilli)

2 garlic cloves, very finely
chopped

1 tbsp brown sugar

4 spring onions, very finely
chopped

Mix the squid with 3 tablespoons of your chosen dipping sauce and leave
to marinate for a couple of hours; if you're hungry, 30 minutes will just
about do.

Carefully heat a deep pan with enough oil to fully submerge the squid pieces.
Add a thin slice of onion, and when it starts to turn brown it will be ready
to fry.

Mix the flours with a big pinch of salt and plenty of pepper, then dredge the
squid thoroughly and fry in batches for 1–2 minutes until golden and crisp,
then drain on kitchen paper and season to taste with salt and pepper. Serve
immediately with your dipping sauce.

SOUSED HERRING ON RYE WITH CHERVIL BUTTER

Once in a while, when the gods are staring down at the tide's turn or at the fishmongers, you may find yourself in the sweet presence of a good deal of oily fish. Buy more than a handful for the day's tea, and make this; it is extra-ordinarily good and comes without the pressure of having to eat it today.

   The brining is the key element here, transforming the texture beautifully, while the vinegar is more about the flavouring. Herring is the classic fish for sousing, but do try this with mackerel or sardines too. If you can't find chervil, dill or chives work really well too.

Serves 4

60g (2¼oz) salt

500ml (18fl oz) cider vinegar or white wine vinegar

200ml (7fl oz) cider or white wine

1 tbsp sugar

1 carrot, peeled and very thinly sliced

1 onion, very thinly sliced

1 tbsp allspice berries

1 tbsp black peppercorns

4 fresh bay leaves

12–16 fresh herring fillets, descaled and pin bones removed

Dijon mustard, for smearing

sliced rye bread, to serve

For the chervil butter

zest and juice of ½ lemon 100g (3½oz) butter, softened

big bunch of chervil, finely chopped

sea salt and freshly ground black pepper

Make the brine by dissolving 50g (2oz) of the salt in 150ml (5fl oz) simmering water before adding 400ml (14fl oz) cold water. Set aside to cool completely.

Meanwhile, put the vinegar, cider or wine, sugar, carrot and onion into a pan and bring to the boil. Add the spices and simmer for 2 minutes. Set aside to cool completely.

Place the herring fillets in a shallow dish and pour over the cooled brine. Chill in the fridge for at least 3 hours, or overnight.

Drain the herring fillets from the brine and dry on a clean cloth. Smear the flesh side of each with a little Dijon mustard and roll them up, skin side out, and pack into a large non-reactive container or jar. Pour the spicy marinade over the herrings.

Place in the fridge for at least 4 days to develop. They will keep for about 2 months, but have the best texture in the first couple of weeks after being ready.

Make the butter by beating the lemon zest and juice and some black pepper to taste into the butter. Stir through the chervil and add salt to taste.

To serve, drain the fillets from their marinade. Spread the butter over the rye bread (toasted if you prefer) and top with the herrings. If you aren't thinking of a stone-cold dry white wine or a sharp cider to go with, have a long hard word with yourself.

PERSIAN FISH STEW

There are so many ways that curries and stews are soured around the world – lemon, tamarind, vinegar (try the pork vindaloo on page 173) and anardana among them – and the black lime here (see page 20) may be swapped out for any of them, but please, at least once, try this with black lime. They are increasingly available in supermarkets and widely online.

Serves 4

5 tbsp vegetable oil

2 onions, finely chopped

3 garlic cloves, finely chopped

1 whole green chilli, left whole but sliced open

3 tomatoes, chopped

2 tbsp tomato purée

2 whole black limes, pierced a few times with a skewer or knife tip

small bunch of coriander, finely chopped

small bunch of dill, finely chopped

4 white fish fillets, such as cod (about 700g/1½lb), cut into largeish pieces

2 tbsp plain flour

sea salt and freshly ground black pepper

For the spice mix

2 tsp ground cumin

2 tsp freshly ground black pepper

1 tsp ground cardamom

2 tsp ground turmeric

Mix together the ingredients for the spice mix and put to one side.

Heat 2 tablespoons of the oil in a pan, add the onions and fry for 10 minutes until soft. Add the garlic, chilli, tomatoes, tomato purée and 2 teaspoons of the spice mix and cook for 30 seconds. Add the black limes, crushing them slightly to let the sauce in and their flavour out. Then add half of each of the herbs and ½ teaspoon of salt along with 500ml (18fl oz) water and bring to a gentle simmer while you cook the fish.

Sprinkle the remaining spice mixture on both sides of the fish with ½ teaspoon of salt and dust with flour. Heat the remaining vegetable oil in a frying pan, add the fish fillets and fry on both sides until golden brown.

Add the fish to the stew, adding more hot water if needed to cover the fish. Simmer gently for 5–10 minutes until the fish is cooked through.

Serve with rice, the whole sprinkled with the remaining herbs.

MACKEREL, GOOSEBERRY SALSA AND HORSERADISH BUTTER

As a kid born and living by the sea, it blew my young mind that the sea never stops, never sleeps, never takes a break. It still seems impossible to me that the crazy moon is what breathes air into its lungs. The sea is still the place I gravitate towards when things are good, bad, indifferent; when I'm looking for answers or in search of none.

A few years ago, in the valley of interesting times, I'd sit on the sea wall and let the breeze push me around, fish bap from the nearby fish shack in hand. For a few minutes, that fish bap – perfectly over-peppered, glittered with salt and running with butter – made everything okay for long enough to remind me that things would again be good.

This has that glorious combination of bread and fish, carb and protein, sharpened joyfully here with gooseberries and kept on the straight and narrow by the horseradish. Next summer, when I snag a mackerel or two at the tide's turn, I'm going to sit on that sea wall and eat this, and smile.

Serves 4

7 tbsp gooseberry salsa (see page 91)

2 tbsp prepared horseradish

half a handful of chives, chopped

100g (3½oz) softened butter

2 tbsp mild olive oil or vegetable oil

600g (1lb 5oz) mackerel fillets

4 buns, sliced in half (or 8 thick slices from a loaf)

a small handful of mint, roughly chopped

a small handful of coriander leaves, roughly chopped

sea salt and freshly ground black pepper

First make the gooseberry salsa (see page 91) so you can refrigerate it for at least a couple of hours before serving.

Mix the horseradish and chives into the softened butter and put to one side.

Heat the oil in a large frying pan. Season the mackerel fillets and pan-fry them skin side down first for 2 minutes over a medium heat. Carefully flip the fillets over with a spatula, add 3 tablespoons of the gooseberry salsa and cook for another minute.

Lightly toast the buns or bread and spread with the horseradish butter. Stuff the buttered buns with the gooseberry-coated mackerel, add another spoonful of the salsa, generously sprinkle with mint and coriander and serve immediately.

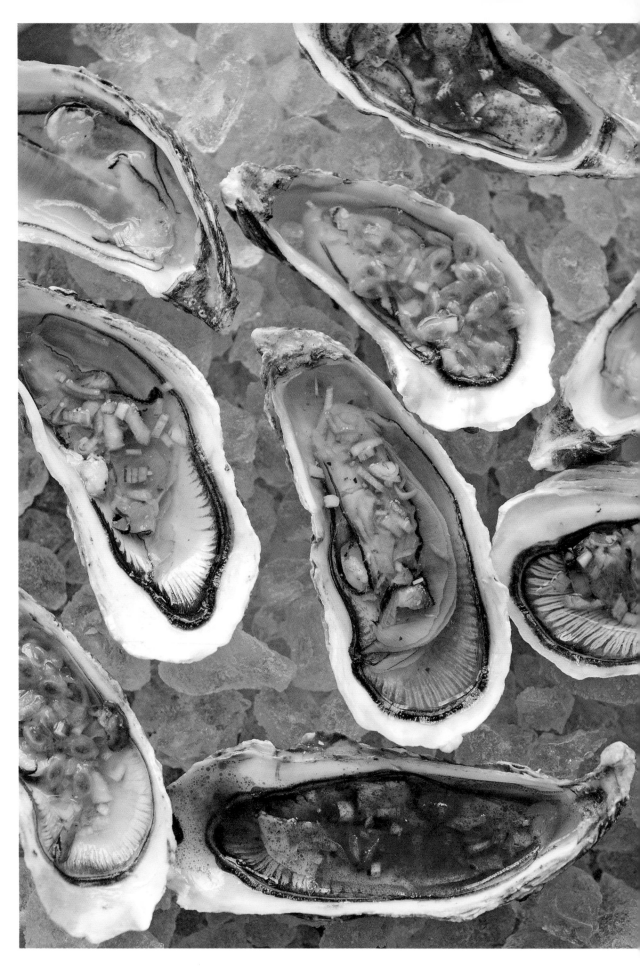

OYSTERS MIGNONETTE, FOUR WAYS

Mignonette is just about the loveliest way with an oyster, the combination of vinegar, shallot and pepper just made for that delightful bivalve. Varying the nature of the acidity makes for all kinds of marvellousness: grapefruit juice, verjuice and Seville orange juice are all superb. By all means use white or Szechuan pepper in place of black if you fancy.

These four ways offer the classic route and three excellent side roads to explore. A few of each is entirely appropriate.

Each dressing makes enough for at least 2 dozen oysters; leftovers will make an excellent salad dressing with a little olive oil.

Classic

5 tbsp white wine vinegar

2 tbsp very finely chopped shallot

¼ tsp coarsely ground black pepper

pinch of salt

Passion fruit

4 tbsp passion fruit pulp

1 tbsp lime juice

2 tbsp very finely chopped shallot

¼ tsp coarsely ground black pepper

pinch of salt

Kombucha

5 tbsp kombucha

2 tbsp very finely chopped shallot

¼ tsp coarsely ground black pepper

pinch of salt

Sambal oelek

1 tbsp sambal oelek (see page 113)

3 tbsp Seville orange juice (or other citrus, if out of season)

2 tsp very finely chopped shallot

¼ tsp coarsely ground black pepper

pinch of salt

For each mignonette variation, stir together the ingredients and let them sit at least 10 minutes and up to 1 hour before serving. Add about ½ teaspoon of the dressing, including a few pieces shallot, to each oyster before eating.

MUSSELS IN BEER

Much as I take some persuading to steer away from my beloved cider when making mussels, I have been turned – at least some of the time – by sour beer. This works perfectly well with many lighter beers, but with a sour beer – especially a Berliner Weisse or Gose style beer, which are made with lactic acid bacteria – it is phenomenal. Food and drink writer Melissa Cole put me on to Magic Rock's marvellous Salty Kiss, delightfully sour and salty, and it is perfect for this.

Serves 4

6 slices of sourdough bread, half torn into chunks

olive or vegetable oil, for drizzling

40g (1½oz) butter

1 celery heart, finely chopped and leaves reserved and chopped

3 garlic cloves, finely chopped

2 shallots, finely chopped

2 bay leaves

1kg (2lb 4oz) mussels, scrubbed and beards removed (discard any that are broken or that remain open when tapped)

330ml (11½fl oz) sour beer

1 tbsp Dijon mustard (optional)

good splash of double cream (optional)

sea salt and freshly ground black pepper

Preheat the oven to 200°C/400°F/gas mark 6.

Tip the torn bread pieces on to a baking tray, drizzle with oil, sprinkle with salt and bake until golden and dry, about 10 minutes. Blitz in a food processor to coarse crumbs and set aside.

Melt half the butter in a wide, shallow pan and cook the celery heart, garlic, shallots and bay leaves over a low-medium heat for 6–8 minutes until soft, stirring occasionally.

Add the mussels, stir well and turn up the heat. Add the beer, cover and cook for about 4–5 minutes until all the mussels are open – discard any that remain closed. Meanwhile lightly toast the remaining bread slices.

Stir the remaining butter, celery leaves and mustard and cream (if using) into the mussels and season to taste. Scatter over the breadcrumbs and serve immediately with chunks of bread.

CRAB WITH PICKLED JERSUALEM ARTICHOKES AND GREEN APPLE

During a spell when life was frantic, my wife and I stole away along the coast for an evening of pints and a day with the sea air blown high to the overlooking hills. Walking is perhaps where we talk most and where we are most silent. Anything big, everything small; it's all okay. She spies leaves, flowers and shoots, identifying; I with an eye alternately on where the sky meets the sea, and where my feet are about to fall. Between us, we miss little.

I'm not sure I've seen a finer view than on that glorious day, from the hills just north of the B3157, looking out over the Abbotsbury, The Fleet and Chesil Beach to the forever. In all substantial ways, that view may not have changed in millennia, while constantly shifting nevertheless.

A long morning's walk ended in the perfect late lunch, almost in the reach of the sea's spray: a whole crab, a salad with a sharp, sharp dressing, and a bright cider. Here is a shell-less re-creation that takes the spirit of that simple, perfect combination of sea and sharp. Enjoy with a cold, dry wine or cider at a time of day you ordinarily wouldn't have one.

By all means try this with pickled salsify, kimchi or even sauerkraut in place of the artichokes. And really, no one's watching if you're using bought mayo, as long as it's a good one.

Serves 4

300g (10oz) white crabmeat

small handful of tarragon and chives

zest and juice of 1 lemon

50g (2oz) brown crabmeat

1 tbsp olive oil

2 Granny Smiths or other sharp apple

100g (3½oz) bold salad leaves, such as watercress or lamb's lettuce

sea salt and freshly ground black pepper

To serve

zest of 1 lemon

kombucha mayonnaise (see page 119)

pickled Jerusalem artichokes (see page 92)

Put the white crabmeat into a bowl, stir in the herbs and lemon zest and season to taste with salt and pepper. Put to one side.

Put the brown crabmeat into a bowl and squeeze in the lemon juice and oil to make a loose dressing.

Core and thinly slice the apples.

Place the apples, artichoke slices and salad leaves in a bowl and add the white crabmeat. Toss lightly with your hands, then transfer to a large serving plate or individual plates. Drizzle with the brown crabmeat dressing, scatter over the lemon zest and some black pepper and dollop with mayonnaise.

TOMATO, CRÈME FRAÎCHE AND MUSTARD TART

Like when you realize that two old friends have been facing the wrong way romantically all their lives, I spent too long not appreciating how happy tomatoes and mustard are together. This tart puts that to rights. I think it works best with a range of tomatoes – bringing variety in texture and flavour – though I tend to roast cherry and other small tomatoes alongside the tart and place them on top to serve. Much of the sweetness of a tomato is in the flesh, with the sour in the juice; the vinegar in the mustard picks out both and makes them sing louder. And as if that's not enough, the crème fraîche's sour tones bring everything together perfectly. One for a sunny day or sleet.

For the pastry (by all means use bought pastry if you are in a dash)

200g (7oz) plain flour, plus more for rolling

pinch of salt

1 tbsp Parmesan cheese (optional)

100g (3½oz) butter, chilled and cut into cubes

For the filling

600g (1lb 5oz) ripe tomatoes, cut in half through the equator

50g (2oz) soft butter

2–3 tbsp thyme leaves

300g (10oz) crème fraîche

1 garlic clove, finely chopped

1 tbsp Dijon mustard

sea salt and freshly ground black pepper

Preheat the oven to 180°C/350°F/gas mark 4 and lightly grease a 28–30cm (11–12in) loose-bottomed tart case.

Put the flour, salt, Parmesan (if using) and butter in a food processor and blend until the mixture resembles fine breadcrumbs. Add cold water, a tablespoon at a time, and pulse bit by bit until the mixture just comes together as a dough. Bring the dough together with your hands and shape into a large flat disc. Clingfilm the pastry and allow it to rest in the fridge for 30 minutes.

Dust a rolling pin and surface lightly with flour and roll out the dough to about 5cm (2in) larger than the tart case. Lift it up by carefully rolling it around the rolling pin and lay it across the tart case. Press the dough into the corners of the case using your fingers, filling any holes or tears as you go. Trim the pastry edges and chill for 30 minutes.

While the pastry chills, toss the tomatoes with a pinch of salt, the butter and half the thyme and arrange cut side up on a baking tray. Roast for 10–15 minutes until they are soft yet retain their shape. Remove from the oven and set to one side to cool, keeping any juices.

Fill the pastry case with a circle of baking parchment and baking beans. Bake for 15 minutes, then remove the paper with the beans and cook the pastry for another 5 minutes. Use any uncooked pastry to patch any holes.

While the pastry is cooking, beat together the crème fraîche, garlic, mustard, the remaining thyme and salt and pepper to taste. Add any juices from the tomato roasting tray and spread the mixture over the blind baked tart case. Arrange the tomatoes over the top – don't be precious here. Bake for 20–25 minutes until the pastry is crisp and the tomatoes are golden.

Leave the tart to cool in the tin for 15 minutes or so before removing and serving warm.

LEEKS 'VINAIGRETTE' PANGRATTATO WITH CHOPPED EGG

This is one of my favourite things in those post-Christmas days, when spring seems a long way off and a simple but satisfying supper is in order. Try this with a few leaves, roast lamb, beef, fish, and/or the shredded sprouts on page 148. This is eminently tweakable too: I love it made with a classic vinaigrette, with a pinch of mixed spice or a generous rasping of nutmeg, and with a little bacon or ham thrown in.

Cook the eggs and make the sour cream dressing while the leeks are cooking, so that you can bring everything together at your own pace.

Serves 4
800g (1lb 12oz) leeks
4 eggs
sour cream dressing (see page 112)
sea salt and freshly ground black pepper

For the pangrattato
2 tbsp olive oil
50g (2oz) panko breadcrumbs
zest of ½ lemon
small handful of flat-leaf parsley, finely chopped

Take care with preparation of the leeks, as this greatly affects the degree to which they fall apart. Slice just enough of the base off so as to remove any straggly roots. This helps to stop the leeks unravelling like the supplements from a Sunday paper. Run a knife down the length of each leek, cutting only halfway through, and not cutting through the base. Peel off the outer layer only and discard. Slice off most of the green – just enough that you leave a V-necked jumper at the top of the outer layer. Run cold water into the long cut and rinse to remove any stray soil.

Bring a large pan of generously salted water to the boil and add the leeks, cooking them for 15–20 minutes until surrendering without resistance to a knife's point. Drain in a wide colander and cover with foil to keep warm.

For the eggs: use a spoon to lower the eggs into a medium-sized pan of boiling water. Boil them for exactly 6 minutes for a hint of molten lava in the centre; 7 minutes for hard-boiled. Drain and set aside. Once easy to handle, peel and chop the eggs roughly – by all means grate the eggs if you prefer.

For the pangrattato, heat the olive oil in a medium-sized frying pan until it shimmers. Add the panko breadcrumbs and stir with a wooden spoon; the oil will absorb quickly and the breadcrumbs begin to colour. The dust goes first: your job is to stir slowly but constantly enough to ensure that all but the largest crumbs colour without the finest burning. Don't push your luck: stop as soon as the finest turn a nutty dark brown. Stir in the lemon zest and parsley.

Lay the leeks in a warmed dish, slicing any thick ones lengthways. Add the chopped egg, pour over the sour cream dressing and scatter with the breadcrumbs.

CRANBERRY JEWELLED RICE

Saffron is a funny thing. Mostly it reminds me of that time I sucked the end of the fountain pen I used for all of a fortnight at school, only to find it was leaking its turquoise (classy) Quink all over my mouth. Happy days. Saffron gives me hope that perhaps there is nothing to which a delicious end cannot be found. Here, its generous nasal bitterness is what creates the alchemy. Sour fruit and nuts are so fine together too, and I think this shows that happy alliance at its best. I'm as likely to eat this as it is – a joyously satisfying bowlful, fork pecking away – as I am to bother with a bright salad to accompany.

Serves 4

300g (10oz) basmati rice

large pinch of saffron (or use ground turmeric)

50ml (2fl oz) orange blossom water

3 tbsp butter, ghee or olive oil

1 onion, finely chopped

2 carrots, peeled and finely chopped

½ tsp ground cardamom

1 cinnamon stick

100g (3½oz) shelled pistachios (or use flaked almonds or pine nuts, or a mix)

100g (3½oz) dried cranberries (or use dried sour cherries)

sea salt and freshly ground black pepper

Wash the rice thoroughly and drain well. Soak the saffron in the orange blossom water.

Heat the butter, ghee or oil in a large pan, add the onion and carrots and cook over a medium heat until soft – this will take 10–15 minutes or so. Add the spices, nuts and 1 teaspoon of salt and cook for 1 minute more.

Add the drained rice and cranberries and cook for a minute to toast the rice, then add the orange blossom saffron water plus another 400ml (14fl oz) hot water and cover. Turn the heat down to low and continue cooking for 15 minutes until all the liquid has evaporated and the rice is tender. Turn the heat up to medium and cook for 5 minutes to develop a crust at the base.

Turn off the heat. Place a clean tea towel between the pan and its lid and let the pan sit and rest for 5 minutes in about 3cm (1¼in) cold water in the sink to help loosen the crust.

Turn the rice out on to a large platter to serve.

MALFATTI

Being more than a little attached to crunch, I have to say I'm more likely to order badger scrotum when eating out than I am gnocchi, but their similarly soft cousins, malfatti, somehow seduce me. They make the perfect home for ricotta's gentle sourness, with the lemon juice in the sage butter giving it the lightest of acidic high fives.

In an ideal world – i.e. when you know 90 minutes ahead that you're going to be hungry – you should leave the just-formed, uncooked malfatti in the fridge for an hour; the chilly pause creates the hint of a skin, and just enough resistance to the bite when cooked to give the impression of a filled pasta.

Malfatti are sneakily rich and filling, especially with the butter, but feel free to scale up the recipe for big appetites. You can simmer the reserved chard or spinach stalks until tender, and chop to serve scattered over the malfatti.

Serves 4

500g (1lb 2oz) chard or spinach leaves

250g (9oz) fresh ricotta

¼ nutmeg, grated

40g (1½oz) Parmesan cheese, plus more to serve

3 tbsp '00' or plain flour

2 large eggs, lightly beaten

100–150g (3½–5oz) semolina flour

50g (2oz) unsalted butter

12 sage leaves

juice of ½ lemon

sea salt and freshly ground black pepper

Cook the chard or spinach in a large pan of boiling salted water for about 1–2 minutes until completely tender. Drain, refresh in cold water to retain colour, then squeeze out all the water. Finely chop and set aside to cool.

Mix together the ricotta, nutmeg, Parmesan and flour. Stir in the squeezed leaves and the beaten eggs and season to taste with salt and pepper. Stir well until mixed.

Form into 20 balls on a surface dusted with semolina flour, coating each ball, then place on a tray dusted with more semolina flour. Refrigerate for cooking later if you prefer.

Melt the butter and fry the sage leaves for 2 minutes, squeezing the lemon juice into the butter as it foams. Set to one side.

Bring a pan of water to the boil, gently add the malfatti and simmer for 2–3 minutes – they will float to the surface when cooked. Drain and serve topped with the sage butter and a bit more Parmesan.

KIMCHI KOREAN TACO

Occasionally, a little bit of rough does you good: a G&T out of a can on the 8.19pm train home, cod and large on the beach, a second Magnum before the bone from the first is cast into the bin. And so too this food truck fusion mash-up from the west coast of the USA. This isn't sophisticated by any means, but it opens the pleasure valve fully: it is like a cold, salty shot of tequila on a hot day; perhaps not the best thing for you but it sure feels like it.

If you have quick pickled red onions to hand (see page 88), then use them and avoid adding the sliced onion/lime juice.

Serves 4

1 red onion, ½ very thinly sliced, ½ finely chopped

50g (2oz) sugar

3 tbsp soy sauce

2 garlic cloves, very finely chopped

2 tbsp finely grated fresh ginger

1–2 tsp chilli flakes (preferably Korean)

juice of 2 limes

400g (14oz) diced chicken (or beef or tofu)

1 tbsp cornflour (or use plain flour)

vegetable oil, for frying

1 tbsp toasted sesame seeds

400g (14oz) cooked rice

3 eggs, beaten

200g (7oz) kimchi, sliced

bunch of spring onions, thinly sliced

sea salt and freshly ground black pepper

To serve

4 corn tortillas

chilli sauce

small bunch of coriander, leaves roughly chopped

150ml (5fl oz) sour cream (optional)

Cover the thinly sliced red onion with hot water from the kettle and leave to steep for 5 minutes.

Mix together the sugar, soy sauce, garlic, ginger and chilli flakes in a pan until fully combined. Add 100ml (3½fl oz) water and simmer for 3–5 minutes or until reduced by half and syrupy. Squeeze in the juice of 1 of the limes and keep warm.

Drain the onions then stir in the juice of the other lime and a pinch of salt and leave to one side.

Toss the chicken (or beef or tofu) in the cornflour and then fry in 2 tablespoons of vegetable oil for 5–10 minutes until just cooked through and starting to brown, then stir into the spicy soy syrup and sprinkle with the sesame seeds. Keep warm.

Heat 3 tablespoons of oil in a large frying pan or wok until smoking hot, add the finely chopped onion and cook for 2 minutes to soften and lightly brown. Add the cooked rice and fry for 5 minutes, stirring until all the grains of rice are coated in oil and the rice is hot through. Add the beaten eggs and kimchi and continue to fry for another 2–3 minutes over a high heat until the egg is cooked. Stir through the spring onions and season to taste.

Warm the tortillas and serve topped with the kimchi fried rice and spicy chicken, then top with chilli sauce, coriander, sour cream (if using) and the lime pickled red onions.

SOURDOUGH, LABNEH, ROAST GRAPES AND STRAWBERRY SAMBAL

You can have this glorious coming-together of simple sours, fruit and heat as an open sandwich – the sourdough as toast or bread – or as here, as canapé-sized double-mouthfuls. If you can get hold of a good organic rapeseed oil such as from Harnett Oils, then the hazelnuttiness is perfect here – organic is especially important, as particularly uncheery chemical levels are the norm for rapeseed otherwise.

Serves 4

200g (7oz) grapes (Fragoli or Vitoria if available)

4 slices of sourdough

200g (7oz) labneh, or more if preferred

strawberry sambal (see page 116)

small handful of mint leaves, thinly sliced

organic rapeseed oil or olive oil, for drizzling

Preheat the oven to 190°C/375°F/gas mark 5 and roast the grapes for 5–15 minutes until they just collapse – you want to retain just enough structure so that the grapes keep hold of most of their juice.

Lightly toast the sourdough and allow to cool. Slice into canapé-sized pieces, slather in labneh, top with the grapes (squeezing a little of the juice out as you do), dot with sambal, sprinkle with mint and drizzle with oil.

DOSA PANCAKES WITH ROAST CAULIFLOWER AND RAITA

This is one of those easy teas that looks like a palaver; it is, I promise, both quick and marvellous. It's also a proper storecupboard recipe, with the pancakes (aka besan puda) forming a lifesaving boat in which to sail whatever's in the fridge. It is infinitely variable: try mint instead of coriander, steamed broccoli in place of the roast cauliflower, etc, etc.

The sourness comes from the fermented batter as well as the liberal use of lemon; you can make the pancakes with fresh batter, but the depth of flavour and bacterial wealth comes with at least half a day's fermentation. The batter only takes the time it takes for the kettle to boil to make, so it's easy to do before work, ready to use that evening.

Serves 4

150g (5oz) gram flour
50g (2oz) rice flour
2 tsp ground cumin
3 tsp ground turmeric
1 tsp ground fenugreek seeds, or ¼ tsp asafoetida
500g (1lb 2oz) cauliflower (about 1 large), cut into small florets
vegetable oil, for roasting and frying
200g (7oz) natural yoghurt
1–2 tsp chilli flakes
1 lemon, cut into wedges
small bunch of coriander, roughly chopped
2 chopped green chillies (optional)
sea salt and freshly ground pepper

Mix the gram flour and rice flour with 200ml (7fl oz) water. Add half the cumin, half the turmeric and the ground fenugreek seeds or asafoetida. Put to one side in a warm place for a few hours until it foams with a fermenting action.

Preheat the oven to 210°C/410°F/gas mark 7.

In a shallow baking dish, toss the cauliflower with 3 tablespoons of oil and 50g (2oz) of the yoghurt and season with salt and pepper and the remaining turmeric and cumin and the chilli flakes.

Roast for 20 minutes, or until the cauliflower is tender and golden in places. Season the remaining yoghurt with a squeeze of juice from one of the segments, and some salt and pepper to make a raita.

Add ½ teaspoon of salt to the dosa batter. Heat a tablespoon of oil in a frying pan and fry the batter in thin pancakes until golden brown on the base. Serve the pancakes topped with the roasted cauliflower, drizzled with the raita, sprinkled with the coriander and the green chilli (if using), and with lemon segments for everyone to squeeze over as they like.

215

TAMARIND CHUTNEY AND QUICK PAKORA

Back in my Years Of Great Idleness, a friend had a flat in town that served as the lets-get-a-few-on-board-before-we-go-out venue, as well as the place-at-which-I-can-sleep-should-I-be-unwilling/incapable-of-making-it-home. At either end of the evening, he would make pakora – the ingredients were cheap and, equally importantly, always there. Now that I have what passes for a job and will do anything to make it home to my own bed, I still love pakora; even more so with this simple, delicious chutney.

Use tamarind block if you can, otherwise deseeded tamarind, at a push the stuff in jars. The chutney keeps for a month or so in the fridge, so I make a batch of this volume, as it loves a cold sausage – by all means do half.

Serves 4

75g (2½oz) gram flour

½ tsp baking powder

½ tsp sea salt

1 tsp curry powder

150g (5oz) coarsely grated carrot or squash, or finely shredded cabbage

1 small onion, thinly sliced

1 fresh chilli, finely chopped (optional)

Vegetable oil, for frying

a few tbsp of chaat masala (optional, see page 96)

For the chutney

400g (14oz) tamarind block (or 200g/7oz deseeded tamarind)

200g (7oz) sugar, or more to taste (this can be very sweet if you prefer)

1 tsp ground toasted cumin seeds

1 tsp salt

½–1 tsp red chilli powder

½ tsp cracked black pepper

½ tsp ground ginger

First make the chutney. Break the tamarind into small pieces and soak in 500ml (18fl oz) boiling water for half an hour or so. Mash it into a pulp with your fingers, removing the seeds as you go. Strain by pushing the tamarind through a sieve into a pan to remove (and discard) all the fibrous pulp and seeds. Add the remaining ingredients and gently cook until the sugar has dissolved. Taste and tweak with sugar, salt or chilli if you like. Transfer to a sterilized jar, allow to cool and then store in the fridge.

Whisk the flour, baking powder, salt, curry powder and 100ml (3½fl oz) water to a smooth batter then stir in the vegetables and chilli (if using). Carefully heat about 4cm (1½in) oil in a wide, deep frying pan until very hot – when you drop in a small piece of the batter it should sizzle straightaway. Drop heaped tablespoons of the batter into the hot oil and fry for a few minutes in batches until brown on both sides and cooked through. Drain on kitchen paper.

Sprinkle over chaat masala (if using) to taste and serve with the chutney.

KIMCHI PANCAKE (CHIJIMI)

Weekend breakfasts are special. I can get by on porridge, toast or whatever in the week but a good breakfast at the weekend says, 'Hang on, today is different'. It might be the full Monty, it might be last night's leftover curry on toast, or it might be this little smasher. This pancake lies somewhere between Shrove Tuesday and a Spanish tortilla, and is everything you might want after a big night – substance, zing and a good bite of spice to get body and soul back on track. For a gentler sourness, sauerkraut works delightfully in place of the kimchi.

These can be fried small and individual, or large and generous, to be cut into smaller pieces. Serve with ketchup, chilli sauce, the strawberry sambal on page 116, quick pickled red onions, or whatever takes your fancy.

The recipe calls for all plain flour as that's what most of us have, but if you substitute 100g (2½oz) for the same of rice flour it adds a little chewy magic that I rather like.

Makes 2 (cooked in a 20cm/8in pan)

400g (14oz) plain flour

2 tbsp sesame seeds

3 eggs, lightly beaten

2 tbsp sesame oil

300g (10oz) kimchi (see page 58)

200g (7oz) thinly sliced spring onions, red onions or beansprouts – your preference

100g (3½oz) thinly sliced bacon, cooked (optional)

vegetable oil, for frying

sea salt

Mix the flour, a big pinch of salt and the sesame seeds in a large bowl. Whisk in 250ml (9fl oz) water, the beaten eggs and sesame oil, making sure there are no lumps.

Gently fold in the kimchi, vegetables and bacon (if using).

Heat a little oil in a medium-hot frying pan and fry a tablespoon of the batter to test the seasoning – add more to taste if needed.

Pour in enough batter to form a 1.5cm (¾in) layer in the pan. Cook for 2 minutes, or until the edges have begun to crisp up and the base is golden. Flip over and cook for another 2–3 minutes.

Serve immediately.

TURKISH EGGS

A fine breakfast for a lazy Sunday, especially if you have someone still dozing who you'd like to impress. A couple of tips: Nigella suggests warming the yoghurt over a pan of just-boiled water, and straining the egg of its runniest white through a tea strainer – it's breakfast, so often I can't quite summon the enthusiasm, but it does make a small difference. And in your snooziness, don't salt the water – it breaks bonds in the egg white and makes them tatty. I like two eggs for this, but for some, as the French say, one egg is *un oeuf*.

Should you be home alone, it is so very worth the bother of making this for one, hence I've written this to serve one – you deserve it (even if you don't). You can easily double up the quantities to serve two.

Dill is the mid-morning pastis of herbs: there are days I like nothing more, and there are days I like nothing less; when it's the latter, parsley steps into its place to no lesser delight. I have cast a handful of diced, fried paneer cubes into the yoghurt when I've had some leftover, and it has been mighty fine.

Serves 1

½ garlic clove, finely chopped

2 tsp olive oil

90g (3 ¼ oz) Greek yoghurt

30g (1oz) butter

1 tsp Aleppo pepper

toasted sourdough, to serve

2 eggs

1 tsp lemon juice

small handful of finely chopped dill or flat-leaf parsley

sea salt and freshly ground black pepper

Bring a pan filled with 10cm (4in) with water to a lazy boil.

Stir the garlic and half the olive oil into the yoghurt and put aside – it's best served at room temperature.

Gently warm the butter in a pan until it becomes nutty brown, remove from the heat, add the Aleppo pepper and swirl the pan gently as it sizzles in the hot butter.

Pop the bread into the toaster.

Turn the heat down on the water until it has the barest shimmer – simmering is too much. Crack an egg into a small cup and add the lemon juice – this makes the egg perk up like that muscly bloke on the beach pretending not to tense, and prevents the egg waving white hands in the water as it poaches. Gently ease the egg into the water (repeat with a second egg if you are as greedy as I am) and poach for 3 ½ minutes. Lift the egg(s) out with a slotted spoon on to kitchen paper – you don't want any water in the bowl.

Spoon the yoghurt into a warmed bowl, place the egg(s) on top, and then spoon the chilli butter over with as much artistic licence as your morning head allows. Sprinkle with dill or parsley, almost over-season, and enjoy with sourdough toast, back in bed.

SON-IN-LAW EGGS

Of the many tales ascribed to the name of this recipe, the story of a mother wanting to subtly convey to her son-in-law what might occur to his own ovate possessions should the treatment of his wife not improve seems most fitting. I ought to make clear that I didn't get this recipe from my mother-in-law: she has been faultlessly generous in Florentines, which leads me to believe that I must be at least an adequate husband.

Serves 4

8 eggs

vegetable oil, for frying

200g (7oz) shallots, very thinly sliced

4 fresh or dried chillies, split in half lengthways (optional)

sea salt

To serve

tamarind chutney, (see page 216)

red chilli sauce, such as sambal oelek (see page 113)

small bunch of coriander, roughly chopped

Lower the eggs into a pan of cold water and bring to the boil. Simmer for 6 minutes then drain, cool and peel the eggs.

Slowly heat 3cm (1 ¼ in) oil in a deep frying pan over a medium heat. The oil is ready when you drop a small piece of shallot into the oil and it sizzles immediately. Fry the shallots in the oil for 3–5 minutes until golden brown and crisp, then drain on kitchen paper and sprinkle with salt.

Fry the whole peeled eggs in the same oil for a few minutes until golden brown all over, then drain on kitchen paper. Fry the chillies (if using) in the oil for about 30 seconds until brown at the edges.

Cut the eggs in half and drizzle with the tamarind chutney and chilli sauce. Scatter over the fried shallots and chillies and the chopped coriander and serve immediately.

PINK EGGS BENEDICT

I once rose at 3.30am to drive with a friend from deepest Kent to furthest Snowdonia for a launch of a work thing at a hotel. We got there road-frazzled, 20 minutes before the start, ready to eat our feet if needs be. We dove into the restaurant in hope of weak coffee and a limp croissant.

'What would you like sir?'

'In my imaginary life, eggs Benedict and excellent coffee please.'

'No problem sir.'

It still ranks as one of the finest three conversations of my life.

This is a fabulous tweak on the classic hollandaise (see page 117), working just that bit better with the eggs and bacon than straight hollandaise. A cabernet sauvignon wine and vinegar are ideal, if you have them.

Serves 4

100ml (3½fl oz) rich red wine, such as cabernet sauvignon

2 tsp sugar

2–3 tbsp red wine vinegar

8 thick streaky bacon rashers

2 large egg yolks, plus 8 whole eggs

150g (5oz) unsalted butter, melted

8 tsp lemon juice (a little less than you'd get from a supermarket lemon)

4 English muffins, split and toasted

sea salt and freshly ground black pepper

Simmer the red wine, sugar and 2 tablespoons of red wine vinegar until reduced to about 2 tablespoons of syrup – it usually takes 10 minutes or so. Allow to cool slightly.

At the same time, fry the bacon to your liking – I like it just threatening to be crisp – then set aside to keep warm.

Set a large metal bowl over a pan of simmering water, ensuring the base doesn't touch the water.

Add the egg yolks and wine reduction to the bowl and whisk for 2–3 minutes until thick. Now add the melted butter very gradually in a thin stream, retaining the white milky solids, whisking continually until thick and creamy. Season with salt, pepper and a little more red wine vinegar to taste. Keep the hollandaise sauce warm over a very low heat, stirring occasionally.

Bring a large, wide pan filled with 10cm (4in) water to a gentle boil, then lower the heat until only the barest surface shimmer tells you it's hot. Crack an egg into a cup, add a teaspoon of lemon juice to tighten the white up, and tip it gently from minimal height into the water. Set the timer to go in 3½ minutes. Repeat for the rest of the eggs, ideally in a circle around the pan. When the alarm goes off, use a slotted spoon to unhurriedly lift the poached eggs out, in order, to a plate lined with a kitchen paper or a clean cloth. Season with salt and pepper.

Arrange 2 English muffin halves on each plate and top each with a rasher of bacon. Place a poached egg on each, spoon the sauce over and serve immediately.

DESSERTS

CHERRY SOUR CREAM CLAFOUTIS

A few years ago, we stayed with friends who live in that part of Aquitaine where the roofs are red, chestnut woods dot the hills, and wild strawberries and their Gariguette cousins sit in punnets in the markets of early May. We next visited only a few weeks later in the year; the scent was like another country. There were almost no strawberries, but the cherries – oh, the cherries. Of all the fruit, perhaps only mulberries can convince me as much that there is an all-guiding hand. On that second visit, the cherries hung from the tree outside their house calling our name like a leftover trifle in the fridge. I feel like I can remember each cherry, they were so good. I pulled the higher branches down for my daughter, already taught by her taste buds to look for the darkest. I reached up and handed down those beyond her grasp. Wordless pleasure.

Sweet as those special cherries were, I crave sour cherries almost as much. This clafoutis works well with either, or with fermented cherries (see page 104) – or even a mixture, for a little Russian roulette.

I don't usually add booze to this, but almonds and cherries were made for each other so a splash of Amaretto in the batter works well, as does Kirsch or crème de cassis. Feel free to make this entirely with milk, to the same joint volume with the sour cream – I just enjoy the layering of sourness with the cream here. Chocolate and cherries go beautifully too, hence the talcing of cocoa to finish – but do try dried raspberry powder too; it's truly special.

Serves 6

75g (2½oz) plain flour, plus a little more for dusting

pinch of salt

½ tsp vanilla extract or seeds from half a vanilla pod

splash of Amaretto, Kirsch or crème de cassis (optional)

230ml (8fl oz) whole milk

2 large eggs

40g (1½oz) caster sugar

120ml (4fl oz) sour cream

300g (10oz) cherries – sour or fermented (see page 104)

20g (¾oz) unsalted butter, cut into small cubes, plus a little for buttering the dish

1 tbsp icing sugar

1 tbsp dried raspberry powder or cocoa

Preheat the oven to 230°C/450°F/gas mark 8. Butter a round baking dish of around 25cm (10in) diameter, or 28 x 20cm (11 x 8in) if rectangular. Dust it lightly with flour.

Sift the flour and salt into a large bowl and add the vanilla extract (or seeds), the liqueur (if using) and half the milk. Whisk into a smooth batter. Add the eggs one at a time, whisking quickly as you add, before whisking in the caster sugar, the rest of the milk and the sour cream until just smooth.

Spread the cherries in the baking dish, pour in the batter and dot the cubes of butter across the top. Place the dish into the oven and cook for about 25 minutes until it is plump and golden. Remove from the oven and, after allowing it to cool a little, dust with icing sugar followed by the dried raspberry powder. Serve warm with double cream.

SUSSEX POND PUDDING

There are some days when the cold and lack of light are such that only some rib-sticking suet will do. For those days, make this marvellously old-school English pudding, first referenced in 1672. It is, essentially, a whole lemon set adrift in a sea of butter and sugar kept in order by a suet case, that's steamed until the lemon's skin almost dissolves, creating a centre of sweet, sour, bitter, fruit fat that can kill me for all I care. A Seville orange or a handful of gooseberries would work well instead of the lemon. Should you still have a functioning artery the day after eating some, the leftovers are extraordinarily good pushed around a pan with butter, as you might Christmas pudding. It is the perfect accompaniment to a rainy Sunday afternoon.

Serves 4–6

120g (4oz) self-raising flour, plus more for rolling

100g (3½oz) shredded suet

pinch of salt

120ml (4fl oz) milk

100g (3½oz) diced cold butter, plus more for greasing

100g (3½oz) soft light brown sugar

1 unwaxed lemon, slashed a few times with a sharp knife (a thin-skinned variety is best)

Preheat the oven to 180°C/350°F/gas mark 4. Grease a 1 litre (1¾ pint) pudding basin with butter and line with baking parchment.

Stir the flour, suet and salt together in a large bowl. Mix in the milk and carefully bring together into a dough firm enough to roll out to line the pudding basin. Don't overmix, and add a little flour if the dough seems too wet.

Roll the dough out on a lightly floured surface until just large enough to line the basin. Cut out one quarter as a wedge and reserve as the lid. Line the basin with the largest piece of pastry, sealing the joins by slightly overlapping, wetting a little and pressing together.

Mix the butter and sugar together, leaving the butter cubes intact and put half inside the pastry. Place the slashed lemon on top and bury in the remaining sugar and butter.

Roll out the remaining pastry to make a lid, wet the edge of the pastry in the basin a little and press the lid on to seal. Cover the pudding with pleated foil or baking parchment and secure with string.

Bring a large ovenproof pan of water to the boil and lower the pudding basin into it; the water should come halfway up the side. Cover and place in the oven to steam for about 4 hours – the surface of the pudding should be golden brown. If the water level falls too low, add more boiling water.

Allow the pudding to rest for 5 minutes, then carefully lift out of the pan and remove the paper or foil. Turn the pudding out on to a large lipped plate or platter (the juices will spill out to form a 'pond' of sauce). It's highly likely that the pudding will partially collapse, but it's part of this puddings rustic charm and lovely texture.

Serve with cold double cream or hot custard.

GRANDAD'S TRIFLE

The first time I made this was one of those peculiar days between Christmas and New Year, which – depending on circumstance and disposition – are either a cheese-filled relief from the everyday, or a discombobulating wave of incoherent mornings and what-day-is-it afternoons.

That evening, my mum called to say that my stepdad and her man of 40-odd years was, finally after his illness, about to discover the answers we're all – in more ways than one – dying to know. We and his son and other half met in a semi-circle of plastic chairs around the hospital bed. What started sombre became more light-hearted as the hours passed. 'Well, at least I kept the receipt from his Christmas present.' 'I haven't given him his Christmas bottle of rum yet.'

When it became clear that perhaps tonight wasn't to be the night, we left agreeing to reconvene in the morning. We had talked about needing a snack to keep us going and I promised to bring in the trifle I'd just made, as it seemed faintly ridiculous to do so, in just the fashion that he might have enjoyed.

My daughter had asked me to say goodbye to grandad for her; when he unexpectedly opened his eyes a little, I said hello and gave him her love instead. We ate the trifle as he slept on a little before slipping away.

For the plums

12 large plums, halved and stoned

30g (1oz) sugar

8 cardamom pods

3 tbsp rosewater

splash of red wine vinegar

For the custard

300ml (10fl oz) whole milk

300ml (10fl oz) double cream

2 bay leaves

2 tbsp cornflour

5 egg yolks

70g (2½oz) caster sugar

4 tbsp cider vinegar

To assemble

50g (2oz) hazelnuts, crushed

250g (9oz) Christmas pudding or cake

Place the plums in a heavy-based pan with 1cm (½in) water and bring to a simmer over a medium heat. Add the sugar and cardamom pods. Simmer until the fruit fall into disrepair but before they lose all composure. Then remove from the heat, allow to cool and stir in the rosewater and vinegar.

To make the custard, warm the milk, cream and bay leaves in a medium heavy-based pan and bring it slowly to the boil. Remove from the heat and allow to infuse as the mix cools a little.

In a cup, use your fingers to blend the cornflour with an equal volume of water until smooth.

Whisk the egg yolks and sugar in a bowl until pale and thickened. Remove the bay leaves from the warm creamy milk. Slowly add the warm mixture to the bowl, stirring it constantly into the sugary egg yolks until well combined. Tip the mixture back into the pan using a rubber spatula to get out as much as possible, and warm over a low-medium heat.

Cook for 10 minutes or so, stirring constantly. You'll feel the custard start to thicken; reduce the heat a touch if this is happening too quickly for comfort. The custard will thicken enough to coat the back of a wooden spoon, at which point turn off the heat.

250g (9oz) mascarpone

250g (9oz) crème fraîche or ricotta

50g (2oz) icing sugar

generous drizzling of pomegranate molasses

a generous sprinkling of passion fruit powder

Use your fingers to blend the cornflour mixture again if it has separated a little, then stir it into the custard. Cook for a couple of minutes more, stirring constantly to prevent sticking and to keep it smooth: the custard will become very thick. Remove it from the heat and, stirring constantly, add the cider vinegar and incorporate thoroughly. Place a damp tea towel over the top of the pan to prevent the custard forming a skin as it cools.

Toast the crushed hazelnuts briefly over a medium-high heat in a dry pan. A little light darkening and intensifying of colour is what you are looking for, rather than scorch.

To assemble the trifle, crumble the Christmas pudding into the bottom of a trifle bowl and drown it in the aromatic plums. Pour the custard over and refrigerate until set.

Whisk the mascarpone, crème fraîche and icing sugar together in a large bowl until combined, then use a spatula to spread it across the custard. Scatter the cream with hazelnuts, drizzle plentifully with pomegranate molasses and dust the entirety generously with passion fruit powder.

Put the trifle somewhere no one else will find it and return regularly to demolish it in instalments.

AUTUMN PUDDING

If I'm going to have a pudding when the cold days are here, I usually want a hot one – this is a happy exception. It's as fine a celebration of the end of summer and the start of winter as there is – sweet, sharp and deep in colour and intent. By all means mess with the proportions and the fruit you choose, as long as the overall weight is retained. This is one to make ahead and allow to settle in for a day or two before the spoon breaks its autumnal seal.

Should it be proper grim outside, you can, as Nigel Slater does with his, scatter a little sugar over the surface and bake for 25 minutes at 200°C/400°F/gas mark 6 and enjoy hot. It may surrender its shape as you ease it out of the bowl, but who cares.

Serves 4–6

150g (5oz) plums, quartered and stoned

100g (3½oz) caster sugar

180g (6oz) raspberries

130g (4½oz) redcurrants

6–8 slices of good white bread, crusts removed

Put the plums and the sugar into a large pan and cook over a gentle heat for 15 minutes or so until the juices begin to run, the sugar has dissolved and the fruit is soft. Add the raspberries and redcurrants and cook for another 4–5 minutes until soft. Remove from the heat.

Line an 850ml (1½ pint) pudding bowl with a double layer of clingfilm that overhangs the side well. Dip the bread slices in the syrup released by the fruit and line the bottom and sides of the bowl with the soaked bread slices, slightly overlapping each – keeping one slice back for the lid.

Spoon the rest of the fruit and its juice into the pudding bowl. Place the reserved slice of bread on top and fold over the clingfilm to seal the pudding. Place a saucer or small plate that fits inside the bowl on top of the pudding and add a weight such as a bag or two of sugar, or some cans of food. Refrigerate overnight.

When you are ready to serve the pudding, lift off the plate and peel back the clingfilm. Place a serving plate over the top of the pudding and invert the pudding carefully. Lift off the bowl and remove the clingfilm.

Serve with thick double cream.

ROASTED APRICOTS WITH CRÈME FRAÎCHE, POMEGRANATE MOLASSES AND FENNEL CRUMBLE

It's often better to play cricket with supermarket apricots than to eat them, however, this is a fine way to coax out their best – the combination of sugar and vinegar drawing out their natural sweet and sour.

Cardamom and apricots are – like Béatrice Dalle and Jean-Hugues Anglade in *Betty Blue* – such a hot combination, but as with those two, things can easily turn a bit much: a couple of cardamom seeds in each apricot is all you need if you want to avoid the culinary equivalent of the bother they got into.

You can play with this all you like – fennel or star anise in place of the cardamom, lemon thyme instead of rosemary, and so on – just keep the cooking of the apricots brief: roast them high and hard like you're trying to get a secret out of them. I haven't included amounts because you don't need them – it's as simple as it sounds, I promise.

I admit, I occasionally over-butter this and end up with golden marbling on the tray as the apricots' juice and the topping bubble over – it's very close to the flavour of the humbugs I used to spend my school dinner money on.

Serves as many as you wish
apricots, halved and stoned
vinegar
cardamom pods, crushed to remove the seeds
butter
soft light brown sugar
a few stems of ginger rosemary (or use regular rosemary)
crème fraîche or yoghurt
freshly ground black pepper
pomegranate molasses

For the fennel crumble
butter
soft light brown sugar
plain flour
fennel seeds

Preheat the oven to 200°C/400°F/gas mark 6.

Arrange the apricot halves on a baking tray, cut side up. To each half add a few drops of vinegar – this is one of those times when an excellent vinegar pays off, but even a plain vinegar makes a difference. Place a couple of cardamom seeds and a thumbnail of butter in each stone dent and sprinkle with brown sugar. Place rosemary (ginger rosemary, if you have it) over the top and roast for 10–15 minutes until succulent but still holding their shape.

They are wonderful as they are, but if you are in the mood for a little crunch, make a simple fennel crumble – one part butter to two sugar to three plain flour, generously riddled with fennel seed – can be baked on a separate baking tray alongside the apricots for 10 minutes, and then atop the apricots for a further 5 minutes.

Serve with crème fraîche or yoghurt, a generous peppering, and drizzled with pomegranate molasses or a good dark honey if straight-up sweetness appeals.

LIME POSSET

There is never a time when this pud is not welcome. I could have (and have had) it for breakfast as happily as after dinner, in summer as often as winter. It is as classy as you like, yet not beyond a crumbled ginger biscuit as a topping of sorts. And the prep is 6 or 7 minutes, tops.

The slice of ginger (and the topping) are very much optional, though ginger and lime go together very well, if you are in the mood. And if you have lemons, Sevilles, grapefruits etc instead of limes, do feel free to go offroad. One thing to try is a dusting of passion fruit powder on the surface. My word.

Serves 4

500ml (18fl oz) double cream

150g (5oz) caster sugar

1 slice of fresh ginger (optional)

3 fresh kaffir lime leaves, roughly chopped

100ml (3½fl oz) lime juice (about 3 juicy limes)

Put the cream, sugar, ginger (if using) and lime leaves in a small pan and bring to the boil, stirring a few times until the sugar has dissolved. Simmer for 2 minutes, then stir in the lime juice and bring back to the boil. As soon as it starts to bubble remove from the heat and then pour through a sieve into a jug.

Divide between ramekins or glasses. Allow to cool, then chill for a couple of hours until set.

ROSEMARY RHUBARB BUTTERMILK PUDDINGS

The buttermilk pudding is so good and delicately flavoured with orange and bay on its own that I almost hesitate to include the way I like it best – with rhubarb roasted with orange and rosemary – but I'll trust you to try it without any fruit too. A cooking apple or two simmered with star anise until collapsed, plums, or even banana slices fried in butter and honey are worthy accompaniments too. And do swap the orange zest for lemon should you fancy.

With fruit or without, these puddings are best served in glasses as they are very wobbly; you can turn them out on to a plate if you want but they are mighty fragile. If you're feeling brave, dip the glass into hot water to loosen the pudding a little. I tend to serve this in sherry glasses – a small sweet finish to a meal – but you can split it just between four larger glasses if you prefer.

Serves 4–6

For the roast rhubarb

5 sticks of rhubarb, cut into 2.5cm (1in) lengths

3 tbsp honey

zest of 1 orange

3 sprigs of rosemary, each cut into 2.5cm (1in) lengths

For the pudding

1 gelatine leaf

100ml (3½fl oz) milk

40g (1½oz) sugar

2 strips of pared orange zest

½ a bay leaf

300ml (10fl oz) buttermilk

100ml (3½fl oz) double cream

Preheat the oven to 180°C/350°F/gas mark 4.

Place the rhubarb in a single layer in a roasting tray. Drizzle with the honey, scatter the orange zest evenly across the rhubarb and dot with rosemary. Cover with foil and roast for 10–15 minutes until the rhubarb's legs just give way. Spoon the fruit and all the juices into a bowl to cool.

Soak the gelatine in cold water in a bowl for 5 minutes until soft.

Put the milk, sugar, strips of orange zest and half bay leaf into a pan and bring to the boil. Remove the pan from the heat.

Drain the gelatine, squeeze dry, add to the warm milk and whisk to melt the gelatine. Let the milk mixture cool down to room temperature then remove the zest and bay, then mix the buttermilk into the cooled milk.

Whip the cream to soft peaks then fold the buttermilk mixture into the cream.

Spoon the rhubarb between as many glasses as you are using, then top with the buttermilk mixture. Chill for at least 2 hours before serving.

KIWI, LIME AND GINGER LABNEH CHEESECAKE

This tastes very much like the eighties just came for tea, exactly as I'd hoped. The sourness and sweetness are distinct – allowed their space in the ensemble, rather than being lost in the mix: the sweet ginger biscuit base and the ginger syrup sandwich the gentle sours of labneh, lime and kiwi. As far as I'm concerned, there is no place for the fudgy heft of cheesecake after a main course, though my 12-year-old self – along with my 13-year-old daughter – is shouting loud disapproval in my ear. The somewhat older me suggests that this should be enjoyed without guilt, in unnecessary slices with mid-morning coffee or afternoon tea. If you are a hog, this is one of those handy puds you can all but make a day or two ahead, and finish just as you serve.

You'll need a 23cm (9in) shallow flan dish – I usually use a fixed ceramic rather than loose-bottomed tin for this.

Serves 8

900g (2lb) Greek yoghurt
270g (9½oz) ginger biscuits
80g (3oz) soft salted butter
2 eggs
zest and juice of 2 limes
1 tsp vanilla extract
4 kiwis, peeled and sliced
3 tsp syrup from a jar of stem ginger

Line a colander with muslin and place it over a large bowl. Pour the yoghurt into the muslin and twist the end so it forms a tightish ball – secure with a peg or some string. Leave it in the fridge overnight, ideally for 24 hours or so. The whey will seep out, and you can persuade it further by twisting the loose ends to squeeze the ball.

Preheat the oven to 170°C/340°F/gas mark 3.

Whizz the biscuits in a blender until they resemble the sand you tip out of your holiday shoes. Melt the butter in a pan over a low heat and pour into the blender, then whizz until it starts to come together just a little. Tip into the flan dish and spread across the base and 1cm (½in) or so up the sides using your hands.

In a medium-sized bowl, mix the labneh, eggs, lime zest and juice and vanilla extract thoroughly. Using a spatula, spread the resulting 'cheese' over the base. Place in the oven and cook for 20 minutes – allow a few minutes more if the centre isn't quite set.

Remove from the oven and allow to cool completely, then refrigerate for a minimum of 2 hours. Just before serving, arrange the kiwi slices over the top and drizzle over the ginger syrup.

GOOSEBERRY AND OAT CAKE

An early morning visit to Honey & Co in London a few years ago cemented my love of the breakfast pudding. A cold walk through streets near where I used to work on the central edges of north London was rewarded by a breakfast that ended with their rightly famous honey, feta and kadaif cheesecake. Last week, perfect cinnamon toast from the excellent Rousdon Village Bakery along the Devon coast from my home finished off a full English in an entirely unnecessary and delightful way that left me forgetting the idea of lunch. 'Breakfast like a king', they say, and why not.

I love this cake for any time of day, but you really ought to try it for breakfast, either on its own or following something good and salty. The oats give a gorgeous porridge backbeat and the gooseberries almost dissolve into wonderful sour pools throughout. A little yoghurt goes well here.

In the unlikely event that you don't see this off quickly, it keeps well too.

Serves 6–8

100g (3½oz) rolled oats, plus more to sprinkle

85g (3oz) plain flour

1½ tsp baking powder

finely grated zest of 1 lemon

1 vanilla pod, seeds scraped out (or use 1 tsp vanilla extract)

250g (9oz) caster sugar

2 eggs

150ml (5fl oz) milk

110g (4oz) melted butter, plus more for greasing

150g (5oz) gooseberries, topped and tailed

2 tbsp demerara sugar

Preheat the oven to 180°C/350°F/gas mark 4. Line a 23cm (9in) cake tin with baking parchment and grease with butter.

Whizz the oats in a blender or food processor for a few seconds to create a coarse flour, then mix with the plain flour and baking powder.

Stir the lemon zest and vanilla into the caster sugar, then beat with the eggs until thick and pale. Slowly add the milk and the melted butter in to the eggs, then fold in the flour mix to make a batter. Add half the gooseberries to the batter.

Pour into the cake tin, dot the rest of the gooseberries over the top, and sprinkle with the demerara sugar and a few more oats.

Bake in the oven for 45 minutes or so – until a skewer comes out clean. Allow the cake to cool in the tin for about 20 minutes before removing. Serve still warm, with crème fraîche or double cream.

SWEET AND SOUR APRICOT UPSIDE DOWN CAKE

The thrill of an upside down cake is all in the reveal: has it stuck, or am I a genius? This has another reveal the first time you make it – will sweet and sour really be nice in a cake? Allow me to coax you, eyes like Kaa, into trying this once: it's all it will take.

Serves 6–8

50g (2oz) unsalted butter

100g (3½oz) soft light brown sugar

150g (5oz) plain flour

1 tsp ground cardamom (or use cinnamon)

1 tsp bicarbonate of soda

½ tsp salt

150g (5oz) caster sugar

one quantity of sweet and sour apricots (see page 98)

4 eggs

100ml (3½fl oz) sunflower oil

Preheat the oven to 180°C/350°F/gas mark 4 and line a 25cm (10in) cake tin with baking parchment.

Melt the butter and the brown sugar together in a pan over a medium heat, stirring to combine.

Sift the flour, cardamom, bicarbonate of soda and salt into a bowl, mix in the caster sugar and put to one side.

Pour the melted butter and brown sugar mix into the cake tin and arrange the apricots on top, cut side down.

Whisk the eggs and sunflower oil together, then combine into the dry ingredients. Pour this batter over the apricots in the cake tin, place in the centre of the oven and bake for 40 minutes, or until a skewer comes out clean.

Cool on a wire rack for 5 minutes, then place a plate on top and carefully turn the cake upside down and out on to the plate. Serve warm or at room temperature, with whichever cream or yoghurt takes your fancy.

BLACKCURRANT YOGHURT CAKE

I have few rules in life, but I won't be moved on the most important: never eat a biscuit that floats. I feel similarly about cakes. I couldn't be less interested in a Victoria sponge; it is the pink wafer biscuit of the cake world. My heart lies with fudgy brownies, gooseberry and oat cake (see page 244) and Nigella's olive oil cake: all tickle my preference for a little weight, a cake of substance and presence, as does this little beauty.

This is entirely foolproof too, so if you are the sort – as am I – who retrieves a delightfully domed cake from the oven only for it to cleave to the concave, this is for you. It's also bloody delicious.

Serves 6–8

225g (8oz) caster sugar, plus more for sprinkling

finely grated zest of 1 lemon

2 eggs

100g (3½oz) self-raising flour

1 tsp baking powder

150g (5oz) ground almonds

225g (8oz) natural yoghurt

pinch of salt

200g (7oz) blackcurrants or any soft fruit (fresh or frozen)

Preheat the oven to 170°C/340°F/gas mark 3 and line a 23cm (9in) cake tin with baking parchment.

Use an electric whisk to combine the sugar, lemon zest and eggs together for 4–5 minutes until the mixture is a thick pale foam.

Sift the flour and baking powder into a bowl and mix in the ground almonds.

Fold the yoghurt and a pinch of salt into the sugary eggs, followed by the dry ingredients and half the blackcurrants, until everything is combined.

Pour into the prepared tin and sprinkle over the remaining blackcurrants and a dusting of sugar.

Place in the centre of the oven and bake for 40–45 minutes until the cake is firm and a skewer comes out clean.

Cool the cake on a wire rack, before eating indecently quickly.

MATT'S NUT GATEAU

The first time my friend Matt made this for me I wanted to shoot him: if I bumped him off, I could pass it off as my own. This is pretty thin – I wouldn't call it a gateau, but Matt is from New Zealand and has questionable footwear: we must excuse him his peculiar ways. The cake has two layers, a crisp base and a cakier top. Excellent with good coffee as it is, I also love this as more of a pud with stewed plums or rhubarb, and with a thick sour cream.

If you have a food processor then this cake is super-fast to make, but it's easy enough without. It's best eaten on the day it is made, just-warm from the oven and still nuttily aromatic.

Serves 6–8

100g (3½oz) walnuts, almonds or hazelnuts, roughly chopped

130g (4½oz) soft light brown sugar, plus 2 tbsp to sprinkle

1 tsp ground cinnamon

pinch of salt

100g (3½oz) plain flour

50g (2oz) cold butter, diced

120ml (4fl oz) sour cream, plus more to serve

½ tsp baking powder

1 egg

Preheat the oven to 180°C/350°F/gas mark 4 and line a 23cm (9in) cake tin with baking parchment.

Use a food processor or rolling pin to crush half the nuts to a coarse gravel. Mix the sugar, cinnamon, salt and flour into the nuts.

Work the butter into the flour mix by pulsing in a food processor or with your fingertips until you have a sandy texture. Spread half this mix into the cake tin and press down slightly to form an even base.

Whisk the sour cream, baking powder and egg together. Add this to the remaining half of the butter-flour mix, then pour over the pressed base. Sprinkle the top with the rest of the chopped nuts and the remaining 2 tablespoons of sugar.

Bake for 40 minutes or so until golden on top and a skewer comes out clean. Serve with good sour cream.

APPLE ZABAGLIONE

Zabaglione is one of those words I can never quite commit to: sometimes I'm
Paulie Walnuts, other times Pam Ayres. Either way, you must make this, it's so
simple yet marvellous. You can make it with any fruit that takes your fancy, but
I think all that sweet richness works best when the fruit is sour. Rhubarb, the
sourest of plums or a few semi-ripe kiwis are equally fine. If you don't have any
Calvados, then brandy or even a smoky whisky will do just fine.

Serves 4

2 cooking apples, cored,
peeled and diced

1 star anise

90g (3¼oz) golden caster
sugar, plus more to taste

a shot of Calvados, apple
brandy, or even use a good
cider

2 eggs, plus 2 egg yolks

4 amaretti biscuits,
crumbled (optional)

Put the apples, the star anise, a splash of water and 50g (2oz) of the sugar into
a pan and cook until just surrendering themselves. Add a splash of apple
brandy plus a little more sugar (if you must) to taste, but allow them to stay
on the sour side. Allow to cool a little before spooning into glasses.

Bring a pan of water to a gentle simmer.

Beat the eggs and yolks together with the remaining 40g (2oz) sugar and the
shot of apple brandy in a large metal bowl that fits over the pan (without the
base touching the water). Place the bowl over the pan of simmering water and
whisk constantly until thick and fluffy – usually 3–5 minutes. Spoon over the
apples and serve immediately, sprinkled with the crumbled amaretti (if using).

KULFI WITH ROSEMARY AND GINGER RHUBARB AND TAMARIND

If, like me, you went in search of one last Kubrick masterpiece in *Eyes Wide Shut*, you may remember Nicole Kidman's character telling her husband – who had just said he thought her too dull to have an affair – of a naval officer walking past her in the hotel lobby and who she later saw on another table at dinner; despite the fleeting moments and no words exchanged, it had left her demolished. 'If he wanted me, even if it was only for one night, I was ready to give up everything. You. Helena. My whole fucking future. Everything.' That is exactly how I feel about this kulfi.

Impossibly laden with a life-shortening combination of sugar and fat as it is, I couldn't care less: take me, I'm ready. Its deep caramel, singed-toffee flavour is the finest accompaniment there is to roasted rhubarb, creating a fabulous clash of sweet, ginger, rosemary, lightly sour rhubarb with full-on tamarind, and it comes without the (pleasurable) faff of ice-cream making.

What kulfi you don't eat with the rhubarb, you'll sneak with a spoon in the night, pyjama-clad knees chilly from the dry ice of the freezer.

Serves 4, with leftovers

2 ½ tbsp maple syrup

1 tbsp pomegranate molasses

80g (3oz) soft dark brown sugar

340ml (12fl oz) evaporated milk

340ml (12fl oz) double cream

good pinch of salt

few drops of tamarind paste, as you like, to serve

For the rhubarb

400g (14oz) rhubarb

1 globe of stem ginger, cut in half, and thinly sliced

15cm (6in) sprig of rosemary, broken into 6 or so pieces

3 tsp syrup from the stem ginger jar

Warm the syrup, molasses and sugar in a pan over a low-medium heat, stirring occasionally, until the sugar becomes molten. Stir in the evaporated milk, cream and salt thoroughly and increase the heat. Bring to an almost-simmer, stirring most of the time, to prevent it catching on the bottom of the pan. Take off the heat and pour into a tub to freeze once it's completely cool.

Preheat the oven to 150°C/300°F/gas mark 2.

Chop the rhubarb into 2–3cm (¾–1¼in) pieces. Arrange them in a roasting dish, inside curve up so as to catch the flavours. Scatter with ginger slices, then the rosemary and finally drizzle with the ginger syrup. You can add a little more syrup if you are having this with yoghurt instead of kulfi, but the contrast with the sweet kulfi is so much the better when the rhubarb is sour.

Cover the dish with foil and cook for 13 minutes: the rhubarb should be soft, but hold its shape.

Spoon a little rhubarb on to a plate. Using an ice-cream scoop, curl the kulfi into a generous coil and place on top of the rhubarb. Fill the inside of the coil with a little more rhubarb, then drizzle over a spoon or two of the rosemary and ginger syrup, followed by a splash or two of wonderfully sour tamarind paste.

BUTTERMILK ICE CREAM AND SORBET

Buttermilk takes equally beautifully to becoming a crystalline sorbet or a richer ice cream. With the ice cream, sometimes I rather like the vanilla to offset the sourness of lemon and buttermilk, sometimes not. If you don't have an ice-cream maker, use an electric whisk; if you don't have one of them, use a fork and plenty of elbow grease.

Makess 800ml (1 ½ pints)

Sorbet

800ml (1 ½ pints) buttermilk

120g (4oz) sugar

finely grated zest and juice of 1 lemon

Ice cream

500ml (18fl oz) double cream

150g (5oz) sugar

4 egg yolks

pared zest of 1 lemon in strips with no pith, and/or the seeds from a vanilla pod

500ml (18fl oz) buttermilk

Sorbet
Whisk together the buttermilk, sugar and lemon zest in a bowl until the sugar dissolves. Stir in the lemon juice and refrigerate for at least 2 hours. Churn in an ice-cream maker according to the manufacturer's instructions. Transfer to an airtight container and freeze for at least 2 hours, until firm, before serving. If you haven't got an ice-cream maker, whisk by hand and freeze, remove the container after 90 minutes, break up the ice crystals and return to the freezer; repeat at least once more after 90 minutes.

Ice cream
Whisk together the cream, sugar, egg yolks and the lemon zest strips and/or the vanilla seeds. Cook over a low heat, stirring constantly with a wooden spoon, until the mixture thickens slightly and coats the back of the spoon. Immediately remove from the heat, strain through a sieve and allow to cool.

Stir in the buttermilk and refrigerate for at least 2 hours. Churn in an ice-cream maker according to the manufacturer's instructions. Transfer to an airtight container and freeze for at least 2 hours, until firm, before serving. If you haven't got an ice cream maker, whisk by hand and freeze, remove the container after 90 minutes, break up the ice crystals and return to the freezer; repeat at least once more after 90 minutes.

MINT AND VERJUICE GRANITA

This is as refreshing as underwear straight out of the fridge in August. If it's not hot enough weather for granita, turn up the heating and put a jumper on until you're sweltering: it's so extraordinarily good you'll want to eat it at any time of year and any time of day.

Makes 900ml (1½ pints)
240g (8½oz) sugar
500ml (18fl oz) water
good handful of mint leaves
230ml (8fl oz) verjuice
2 tbsp white rum

Add the sugar and water to a medium-sized pan and bring to a simmer, stirring to dissolve the sugar. Remove from the heat, add the mint and allow to cool. Strain the syrup through a sieve into a plastic container; discard the mint.

Stir in the verjuice and rum. Freeze for 6 hours or so until part frozen. Break up the ice crystals with a fork and stir well, then refreeze.

CRANBERRY AND RED VERMOUTH SORBET

This is not a sorbet for lying in the sun with, deploying a spoon of a size inversely proportionate to the frequency with which it is used: this is for when you want to wake everyone up at the end of a meal to send them off home to their own beds. It tastes like the run-up to Christmas through a loudhailer. If you are after more of a summery zing, add 3 tablespoons of lime juice when blending for the final time; for winter, try Seville orange juice.

Make 900ml (1½ pints)
300g (10oz) cranberries (frozen or fresh)
300g (10oz) sugar
530ml (18½fl oz) water
7 strips of pared orange zest
240ml (8fl oz) red vermouth

Add all but the vermouth to a pan and bring to the boil, stirring to dissolve the sugar. Simmer until the cranberries are tender, about 15–20 minutes. Discard the zest.

Zap in a blender until smooth – if you have a high-powered blender, ease back on the speed: you want it smooth, but whizzing too powerfully creates a pale froth on the surface. Strain through a sieve into a plastic tub and allow to cool, then stir in the red vermouth.

If using an ice-cream maker, follow the instructions that come with it. Otherwise, freeze for 6 hours or so, or overnight, then transfer the sorbet to a blender and whizz briefly to create a smoother consistency before returning to the freezer.

SOUR CREAM, APPLE AND BLACKBERRY TART

Is there a lovelier feeling, a happier sight at the close of summer than, as Sylvia Plath wrote: 'Nobody in the lane, and nothing, nothing but blackberries'; picking with no one and nothing to hurry you in the precious dimming days, when your skin knows the holidays are coming to an end.

Autumn prefers tarts to unfurl a roof to become pies, so this is for days when you need a little summer, even in October.

Serves 6–8

225g (8oz) cold butter, diced

250g (9oz) plain flour, plus more for rolling

4 tbsp sugar

120g (4oz) sour cream

5 Bramley apples

100g (3½oz) blackberries

Place 200g (7oz) of the butter, the flour and 1 tablespoon of the sugar in a food processor and pulse a few times until the mixture resembles coarse breadcrumbs. By all means, rub the ingredients together in a bowl using your fingertips instead, if you prefer.

Add the sour cream and pulse or mix until the dough starts to come together, stopping just before it forms a ball. If it is still crumbly and does not bind add a little cold water.

Form the dough into a flat disc, wrap in baking parchment and chill for 20–30 minutes before using.

While the pastry is resting, core, peel and dice 3 of the apples. Place them in a pan over a medium heat with the blackberries, the remaining 25g (1oz) butter, 2 tablespoons of the sugar and 1 tablespoon of water and cook for 5–7 minutes until the apples are tender. Remove from the heat and mash everything roughly with a fork.

Roll the pastry on a surface dusted with flour to about 3mm (1/8in) thick. Line a 25cm (10in) tart tin with the pastry, leaving about 5mm (¼in) hanging over the edge of the tin, then allow it to rest for 20 minutes in the fridge.

Preheat the oven to 190°C/375°F/gas mark 5.

Cover the base of the pastry with a circle of baking parchment and fill with baking beans, then bake for 5 minutes. Remove the baking beans and parchment and return the tart case to the oven for 5 minutes until lightly golden and dry to the touch. Trim the edge of the pastry to make it neat, or leave it rough and ready if you prefer.

Core, peel and thinly slice the remaining apples. Spread the apple and blackberry purée over the base of the tart, then arrange the apple slices over the top and sprinkle with the remaining tablespoon of sugar.

Bake for about 20–25 minutes until the apples are just golden brown at the edges but not collapsing. Remove from the oven and serve with whichever form of cream or yoghurt takes your heart's desire.

SHERBET LEMONS

One Christmas as a kid, I did a friend's paper round. A freezing start had the comfort of a forgotten sherbet lemon in my school blazer pocket. Every bike journey had an absent-minded challenge I set myself – longest wheelie, go no-hands between the factory and the turn-off, get up the hill in second gear. That morning's: to not finish the sweet before I got to the newsagent.

    I cycled the six minutes, the sherbet lemon a barely dissolving oyster of the most incredible sweet–sour, unswallowed. I span the pedals to vertical and stood the bike on the kerb. A friend ran out of the shop: 'John Lennon's been shot!' I loved The Beatles, playing my dad's Best-of constantly. I involuntarily swallowed the best lake of sweet–sour I'd ever tasted with a 'NO!', and what was left of the sherbet lemon fell from my mouth in slow motion, cracked in two on the kerb, the largest part slipping into the drain, the smallest sitting in an oily puddle. I almost salvaged it. A little part of me has been chasing that sherbet lemon ever since; this is the closest I've got.

Equipment
kitchen thermometer
silicone mat
marble work surface or oiled sheet of foil wrapped around a chopping board
kitchen scissors
spatula

Makes 30 or so
180g (6oz) sugar
120ml (4fl oz) water
½ tsp cream of tartar (to prevent crystallization)
½ tsp lemon extract
2 tsp citric acid
yellow gel food colouring
icing sugar for dusting
a little vegetable oil

Get everything ready and measure all the ingredients before you start, as when it happens with molten sugar, it happens quickly. Oil the surface of the mat, the blades of the kitchen scissors, and a spatula. Spoon icing sugar in a layer a few millimetres thick on to plate (unless you like breathing in a dense cloud of sugar).

Add the granulated sugar, water and cream of tartar to a small pan – 15cm (6in) across is good, as it gives enough depth of syrup for the thermometer to work well. Place over a high heat, stirring to dissolve the sugar. When the temperature reaches 149°C (300°F), remove the pan from the heat and pour on to the silicone mat.

Stir in the lemon extract, citric acid and a 3cm (1¼in) line of yellow food colouring, until fully incorporated. The mixture will cool quickly from this point, so be ready.

Use the spatula to pull the mix into a long thin mass on your mat, using your hands to form a rope around 1.5cm (¾in) in diameter. Don't worry if it's a little uneven. Use the scissors to cut the rope into 2–3cm (1in) pieces, at a 45-degree angle. Toss the sweets in the icing sugar to prevent them sticking together. They'll harden as they cool.

Variations
Sherbet rhubarb – you'll find rhubarb extract in most supermarkets; use a teaspoon of it plus a dash of green food colouring in place of the lemon extract and yellow colouring.
Sherbet raspberries – you can get dried raspberry powder online (see page 282 for suppliers); use 5 teaspoons of it, plus a few drops of red food colouring in place of the lemon extract and yellow colouring.

DRINKS

TEPACHE

When something has a name as beautifully ricocheting as tepache, phonology compels you to indulge. At first taste it even had me thinking of tequila, something that hasn't happened since a most unfortunate Christmas Eve three decades ago.

It is, I confess, not wildly sour but make it once, and marvel that we aren't all making this weekly as a matter of national institution.

Expect a sweet, heady aromatic juice that sends cocktail ideas Catherine-wheeling from your mind: a shot of rum or tequila, a little sparking water to taste, or just straight up, as I drink it most. Try it and see what you like.

This is definitely one to play with: cinnamon works well, though you might also explore freshening the flavours away from the Christmassy by using lemon verbena, lemon zest, lemongrass and even get spicy with chilli.

Make sure the pineapple is truly ripe; if it's one of those that you've forgotten about and it has started to glue itself to the kitchen counter, so much the better. Tepache is equally good made with scraps – most of the good stuff is in the peelings – so if you're eating pineapple in any other recipe, here is the home for what might otherwise go to compost. And you can make a second batch using the same pineapple and spices – just add more sugar and water.

Makes around 1 litre (1 ¼ pints)

1 large very ripe pineapple
180g (6oz) raw cane sugar
thumb-sized piece of fresh ginger
5 cloves
4 star anise

Unenthusiastically wash the outside of the pineapple to remove any dust etc, but not too thoroughly, as you'll risk ridding the fruit of its natural microbes. Top and tail the fruit.

Slice the pineapple vertically through the centre into 8 wedges, then slice off the thinnest 1cm (½in) of each wedge to do away with the toughest part of the core.

Add the sugar and 5cm (2in) or so of water to a sterilized 1.5 litre (2½ pint) Kilner jar and shake to encourage the sugar to start dissolving. Place each pineapple wedge in the jar with as much Stonehenge-like or Jenga-esque finesse as you fancy. Add the remaining ingredients, then fill with water leaving an inch or so of headspace at the top of the jar. Fix a piece of muslin in place over the top using an elastic band.

Allow this to ferment at room temperature for 3½ days, checking a few times in the last day and a half to skim off any white fug that may have formed on the surface. It will gradually develop a light fizz as fermentation develops.

Strain and bottle the aromatic juice in bottles with a flip-top lid, chilling it before serving. I often leave a few bottles out of the fridge to ferment a little longer, developing more of a sparkle and becoming less sweet as the sugars are devoured by the fermentation process.

LIME AND GINGER SHRUB

This is a delicious, refreshing shrub that makes a fine, squinty, down-in-one nip, a wonderful variation when added to a gin and tonic, a staggeringly good mojito (add rum, mint and soda water), or just as it is lengthened with a little soda water. The leftover sugary fruit – including the ginger here – can be swizzed in a blender or bashed with a wooden spoon and topped with boiling water for a refreshing tea.

Makes about 400ml (14fl oz)

6 limes

200g (7oz) demerara sugar

80g (3oz) white caster sugar

60g (2 ¼ oz) fresh ginger, peeled and finely chopped

about 280ml (9 ½ fl oz) cider vinegar

Microplane the zest of the limes into a glass or other non-reactive bowl, avoiding any of the bitter pith. Using a very sharp knife, peel off the pith and discard, then cut the fruit through the equator and then into sixths through the poles.

Thoroughly combine the lime flesh, sugars and ginger in the bowl, cover and leave to ferment for 12–48 hours; the longer you leave it, the more complex the flavour.

Strain the mixture through a plastic sieve into another non-reactive bowl, gently pressing the mix to extract as much liquid as possible. Allow to drip into the bowl for a couple of hours if you have more patience than I do. Discard all but the liquid.

Combine an equal volume of vinegar with the juice, and pour into a sterilized bottle. Refrigerate for 3 weeks, shaking the bottle whenever you get something from the fridge. Store in the fridge and use within 6 months.

THAI BASIL AND CUCUMBER SHRUB

This is one of those drinks that you can really get a taste for as an enlivening mid-morning nip, or try with equal volume of gin and perhaps a little tonic if you're inclined to drink more quickly than is good for you.

Makes about 250ml (9fl oz)

200g (7oz) caster sugar
240ml (8fl oz) rice wine vinegar
25g (1oz) Thai basil
1 large cucumber, peeled

Dissolve the sugar in the vinegar in a pan over a medium heat, stirring frequently. Take the pan off the heat.

Place the basil in a non-reactive bowl and pour the warm, sweet vinegar over it. Allow to cool.

Grate the cucumber into the bowl, stir and cover with a tea towel. Leave it to infuse for at least 12 hours, and up to 24.

Pour through a strainer into a jug and decant into a sterilized jar or bottle. You can use it immediately, but it's better off left to mature for a week in the fridge. It will last for 3 weeks or so in the fridge.

HIBISCUS AND RASPBERRY WATER KEFIR

In that way *Kind of Blue* or *A Love Supreme* has convinced generations of the deeply disinterested that not all jazz is the right notes in the wrong order, this water kefir is the passport for the uninitiated into the beautiful world of fermenting. It is utterly delicious, wildly addictive and really really simple to make.

Of all the superb variations on water kefir, this is the one I make most. Follow the core kefir recipe (see page 64), using 15g (½oz) dried hibiscus flowers and a handful of raspberries instead of the dried fruit. Over the course of a few hours, the liquid will blush heavily pink with the hibiscus.

Decant into a flip-top bottle when it is the flavour you like, and do a second fermentation if you fancy – add a little honey and/or lemon for flavour and fizz.

SWITCHELS

Go easy on the sweetness here: there should be enough to refresh and revitalize, rather than be a sore throat remedy. By all means play around with the ingredients – many variations exist, as outlined on page 52.

Makes 1 litre

Classic switchel

20g (¾ oz) fresh ginger, peeled and finely chopped

2 tsp lemon juice

70ml (2½ fl oz) apple cider vinegar

3 tbsp honey (raw, ideally)

Turmeric switchel

1 tsp grated fresh turmeric or ½ tsp ground turmeric

20g (¾ oz) fresh ginger, peeled and finely chopped

2 tsp lemon juice

70ml (2½ fl oz) apple cider vinegar

3 tbsp honey

Cranberry switchel

large handful of dried cranberries

20g (¾ oz) fresh ginger, peeled and finely chopped

1 tsp lemon juice

70ml (2½ fl oz) apple cider vinegar

3 tbsp honey

Blackberry and lavender switchel

large handful of blackberries

20g (¾ oz) fresh ginger, peeled and finely chopped

2 tsp lemon juice

2–3cm (1in) sprig of flowering lavender (ideally just as it begins to open for the cleanest flavour)

70ml (2½ fl oz) apple cider vinegar

3 tbsp honey

Add the ginger, lemon juice and vinegar to a sterilized 1 litre (1¾ pint) jar and stir to encourage the ginger to start releasing its flavour. Add the honey and stir until it is dissolved. Fill the jar with water, leaving about an inch at the top of the jar. Seal.

Ideally, leave this overnight to infuse and let the flavours develop, then refrigerate. Pour through a sieve when you want to drink it – as it is, with ice, or however the urge takes. As a mixer for Irish whiskey, it has more than a little merit.

Other switchels

Don't tell anyone I told you, but there's nothing to stop you taking an eraser to the line between a shrub and a switchel and using fruit or other flavourings that take your fancy.

It may not have escaped your notice that the recipes for classic switchel and water kefir bear a healthy resemblance, with vinegar bringing sourness to the switchel, and bacterial grains do the acidifying work in water kefir.

Unsurprisingly, many of the embellishing flavours that work for kefir work equally well with switchels: adding a handful or two of raspberries and/or hibiscus flowers when you add the honey is a great variation to begin with.

Here are three more switchels that follow the core recipe:

Turmeric switchel
Fresh turmeric is the ideal here but ground makes a decent alternative.

Cranberry switchel
You can do a passable impression of this by adding a good slug of cranberry juice to the classic switchel when serving.

Blackberry and lavender switchel
I'd recommend removing the lavender after an hour of infusing, unless you want to drink pot pourri.

BLACK LIMEONADE

On the first day of the year where I get in the car to be welcomed by the smell of sun-warm interior, I make this most refreshing of sunny-weather drinks. The triple sours of black lime (see page 20), citrus and hibiscus make for a beautifully complex lime-lemonade that never oversteps the mark. If you were to try an equal measure of gin to limeonade, and tonic in place of the sparkling water, you may find that your disposition improves.

Makes 400ml (14fl oz)
400ml (14fl oz) water
250g (9oz) sugar
2 black limes, punctured
zest of 2 lemons
zest of 1 lime
6 dried hibiscus flowers
sparkling water and ice, to serve

In a medium-sized pan, bring the water to a simmer and stir the sugar in until it has dissolved. Add the black limes, citrus zest and hibiscus flowers and gently simmer for 15 minutes. The liquid should have become more syrupy, and the colour a pleasing crimson. Allow to cool a little, strain through a sieve into a jug, before pouring into a sterilized bottle (use a funnel if you are as messy as I). Once cool, refrigerate.

Serve diluted with sparkling water: 1:5 limeonade to water is a good place to start. In the unlikely event that you don't finish this within a day or two, it will keep for a couple of weeks in the fridge.

SOL KAHDI

This is a creamy, spicy, weirdly refreshing drink that's hugely popular on India's west coast. It may be the first recipe I have put in a book of which I'm not entirely convinced. I include it because I sort-of quite like it and my wife and daughter – whose taste in most things is superior to mine – really like it. I want to love it: like my lack of enthusiasm for rainy camping and indifference to negronis, I feel that I am a lesser person for it. But there we are. It's here – like putting a track by The Band on a compilation – because I like it enough but many love it, and you might love it too.

Makes 1 litre (1 ¾ pints)
14 dried kokums
1 tsp sea salt
1 tsp mustard seeds
1 tsp cumin seeds
10 curry leaves
½ tsp asafoetida
2 garlic cloves, chopped
1 tsp Kashmiri red chilli powder
good handful of coriander, chopped
300ml (10fl oz) coconut milk

Pour 500ml (18fl oz) boiling water over the kokum pods and allow them to infuse for 45 minutes or so, squishing the pods with a wooden spoon once in a while to encourage the flavour to flow.

Squeeze and break up the pods and strain through a sieve, retaining the liquid.

While the kokum is infusing, combine the salt, spices, garlic, chilli powder and coriander in a pestle and mortar, and work into a smooth paste. Transfer to a jug.

Whisk the kokum liquid a little at a time into the spice paste until fully incorporated. Add the coconut milk, then make up to 1 litre (1 ¾ pints) with cold water. Taste and adjust the seasoning if required. Refrigerate – I think it's at its nicest stone-cold.

ZOOM KOOM

The pleasure of writing a book about all things sour is that everyone has an uplifting sour tale they drift off into: sour plums from their childhood, the greatest pomegranate sour cocktail, pickled onion Monster Munch under the duvet, and so on. This, passed on to me by Peter Weeden, chef at the Duke of Cambridge pub in London, is apparently the national drink of Burkina Faso. I've not googled whether that's true as I don't want to know if it's not.

I've included quantities here as that's what you're supposed to do, but do play with this as you fancy. Really, it's just two complementary sours, a blind cobbler's thumb of ginger, a little sugar for balance and a flavourless, fine flour to add a little creamy silk (millet flour is traditional, but quinoa flour is usually easier to find), plus a pineapple – all in a blender on 'let's destroy all the evidence' setting.

Superbly sour and sweet as this is over ice, drinking it is like sitting at a crossroads, pondering which route to take: a cocktail with rum and kombucha, just lengthened out with sparkling water, or perhaps turned into even more of a smoothie with milk and a little milk kefir.

Makes around 700ml (1¼ pints), depending on the size and ripeness of the pineapple

100g (3½oz) tamarind block (with seeds in)

thumb of fresh ginger (about 30g/1oz), peeled and chopped

1 pineapple, peeled (optional – I have made without the pineapple and it is still delicious)

40g (1½oz) sugar

125ml (4fl oz) lemon juice

80g (3oz) quinoa flour

Crumble the tamarind into a medium pan, add 380ml (13fl oz) boiling water and bring to a simmer, stirring to dissolve the tamarind as much as possible in the water. Simmer for 10 minutes or so, then pass through a sieve and discard the solids.

Allow to cool, then blitz everything in a blender, holding back a quarter of the sugar and lemon juice to allow for adjustment later. Taste – it should be pretty full-on – and adjust the sweet/sourness to taste with sugar or lemon juice then pass the liquid through a fine sieve. Chill in the fridge before serving over ice.

SEVILLE ORANGE AND CARDAMOM GIN

If you are prone, as I am, to buying a skipful of Sevilles for the pleasure of marmalade-making, before remembering that you only get through three jars a year, this is the most pleasing of homes for those leftover fruits. A couple of star anise work well in place of the cardamom, but it has a touch too much Christmas for me as I'm all New Year-y when the Sevilles are about.

Makes 1 litre (1¾ pints)
5 Seville oranges
8 green cardamom pods
1 litre (1¾ pints) gin

Cut each orange in half, and then slice each half into half-moons about 4mm (⅛ in) thick. Place them in a 1.5 litre (2½ pint) Kilner jar and add the cardamom pods.

Pour the gin into the jar – you may end up with enough of a tot left in the bottle to reward you for your hard slicing labours.

Leave this for a couple of weeks; a couple of months if you can. Enjoy with tonic, or ginger ale, and plenty of ice.

GINGER ROSEMARY TOM COLLINS

It'll be 3.30pm, a Sunday, and all you want to do is lie there after a good lunch and watch an old film or embarrass someone at Scrabble, and yet some inconsiderate devil has invited you to a barbecue. I tell my teenage daughter that such tyrannies are one of the awfulnesses of being a grown-up. Poor thing; she still loves being sociable.

And once you go, there's the dark expectation of reciprocation. When it is your turn – and you know that almost everyone coming is feeling the same as you were – this cocktail is the remedy, the way to convince unwilling arrivals that being vertical this afternoon wasn't all a waste.

Make this just before serving, as the sourness fades a little, and it must be full-on. I know you might be thinking 'that sounds like too much lemon' but go with me: it should feel as if someone has taken your teeth out while you were asleep, polished them, put them back in and slapped you awake. Be careful: after one you feel you can do anything, after two you can do nothing.

Serves 1

1 part ginger rosemary
syrup (see method)
1 part gin
1 part lemon juice
a great deal of crushed ice

For the syrup, simmer sugar in an equal weight of water, stirring to dissolve. Add a few sprigs of ginger rosemary and remove the pan from the heat. Taste as the syrup cools, removing the rosemary when it is the strength you like. If you don't have ginger rosemary, use regular and add a little of the syrup from a jar of crystallized stem ginger. The syrup will keep for a few weeks in the fridge.

Combine the ginger rosemary syrup, gin, lemon juice and crushed ice in a cocktail shaker and shake until chilled, or use a jug with a spoon to stir. Strain into a chilled cocktail glass.

MOSCOW MULE

A cocktail that's very much like The Smiths: at first, you think it's all about the vodka/Morrissey, then you realize it's really the ginger beer/Johnny Marr, and later it hits you that the heart of the whole thing is actually the lime/Andy Rourke.

If the sun is high, try this with the juice, strained of seeds, of two passion fruit too.

Serves 1
crushed ice
50ml (2fl oz) vodka
juice of 1 lime
140ml (5fl oz) ginger beer

If you need instructions of how to put this all in a glass, you don't deserve one.

ZOBO

Of all the mulled drinks, this is the one I lean towards when circumstance prevents me tucking into my beloved mulled cider. Sharp, sweet, a little on the festive side without going the whole pot pourri, this is as welcome in midsummer as when in need of a refresher after a brisk winter walk.

So many cultures have their version of this – it's zobo in Nigeria, sorrel in the Caribbean – and it is most certainly one to embellish and tweak as you like: cinnamon and cardamom are good, pineapple excellent, and some swear by chilli and garlic in the mix, though not I.

Rinse the flowers first in cold water; don't worry about losing colour – they're an almost inexhaustible ink cartridge – there'll be plenty for the drink itself.

Makes 1 litre (1¾ pints)
20g (¾oz) dried hibiscus flowers
2 juniper berries
3 star anise
20g (¾oz) fresh ginger, peeled and finely chopped
100g (3½oz) sugar

Put all the ingredients into a medium pan with 1 litre (1¾ pints) water and bring to a gentle boil. Simmer over a medium heat for 10 minutes. Strain, allow to cool and refrigerate. Try it neat, over ice, or diluted with sparkling water if you prefer.

PICKLEBACK

This is a total non-recipe; more of a suggestion, like 'Wear a hat when it's sunny', or 'Don't be the only person who pays full price for an electric toothbrush.' Attributed to a Reggie Cunningham of Bushwick Country Club in Williamsburg, Brooklyn in 2006, a pickleback is a simple succession of a shot of whisky followed by a shot of pickle juice, which may appeal to your frugal side when a jar of pickles is emptied of its objects of preservation. As much as I generally favour an excellent smoky Islay whisky to sniff as much as sip, I'm not about to neck a Lagavulin in a hurry, so likely as not I'll have this with Jameson.

Serves 1

1 shot of whisky

1 shot of pickle juice

Ensure you've eaten something relatively recently. Down the whisky as quickly or slowly as you fancy, then immediately neck the pickle juice. Face the world refreshed and taking no nonsense.

CRANBERRY SOUR

The first kitchen I ever worked in was shared with as fine a bunch of new friends as you might reasonably hope for, randomly thrown together as we were. Almost all of us are still in touch. That first sunny summer, most of us newly flushed with our own money, was a time of red-cheeked freedom. When I asked Mike if he fancied a midweek pint after work, he looked me square in the eye and said, 'Yes, but don't forget: one is one, two is ten.' I never have forgotten, and when it comes to this little chappy, neither should you.

Serves 1

4 tablespoons vodka (some prefer their sours with bourbon; give it a whirl)

2 tablespoons lemon juice

2 tablespoons cranberry juice

1 tsp sugar

soda water (optional)

crushed ice

If you have a cocktail shaker, pour all the ingredients in except the soda water, along with a generous amount of crushed ice and shake for 15 seconds. Decant into a glass, top with some soda water (if using) and wonder why you don't drink this most nights. If you are without a shaker, stir the sugar into the lemon juice in a glass, add the rest of the ingredients and stir and wonder why you don't have a cocktail shaker.

MINT KEFIR MOJITO

This little smasher works with pretty much any water kefir – from blackcurrant to lemon and ginger to raspberry and hibiscus – though if you want to add mint to the kefir as it ferments, it will add another layer of mintiness. If you have a sweet tooth, I will reluctantly allow you to stir in a teaspoon of sugar into the minty lime juice, before adding the ice.

Serves 1

12 mint leaves (ideally Moroccan mint)

juice of 1 lime, plus the squeezed-out skin, quartered

handful of crushed ice

50ml (2fl oz) white rum

water kefir, to taste (see page 64)

Place the mint leaves in a tall glass with the lime juice and the quartered skin. Bash the skins and mint gently with the handle of a wooden spoon to release the scent and oils a little. Add a generous handful of ice, the rum and as much water kefir as takes your fancy.

DOUBLE GINGER TAMARIND MOJITO

A good mojito shows just how much a cocktail really is little more than an alcoholic salad dressing. Sweet, sharp, aromatic and punchy must all be in complementary attendance, and with this mojito they most certainly are. Here, the classic lime is substituted for tamarind, with the double gingers riding side-saddle in place of the sugar and soda water. You can make this with tamarind paste from a jar – it is really pretty good if you do – but if you bother with the tamarind block that comes with the seeds, the few minutes of faff will be amply rewarded in the results.

Serves 1

20g (¾oz) tamarind block

15g (½oz) sugar

good slice of fresh ginger

good handful of mint leaves (ideally Moroccan mint)

good handful of crushed ice

40ml (1½fl oz) white rum

140ml (5fl oz) ginger beer, or to taste

In a cup, add 50ml boiling water to the tamarind, along with the sugar and ginger, and jab and stir with a spoon to break up the tamarind, bruise the ginger and dissolve the sugar.

Place the mint in a tall glass and use the thin end of a wooden spoon to bruise the mint gently – the aim is to release the scent and oils a little, not make pesto. Add a generous amount of crushed ice to the mint, pour the gingery tamarind syrup through a sieve into the glass. Add the rum, stir well, then add ginger beer to taste. Stir and relax.

RESOURCES

Should this book have made you inquisitive for more, here are some places to investigate:

The Art of Fermentation – Sandor Katz
The Cultured Club – Dearbhla Reynolds
Food For A Happy Gut – Naomi Devlin
How To Make Sourdough – Emmanuel Hadjiandreou
Vinegar Revival – Harry Rosenblum
Acid Trip Michael – Harlan Turkell
The Vinegar Cupboard – Angela Clutton
Salt Sugar Smoke – Diana Henry
Pam The Jam: The Book Of Preserves – Pam Corbin
The Beer Kitchen – Melissa Cole

www.neantog.com – Gaby and Hans Wieland's fermentation courses and more
www.sourdough.co.uk – Vanessa Kimbell's school of sourdough
www.naomidevlin.co.uk – for all things fermented and more besides
www.foragefinefoods.com – Liz Knight's foraging courses
www.schoolofartisanfood.org – preserving and fermentation courses
www.happykombucha.co.uk – kombucha SCOBYs, water and milk kefir grains, starters and more
www.souschef.co.uk – natural sours, vinegars, verjuice and other excellent ingredients
www.artisanmaltvinegar.co.uk – excellent malt vinegar from Cornwall
www.cultvinegar.co.uk – special, small batch, unpasteurised vinegars, and vinegar vases for making your own
www.womersleyfoods.com – excellent flavoured vinegars
www.burrenbalsamics.com – superb infused balsamic vinegars
www.willysacv.com – wonderful apple cider vinegar with mother

INDEX

ACKNOWLEDGEMENTS

I am enormously grateful to Sarah Lavelle and Susannah Otter at Quadrille for their enthusiasm for me and the idea, and to Susannah for her dedication, skill, liveliness and excellent humour in overseeing the creation of such a beautiful book. To Claire Rochford, Head of Design at Quadrille, for being the perfect blend of clear and definite ideas as well as openness to others, thank you. To Matt Cox, the best designer with such a sweet eye and excellent taste, thank you. To Clare Sayer, thank you so much for your incisive and sensitive copy editing. I worked with Matt Williamson on getting on for half of the recipes – thank you for the laughing, and your brilliance on the photoshoots.

Thank you all for making it such huge fun: it is criminal that only my name makes the cover.

Thank you also to Becky Smedley, Laura Willis and Laura Eldridge at Quadrille for their brilliant and lively marketing and publicity.

As ever, thank you, Caroline Michel at PFD, who couldn't be more enthusiastic or supportive.

There is usually a rickety train journey from initial idea, via side alleys and dead ends, that leads – if you are lucky – to the final book; that it reaches that destination almost always owes much to a few who dispense insight and wisdom on the way. Diana Henry, Catherine Phipps and Lia Leendertz, thank you for helping germinate the seed of an idea when your bright minds were needed.

Others leant me their ear on elements within the book: thank you in particular to Vanessa Kimbell of the Sourdough School, and Angela Clutton, author of *The Vinegar Cupboard*. Many others gave me inspiration via their writing, acknowledged in these pages where they are most relevant. Thank you especially, to Hans and Gaby Weiland and Naomi Devlin for doing so much to help me to realise my enthusiasm for all things fermented.

Thank you to Candida and Nell for being chief tasters, as well as making it all worthwhile. And lastly, to Antony and Sarah, Cinead McT, Debora R, James AS, Joe S, Tim B and all those who step forwards for people during the big times.